Lucid Exposition of the Middle Way

Lucid Exposition of the Middle Way

The Essential Chapters from the *Prasannapadā* of Candrakīrti

Translated from the Sanskrit

by

Mervyn Sprung

in collaboration with

T. R. V. Murti *and* U. S. Vyas

Prajñā Press Boulder 1979

Prajñā Press
Great Eastern Book Company
1123 Spruce Street
Boulder, Colorado 80302

Printed in Great Britain

Library of Congress Cataloging in Publication Data

Candrakīrti.
Lucid exposition of the middle way.

Bibliography: p.
Includes index.
1. Nāgārjuna, Siddha. Madhyamakakārikā.
2. Mādhyamika (Buddhism)   I. Sprung, Mervyn.
II. Murti, Tirupattur Ramaseshayyer Venkatachala.
III. Vyas, U. S.   IV. Title.
BQ2868.E5S66 1979   294.3'8   79-13033
ISBN 0 87773 711 8

Contents

Preface: Text and Translation

This translation of the essential chapters from the *Prasannapadā* rests on the work of several scholars in different ways. The English of the translation is, throughout, my own, but the reading of the Sanskrit is very much the result of close and repeated collaboration with Indian and Japanese scholars. During the winter of 1965, after reading the *Baghavad Gītā* with my Sanskrit tutor, U. S. Vyas, I happened on some passages from the *Prasannapadā* which concerned the mystifying Mādhyamika theory of two truths, and read several pages with Tervyoshi Tangi of Kyoto, at that time a fellow student at Banaras Hindu University. A year or two later, still pursuing philosophical ideas and without the remotest thought of translation, I read the whole of the chapter on the 'Four Buddhist Truths' with Professor T. R. V. Murti of Banaras while he was a visiting professor at Brock University. This led on to a reading of the *Nirvāṇa* chapter with him the following year and I became strangely seized with the way of thinking of Candrakīrti and Nāgārjuna. By the time I returned to India in 1970 the thought of translating, and not just reading, the *Prasannapadā* had occurred to me. I read the chapter on 'The Perfectly Realized One' with Professor Murti and, with my former tutor, U. S. Vyas, who was now at the Buddhist Research Institute in Nālandā, I read the chapters on 'Vision and the Other Sense Faculties', 'The Factors of Personal Existence', and 'Self-Existence'. In the spring of 1971, in Kyoto, for two months Professor G. Nagao and Dr N. Aramaki painstakingly and enjoyably worked through the chapter on 'Self and the Way Things Really Are' with me. In the summer of 1975, again in Banaras, I read the chapter on 'Motion and Rest', the most difficult of all to translate, with Professor Murti, and the chapters on 'Time', 'Fire and Fuel', 'The Agent Subject and his Doing' and 'The Absence of Being in Things' with U. S. Vyas in Simla and Nālandā. The remaining chapters given here I struggled with on my own. Even so the fine translations available in French and German were always a help. The *Douze Chapitres* of Jacques May was the best model. The sometimes quixotic, but always inspired translations of T. Stcherbatsky were more than a help: I must regard him as a tutor. Without his pioneer work in Buddhist logic I do not believe

I could have risked a translation of the chapter, 'Attack on the Possibility of Knowledge'.

The present translation has, in these ways, emerged from the closest working together of four or five scholars over some ten or twelve years. I stumbled into the task, unaware of what I was doing, and then found it unthinkable to desist before the Mādhyamika philosophy had been presented to Western readers in English. Without my tolerant and gifted friends, my collaborators, the thought of translating the *Prasannapadā* could never have entered my mind; yet the interpretation of the middle way philosophy is my own and I ask no one to share that responsibility with me.

Aim of the translation

This translation was undertaken and is presented with one single purpose in mind: to make an important work of Indian philosophy available to philosophers who read English. It is not directed at Sanskritists who themselves have access to the original and whose interest would be more in the translation of technical terms and in the interpretation of the *Prasannapadā* within Buddhist and Indian philosophy. My concern is to place the *Prasannapadā* squarely within the live philosophical thought of our own time. This concern determined the choice of chapters for translation, the writing of footnotes, and the relatively austere bibliography. For this reason there are no Sanskrit words left untranslated in the English text (*nirvāṇa* is the sole exception) though this sometimes results in a regrettable prolixity. I have attempted to expound the middle way philosophy in plain, non-technical English. My model was Richard Wilhelm's translations from the Chinese. Wilhelm is not afraid to make every sentence perfectly intelligible to the contemporary reader: obscurities or difficulties in the original are no excuse for an obscure translation.

It is, I believe, widely accepted that literal translations tend to obscure the sense of the original, being unfaithful to the sense through being lexicographically exact. The widespread, though not universal, practice among Sanskrit translators has been to proceed as if translation were a matter of finding the most precise European equivalents for Sanskrit technical terms. This is understandable in a pioneering phase of the exploration of a strange tradition, and there is no doubt much of this still to be done. Yet this approach permits certain stultifying abuses. One such idiosyncrasy is the practice of bracketing,[1] a device which

[1] An example: 'But how can we (Mādhyamikas who do not believe in logic altogether) produce an argument (like the one produced by Bhāvaviveka) about the (transcendental) reality (of all mental phenomena)?' T. Stcherbatsky, *The Conception of Buddhist Nirvana*, p. 97.

tends to obscure the relationship of the two languages. It implies that what is outside the brackets tells us what is factually said in the Sanskrit, and what is inside is missing and must be gratuitously added in order to make sense in the language of translation. As there are very few precise word-to-word correspondences between Sanskrit and other languages, especially English, two faults ensue: on the one hand the translator implies the claim of finding an illusory precision, and, on the other, he often includes explanatory or paraphrase material within the bracket which is not to be found in the Sanskrit. One is often left with crippled sentences outside the bracket and unjustified material within. It does seem more suited to the purpose of making a Sanskrit text available to those who do not read Sanskrit to drop the bracketing practice and to attempt to say in the plainest, most intelligible way what the translator thinks is being said in the Sanskrit. However that comes out in the language of translation – longer or shorter, altered in syntax, adapted to a new vocabulary – that, just as it stands, will be the *translation*. It will not be a 'free' translation, nor a paraphrase, nor an 'interpretation'; it will be a translation.

Yet this is not offered as a defence of my own English style. There could be many different kinds of English used to convey the meaning of the Sanskrit of the *Prasannapadā*, and some would be closer to the style of Nāgārjuna and Candrakīrti than my own. By the second century AD – Nāgārjuna's time – Sanskrit had become a delicately sophisticated medium for philosophers, poets, religious writers, scientists and bureaucrats. Its elaborate syntax permitted the tersest of formulations and favoured aphorisms and witty paradoxes expressed in verse. Nāgārjuna was a master of this literary Sanskrit and composed his philosophical works in metred couplets (*kārikās*). At times these are so open and clear that they lend themselves to verse translation. At all times they are balanced in sense but often so terse as to be cryptic, worthy to be treated as word puzzles. Here is one of the most cryptic (p. 133, *kārikā* 5): *ajyate kenacit kascit kimcit kenacid ajyate; kutaḥ kimcid vina kascit kimcit kamcid vina kutaḥ*. Word-for-word it must go like this: 'Something (masculine) becomes evident because of something; because of something, something (neuter) becomes evident. How something (masculine) without something? How something (neuter) without something?' From the thought context, however, the *translation* must go like this: 'Every effect implies a cause; every cause implies an effect. How can there be an effect without a cause? How can there be a cause without an effect?' The word-for-word approach, eked out by bracketing, breaks down, I believe, in the face of such a text.

At the present stage of our penetration into the thought world of Mādhyamika Buddhism it appeared to me better to try to make the sense of the Sanskrit as plain as possible even at the cost of losing the brevity and balanced elegance of the original. Subsequent translators, when the sense of Mādhyamika is no longer the central issue, will certainly achieve translations which more adequately capture the literary form of the original. Candrakīrti, writing at least 400 years after his master, no longer is capable of the youthful power of expression which marks Nāgārjuna, but his Sanskrit is no less crisp and economical though it is argumentative prose and not verse. By Candrakīrti's time the art of disputation according to strict rules was dominant in Indian philosophy. Very often, in passages which enter into direct controversy with opponents of Mādhyamika, Candrakīrti will compose his sentences on an implicit syllogistic model without however doing this formally. I have not supplied the missing syllogistic terms in this translation and hope I do not disappoint the logicians too much by doing this.

What the reader who knows no Sanskrit can most usefully realize is that the Sanskrit language and the English are as far apart as it is possible for two languages within the Indo-European family to be. Sanskrit is highly articulated (eight cases of declension), is not dependent on word order and, being a literary language, uses very little everyday idiom. English is the opposite. In consequence any attempt at word-for-word translation is quite futile and even misleading. Certainly it has been my purpose throughout, after doing everything possible to grasp the sense of Nāgārjuna's or Candrakīrti's Sanskrit, to re-formulate this sense as simply and as expressively as I can in twentieth-century English. I have tried to eschew the technical vocabulary of professional philosophers and most certainly the technical language of any contemporary school of philosophy. So far as I was able I have expressed my understanding of Mādhyamika Buddhism in an English that makes available as many senses and meanings as I find there are in the *Prasannapadā* itself.

I have not heavily footnoted the translation. The translation itself says as clearly as I am able what I think the text means; to add commentary in the guise of footnotes would presume on the freedom of the reader.

The text

The Sanskrit text used for this translation is Louis de la Vallée Poussin's Mūlamadhyamakakārikās *de Nāgārjuna avec la* Prasannapadā *de Candrakīrti*, published from 1903 to 1913 in St Petersburg. This great scholar used three Sanskrit manuscripts – one each in Paris, Cambridge, England, and Calcutta – as the basis of his published text and compared them with a Tibetan translation of a much earlier date. The manuscript I have seen, the one in Cambridge, is in excellent condition but is replete with scribe's errors and, in Poussin's view, is not as reliable as the Tibetan translation. None the less, I have throughout used only the Sanskrit text as edited by Poussin, even though at many places the Tibetan text is said to be clearer.

Omissions and abridgements

Ten chapters of the *Prasannapadā*'s twenty-seven are not included in this translation. Perhaps my energies ebbed, but it seemed to me that the text is both formally and substantially repetitive in such degree that it should be easily possible to present all facets of the middle way philosophy in the seventeen chapters which were selected for translation.

The only passages omitted from the chapters translated consist of Buddhist scriptures – *sūtras* – which Candrakīrti quotes and which bestrew an otherwise clean and precise commentary. This procedure will seem a sacrilege to many and an impropriety to others. I decided, with a view to presenting as closely knit and persuasive an English text as possible, to omit those quotations from the Buddhist scriptures, whether short or long, which in my view slowed and complicated the flow of Candrakīrti's thought for the English language reader. The *sūtras* Candrakīrti quotes, do not, with only rare exceptions, clarify or advance his argument in any way. With virtually no exceptions the first sentence of the commentary which follows a *sūtra* explicitly and unmistakably picks up the argument at precisely the point it had reached immediately before the quotation. This, it seems to me, tells us quite clearly that the scriptural quotations do not contain material indispensable to establishing the point at issue. They do, of course, often bring illustrative material of interest and value for the contemporary reader; where I found this to be so they have not been omitted.

At some points in the text the quoted *sūtras* accumulate at a disturbing rate: the fact that some are not found in the Tibetan translation lends weight to the possibility that later hands than Candrakīrti's may have been at work. The purpose of the elaborate and often too weighty embellishments from the Mahāyāna scriptures is clearly to generate credence for the Mādhyamika understanding of Buddhism. This understandable device was probably essential to Candrakīrti's purpose when we reflect on the almost heretical character of much of Nāgārjuna's thinking. It may or may not have been effective in this sense, but in any case it is irrelevant to the contemporary reader – unless he is interested in sectarian controversy. The philosophy of the middle way will establish itself on its own merits, or fail to do so, quite without regard to its Buddhist orthodoxy. The only remaining reason for not omitting any of the quoted *sūtras* would be to contribute to the study of extant Buddhist literature of the seventh century AD. But as students of Buddhism can use the Sanskrit text this would hardly justify detracting from the economy of the English translation.

Further, some passages have been abridged. Except for the lengthy, rambling account of the Buddhist soteriological path given at 479.1 to 487.4, an account which is effectively re-stated in brief by Candrakīrti himself subsequently, and which is thus of no interest for the rising pitch of the attack on Nāgārjuna developing at just that point, all the passages abridged are in the first chapter of the translation. They are, without exception I believe, concerned with Candrakīrti's controversy with Bhāvaviveka, his rival commentator within the Mādhyamika school, or with his support of Buddhapālita, a commentator he attempts to follow, or else with traditional arguments of the Sāṁkhya school having to do with causation. These controversies are important, obviously. Yet to place them with all their meticulous, Indian love of syllogistic detail, in what is otherwise a finely targeted introduction to the entire *Prasannapadā*, however natural they were to Candrakīrti's contemporaries, is to make access to the work for contemporary readers difficult and discouraging. The abridged translation of such passages, it is hoped, contains the essential point of the argument being given and in this way permits the forward movement of thought without gap or soft spot.

Table 1 lists all passages abridged or omitted.

Table 1

Text Page and line reference	Translation Omissions and abridgements
3.8 to 3.10	Nāgārjuna's dedication is given in full from ll. 13–16
5.7 to 10.10	abridged
14.4 to 16.1	"
16.11 to 18.5	"
19.8 to 23.2	"
28.4 to 29.7	"
31.1 to 34.5	"
34.13 to 35.9	omitted
36.13 to 37.5	abridged
38.13 to 39.4	"
47.1 to 48.14	"
50.1 to 50.3	omitted
50.12 to 52.12	"
53.6 to 54.4	"
109.4 to 112.4	"
122.3 to 122.7	"

Text Page and line reference	Translation Omissions and abridgements
128.5 to 128.14	omitted
Chapter VII	”
191.1 to 191.9	”
200.4 to 201.8	”
215.10 to 217.14	”
Chapter XI	”
Chapter XII	”
Chapter XIV	”
277.5 to 278.4	”
Chapter XVI	”
Chapter XVII	”
354.10 to 355.2	”
361.1 to 363.12	”
374.5 to 374.14	”
377.6 to 378.2	”
387.15 to 389.6	”
Chapter XX	”
Chapter XXI	”
461.1 to 461.2	”
463.10 to 464.20	”
472.7 to 474.10	”
479.1 to 487.4	abridged
516.1 to 518.6	omitted
520.4 to 520.5	Adapted from Stcherbatsky (p. 184)
524.1 to 524.4	” ” ” (p. 189)
Chapter XXVI	omitted
Chapter XXVII	”

Correlation of chapters in the text and in the translation

The lengthy and unfocussed first chapter of the Sanskrit is so unmistakably composed of discrete sections that we must suspect careless editing some time before the extant manuscripts came into being. This is especially so as all other chapters are structured with nothing less than an artistic sense of theme development. With a view to presenting the work in appropriate contemporary form it was important, in the first place, to separate out the middle section (58.14 to 76) which begins and ends without any internal relation to the commentary preceding and following it. This is the controversy with the Buddhist opponent, either Dignāga or Bhāvaviveka, and forms Chapter II of the

Table 2

Sanskrit Text	Translation
I	I, II, III
II	IV
III	V
IV	VI
V	VII
VI	VIII
VII	omitted
VIII	IX
IX	X
X	XI
XI	omitted
XII	omitted
XIII	XII
XIV	omitted
XV	XIII
XVI	omitted
XVII	omitted
XVIII	XIV
XIX	XV
XX	omitted
XXI	omitted
XXII	XVI
XXIII	XVII
XXIV	XVIII
XXV	XIX
XXVI	omitted
XXVII	omitted

translation. From p. 76 to the end of the first chapter of the Sanskrit the text is a normal commentary on Nāgārjuna's *kārikās* concerned with causal conditions and is Chapter III of the translation. The opening sections of the first chapter of the Sanskrit are Candrakīrti's introduction to the *Prasannapadā* as a whole and as a major work in Buddhist philosophy. In these sections Candrakīrti sets Nāgārjuna's thought in historical perspective, singles out its central theme and uses the first *kārikā* as a vehicle to raise the critical questions concerning Mādhyamika as a school of Buddhism and as a philosophical method. These first sections, which close with the words 'in the remaining chapters' and so appear to have been, at one time, an introductory chapter in their own right, form Chapter I of the translation.

Table 2 shows how the chapter numbers of the translation relate to the chapter numbers of the original.

Miscellaneous

The chapter headings of the translation are not always those of the Sanskrit. I permitted myself this latitude because the contents of many chapters are not adequately, indeed are even misleadingly, indicated by the Sanskrit headings and because the Chinese and Tibetan translations use headings which vary considerably from those in the extant Sanskrit manuscripts and are based on manuscripts much earlier than these.

Because ten chapters of the original have been omitted the chapter numbers of the translation do not agree with those of the Sanskrit text. To avoid the confusion which might easily result, all references to chapter numbers which occur in the translation or in the footnotes are to the chapter numbers of the English translation; and all page references which occur in the footnotes and in the translation apply to the pagination of the translation. The arabic numbers carried in the margin of the translation give the pagination of Poussin's Sanskrit text. Omissions and abridgements in the translation are readily recognizable by the gaps and crowdings in the marginal numbers.

Nāgārjuna's *kārikās* are numbered arabically, beginning with 1, in each chapter and are inset for easier recognition. Sometimes Candrakīrti chooses to comment on one portion of a *kārikā* before taking up later portions. To indicate how *kārikās*, in such a circumstance, are broken up, the letters a, b, c, d, are used. Nāgārjuna's verse form consists of four half-lines and these are indicated by the letters a, b, c, d, used serially.

Acknowledgments

This translation could hardly have taken its present form except under assistance of different kinds from various sources:

1 A Government of India Commonwealth Fellowship 1964–5.
2 A Shastri Indo-Canadian Institute Fellowship 1970–1.
3 A Canada Council grant to visit Kyoto, spring 1971.
4 A Canada Council grant to visit India, summer 1975.
5 A Brock University grant for clerical assistance.
6 The patience of students to study many of the chapters in various drafts through several years.
7 The kindness of colleagues, as philosophers, to test selected chapters.
8 The long-sufferance of Mrs Irene Cherrington and Mrs Jenny Gurski who deciphered handwriting and typed drafts, endlessly, as it must often have seemed.

The Thought of the Middle Way: Translator's Introduction

The work whose essential and major portions are presented here in translation from the Sanskrit is, in form, and in the Buddhist tradition, a commentary on an earlier treatise, but in substance and for Western readers, it is, in its own right, a philosophical work of originality and rigour. The author, Candrakīrti, a Buddhist monk writing probably during the first quarter of the seventh century AD, undertakes to expound the thought of Nāgārjuna, himself a Buddhist monk, one great in legend and performance, who had, probably in the second century AD,[1] with a lion's roar second only to that of Buddha, flung the philosophy of the 'middle way' at his receptive, dumbfounded, and outraged contemporaries. In his treatise, which comes to us without a title but which is referred to as a *Treatise on the Middle Way (Madhyamakaśāstra)*, or *Verses on the Principles of the Middle Way (Mūlamadhyamakakārikās)*, Nāgārjuna, generally agreed, whether grudgingly or admiringly, to be the acutest intellect in Buddhist history, thinks his way relentlessly through to the conclusions he found implicit in Buddha's promise of freedom (*nirvāṇa*) for all beings. Gathering into rigorous thought some of the spiritual currents of his time in India (and not merely among Buddhists) he became the founder of the Mādhyamika[2] school of Buddhism – the school of the middle way – and made it impossible for Buddhist religious and philosophical thinking ever again to turn back to earlier conceptions. Nāgārjuna marks, for philosophy, the historical realization of the later phase of Buddhism known as the Mahāyāna.[3] After Nāgārjuna some form of Mahāyāna was irrevocable.

Four or five hundred years later a monk, presumably resident in the then, and today even in its ruins still, fabulous university at Nālandā in northern India, undertook to expound and defend the terse and many-faceted verses of Nāgārjuna. Disputes had naturally arisen among Nāgārjuna's Mādhyamika followers[4] concerning their interpretation and there had been earlier commentators, Buddhapālita and Bhāvaviveka being the best known; Candrakīrti, so far as we know the last to deal exhaustively with Nāgārjuna's treatise, claimed that his exposition was *prasannapadā* – clear-worded, or lucid, or serene – and it is commonly known by that Sanskrit designation. Nāgārjuna's work ran to some 450 couplets, which, printed consecutively, might fill 65 or 70 pages; the *Prasannapadā* in its European edition runs to nearly 600 pages; the difference is Candrakīrti's own work. In what ways Candrakīrti might differ from his master – in how far we should attempt to free Nāgārjuna from his commentator's embrace – is an important question and one so difficult that no one has as yet tried his hand at it. This introduction and the footnotes throughout the translation treat the *Prasannapadā* as a homogeneous work and ignore the problem. For the contemporary reader, whose interest is in the relevance of the thought developed and not in the history of Buddhism, it is a matter which may be overlooked.

The invocation to the *Prasannapadā*, the body of literature from which quotations are drawn in every chapter, and Buddha's easy coming and going from page to page throughout the work, leave us in no doubt about its cultural origins and about the faith – philosophical and religious – of the author. It is, indeed, a key work in the development of Buddhist thought – and a bright jewel in the rich crown of Indian philosophy. It is presented here, however, not primarily as a contribution to Buddhist studies or to the history of Indian philosophy, though it cannot of course be separated from these concerns, but as a work relevant to the most vital problems of philosophy as these engage thinkers of our own time, whatever their language and cultural background. Its thought is rigorous, fresh and often disconcertingly contemporary. If we can treat the details of the historical matrix of the *Prasannapadā* with the tolerance we exercise toward ancient and medieval Western philosophical writing, there should be no insuperable difficulty in seeing its incisive relevance to the questions now obsessing us in the West. That this is possible is the conviction behind this translation as it is behind the approach to philosophical and religious thought often calling itself comparative philosophy, or comparative thought. Those who have penetrated even a short way into Sanskrit and Chinese find that the great questions which frame the religious sense and the intellectual wonder of these cultures are, however different from those of Greece and Europe, still indefeasibly cognate with them so that we can move from one tradition to another without ever leaving the human scene. If this were not so then works like the *Prasannapadā* would be of antiquarian interest only.[5]

Mādhyamika thought has been virulently controversial from the beginning, arousing misunderstanding, disbelief and outrage in roughly equal measure. Classical Indian opponents frequently repudiated it as nihilist, as did E. Burnouf,[6] the first European scholar to study the *Prasannapadā* when it arrived in Europe in manuscript form from Nepal about the middle of the nineteenth century. Burnouf pronounced it 'nihilisme scholastique' and suggested that Hindu opponents of Buddhism could not do better than adopt its negative arguments. Mādhyamika does deny our most deeply rooted intellectual and vivial habits, holding that nothing, whether metaphysical or everyday, can be known in an unequivocal sense; holding that, hence, measured by knowledge, there is no difference between truth and falsehood, that no one, including all the Buddhas, has ever uttered one true word, that all conceptions, including that of an enlightened human being (*buddha*) fall short of the truth.

A century ago Europeans and Americans had, within their tradition, no way of comprehending such seeming nonsense. Today, thanks to the crumbling of some traditional habits of thought and to the pioneering work of some Western philosophers – Nietzsche, Heidegger and Wittgenstein to mention the best known – we can attempt once again and in fresh terms to learn what we may from Nāgārjuna and his school about the puzzlements and conundrums of human existence. Nietzsche attacked the capacity of human reason to yield knowledge much as Nāgārjuna had done, if not quite so thoroughly, and was the first of the Europeans to suspect that the reality of a human being did not lie in his individuality understood as ego. Heidegger has tried to think his way in under the traditional conceptions of the self-contained subject and an objective world and so to understand truth as trans-objective. Wittgenstein has laboured to show that language is not cognitive in the accepted sense, but functions as an integral element in complex human situations. None of these ideas will be strange to Mādhyamika and, I believe, none of the ideas of Mādhyamika will any longer be strange to us – whatever we may think about their tenability.

The first phase of the thought of the Prasannapadā

The *Prasannapadā* remains, for all this, a work of formidable strangeness, unlikely to yield its most interesting insights easily or swiftly. There is no preferred way of taking it up. The great chapters are those on 'Self-Existence' (XIII), 'Self and the Way Things Really Are' (XIV), 'The Four Buddhist Truths' (in substance about the absence of being in things and the two levels of truth) (XVIII), and '*Nirvāṇa*' (XIX). The key to what may otherwise be persistent bafflement is given in the first chapter, 'The Concern, Method and Assumptions of the Middle Way Philosophy'. This is Candrakīrti's introduction to the commentary as a whole and is a statement of his understanding of Nāgārjuna's thought. None of the other chapters will make good sense without it, and yet it will not make good sense until its application has been tested in the major chapters.

There may or may not be a dramatic structure in the *Prasannapadā*, but the investigation proceeds, with some zigzagging, through several discernible stages. The first chapter explains and defends Candrakīrti's understanding of Nāgārjuna's purpose and the principles of his procedure. This purpose (p. 33) is to give a fresh interpretation of the Buddhist term 'dependent origination' in furtherance of the enlightenment of all beings. Dependent origination will come to mean the absence of both being and non-being in particular things (*śūnyatā*); *śūnyatā* will be understood as the true nature of things which cannot be expressed in assertions making cognitive claims but can only be realized in the life of an enlightened being, which is *nirvāṇa*. Nāgārjuna proceeds, so Candrakīrti maintains, without making a single claim to knowledge (p. 37), but simply by persuading those who do make such claims, whether rival Buddhists or spokesmen for the Hindu schools of philosophy, that nothing they say is, in the end, intelligible (p. 37). He shows that every position taken up, every view (*dṛṣṭi*) held, entails claims that are either self-contradictory (pp. 37-9), or false in the face of everyday experience, or incompatible with the possibility of enlightenment – a possibility which neither Nāgārjuna nor Candrakīrti ever questions and which, therefore, serves as a devastating condemnation of inadequate philosophy.

Following this general introduction by Candrakīrti, Nāgārjuna's own inquiry moves through what may be seen as two phases. In the first phase he examines a series of concepts and theories advanced to establish everyday experience on an intelligible and acceptable basis. These concepts and theories are for the most part Buddhist and yet include all the metaphysical possibilities known at that time in India. Causality, the first and most fundamental way of bringing order into experience, is found to be unintelligible (Chapter III), because it presupposes effective entities which, on examination, prove to have merely nominal, not effective, status. Then motion, an assumption no less basic and indispensable, is taken up and dropped in a hopelessly shattered state (Chapter IV); motion cannot be conceived separately from the object or person moving (for then what would move?) nor these from motion (for then how could they be in motion?). In rapid and ruthless succession other possibilities of understanding experience are rejected: perception is unintelligible (Chapter V) because an agent cannot be related to an activity; perceived objects cannot be understood as external and material objects cannot be understood as perceived (Chapter VI); ordering the world into things with attributes is fictitious because neither thing nor attribute makes sense without the other (Chapter VII); affective involvement of persons with people and things is a puzzle because the affections – desire, hatred and so on – are inconceivable without the affected person who in turn is meaningless apart from the inconceivable affection (Chapter VIII); a subject of perception apart from the activity of perceiving is impossible otherwise one could be a perceiver without bothering to perceive (Chapter IX); persons and their actions and any other relation of agent and product are equally fictitious because to *be* an agent entails the *activity* of agency and this makes nonsense out of both concepts (Chapter X). This series of enquiries into the possibilities of ordering a world is concluded by a treatment of the ungraspability of all process, using fire and fuel as the paradigm (Chapter XI). The rigour and imaginativeness of this last investigation is matched in the entire work only by the enquiry into motion and rest. Though fire is accepted as obvious in ordinary experience, we cannot *think* the relationship of *what* is burning (fuel) and the *burning* of it (fire). The unflamed process is overlayed and falsified by the concepts of 'fuel' and 'fire'.

Up to this point Nāgārjuna and Candrakīrti have attempted to invalidate, not to say shatter, any or all sets of concepts designed to give an intelligible account of the everyday world. The first phase of the enquiry is rounded off with a summary statement of the conclusion reached and a hint of the Mādhyamika resolution to be worked out in the later chapters. In the chapter 'The Absence of Being in Things' (XII) the conclusion is given in this way: 'Whatever is not what it pretends to be, is unreal.' All proffered concepts have shown themselves to be pretence, and it is bluntly claimed that all concepts (*dharmas*) are pretence by nature (p. 144); from this it follows that the everyday world, which is a network of concepts, is unreal. *Nirvāṇa* alone does not pretend to be what it is not. But how can everything pretend? How can all Cretans be liars? Must there not be something which does the pretending and is not itself pretence? At this point Mādhyamika briefly displays its crucial notion, *śūnyatā* – the absence of being in things – and hints at the way in which in later chapters (especially XIII, XIV, XVIII and XIX) it will be introduced to show the way out of the jungle of entangling concepts and theories so far encountered. In this chapter (XII) *śūnyatā* is said to be 'the exhaustion of all views', that is, the dissipation (intransitive) of all views, but not itself another view, nor even a predicate which might be attributed to things.

In the remaining chapters, in what may, very loosely, be called the second phase of the investigation, the term *śūnyatā* gains increasing importance as Mādhyamika thought moves explicitly into the great controversial issues: being and non-being, self and the way things are in truth, the nature of an enlightened being, the relationship of the everyday world and the surpassing truth, the distinction, subtle but fundamental, between nihilism and Mādhyamika and, finally, *nirvāṇa*. In these investigations the radical mind of Mādhyamika becomes more recognizable, and the ways in which it may possibly throw some light on issues with which Western philosophers are familiar become more testable.

Some general characteristics of Mādhyamika thought

At this point in the *Prasannapadā*, even before discussion of these major questions, some pervasive characteristics of Mādhyamika thought will have become apparent, possibly estranging. Most obvious, probably, will be the formal, not to say rigid, way of proceeding with the analysis of each of the chosen topics. As most of us assume we can find some good sense in our everyday categories, we prefer to search more informally, more openly, somewhat in Aristotle's manner, for aspects or uses of them which are worth retaining; but, as Mādhyamika was convinced that the categories of our everyday thinking were lacking in ultimate sense, it proceeds more swiftly and more ruthlessly. The forked stick which they used to destroy every proffered view consists, quite simply, and contrary to certain prejudices, of the Aristotelean principles of contradiction and excluded middle. These principles lie so deep in the minds of Nāgārjuna and Candrakīrti that, though operative at every turn of their serpentine arguments, they are not explicitly enunciated as principles of method, though they are adduced as reasons in argument. 'As to exist and not to exist are reciprocally contradictory how can they hold of one and the same thing?' Nāgārjuna asks (p. 120, 7cd) and Candrakīrti adds that this would be 'clearly nonsensical'. Even deeper lies the law of excluded middle. Mādhyamika cannot proceed into an enquiry without applying it: an object is either in motion or it is not; an object is either external to perception or it is not; an agent is either in action or he is not; fuel is either burning or it is not; and so on.

These two principles are the bedrock of what is often called the Mādhyamika dialectic.[7] The procedure is to dichotomize the possible views on any matter into a formal, and final, either/or: the one in motion is either identical with or entirely other than motion itself; the subject of perception must be either identical with perceiving or wholly other than it; an agent subject must either be identical with his activities or wholly other than them; and so on. Either of the two, mutually exclusive, ways of taking any matter must, Mādhyamika insists, be intelligible in itself without reference to its opposite. This contrasts with the everyday way in which sense is sustained by ignoring such a dichotomy, by unknowingly fusing the two possibilities into one workable, if imprecise, concept. Having set up a rigid either/or, Mādhyamika then exhibits the untenability of both, either by showing each to be self-contradictory, or contrary to experience or incompatible with the possibility of enlightenment. In the last analysis the endeavour is to convince that the ideas in question are, in rigour, *unthinkable.* Nāgārjuna's rampage through the notions of the philosophers is directed at uncovering their ultimate nonsense with a view to releasing men from humiliating bondage to them.

This aspect of the method of Nāgārjuna and Candrakīrti has been obscured in some modern treatments of the *Prasannapadā* by a fascination with a feature of their thought which they speak of explicitly, which is traditionally Buddhist and which holds out some promise of logical novelty. This feature, as old as Buddha himself and no doubt much older, is the insistence that assertions about any matter have four possible forms (*catuṣkoṭi*):[8] (1) that it is; (2) that it is not; (3) that it both-is-and-is-not; (4) that it neither-is-nor-is-not. One may be tempted to see in this recurring thought pattern an alternative logic, a novel evasion of the principles of excluded middle and non-contradiction. It may indeed have some logical interest; certainly it is interesting to relate the four types of assertion to one another for their value and force in argument. Whatever one concludes, however, it will have little, virtually no, bearing on Mādhyamika method, for, with one egregious exception the *catuṣkoṭi* is not used as a means of investigation or of argument throughout the *Prasannapadā*. The exception is the enquiry into *nirvāṇa* (Chapter XIX) where the untenable views are rejected in order as they hold that: (1) *nirvāṇa* is something real; (2) is something unreal; (3) is something both-real-and-unreal; (4) is something neither-real-nor-unreal. Nāgārjuna was surely wise not to have applied this formula more often; it proves in its *nirvāṇa* application unhelpful and misleading. The first two alternatives make sense; but the third surreptitiously repeats the first; and the fourth (which is in fact a formulation normally reserved by Mādhyamika for its own position) is refuted on the, logically, arbitrary ground that no one could possibly know that *nirvāṇa* was neither-real-nor-unreal, a point equally valid against the other three alternatives as well.

Though the *logical* importance of the four alternative assertions may be, and has been, exaggerated, its importance for Mādhyamika philosophy of language, and hence ontology, and hence understanding of human freedom, is great. The *catuṣkoṭi* exhausts the ways in which the verb 'to be' may be employed in assertions: one may affirm the 'is' of something, or affirm the 'is not', or 'both-is-and-is-not', or 'neither-is-nor-is-not'. In all four ways language is being used ontologically; the verb 'is', in whatever variation, implies the being or non-being of what the assertion is about. Nāgārjuna and Candrakīrti repudiate all of the four alternatives: they repudiate the ontological implications of the verb 'to be'. They virtually never use the four alternatives as a logical tool, but they introduce them (at times just the first three) in order to make their repudiation of any conceivable implication of the ideas of being or non-being unquestionable and unconditional. How it may be acceptable for them to invalidate the arguments of their opponents by a rigid, non-contradictory logic, and repudiate all ontological assertions, and still speak meaningfully about human bondage and freedom is, obviously, a matter which requires further discussion.

One taking up the *Prasannapadā* for the first time must be struck by the seeming perversity of its refusal to enunciate precise theories in opposition to the theories which it so mercilessly denounces. Nāgārjuna says: 'I advance no thesis and so cannot be faulted' (p. 37). Whatever one thinks about the justification offered for this statement, it is not irresponsible sophistry. Candrakīrti's explanation runs: 'But the Mādhyamika brings no reason or ground (*hetu*) against his adversary; he makes no use of reasons and examples but pursues his own thesis only until the opponent gives up his' (p. 38). Mādhyamika, according to Candrakīrti, could not, in good sense, advance arguments claiming to have a ground, for this would imply the ontological basis of logic and language. It is enough, in the interest of freeing the mind from its obstructive lumber, to convince the opponent that his theory entails, by logical consequence (*prasaṅga*), conclusions which are unacceptable to reason, or to common sense, or to Buddhist axioms. Because of this conception of the function of argument, Candrakīrti is accounted a spokesman for the *prāsaṅgika* branch of the Mādhyamika school. His rival commentator on Nāgārjuna's *Middle Way Treatise*, Bhāvaviveka, because he held that a Mādhyamika could and should advance self-contained, autonomous (*svatantra*) arguments, is regarded as a spokesman for the *svātantrika* branch of Mādhyamika.[9]

Candrakīrti's seemingly untenable claim that the negation of an opponent's point of view does not commit one to the point of view from which the negation was made (pp. 36, 38) must provoke puzzlement and certainly requires some study. It may be understood within the logic of negation with at least partial approval[10] though the Mādhyamika understanding of its own procedure is not primarily logical. It presupposes that language is not ontologically bound, that assertions function within a jungle of infinitely articulable conceptions, and serve to promote or hinder the vivial energies latent in these. The attack on concepts, on points of view, is aimed at the vivial energies to which they are wedded, though it must strike the ideas en route.[11] The success of the attack is measured by the lessening of the clutter of ideas which blocks the way to clarity of mind and to a grasp of the way things really are. The *prāsaṅgika* understanding of the purpose of thought does not prevent Candrakīrti from giving a Mādhyamika resolution of the major questions facing Buddhist philosophy. In each case, however, he does decline to offer one more theory in addition to and in competition with, and of the same order as, the theories advanced by other schools. The Mādhyamika attitude, when it is given positive expression, never takes the form of a metaphysical theory (which would be a self-contradiction) but is offered as an interpretation of

Buddha's words in the interests of bringing the way of enlightenment closer to listeners and readers. Dependent origination is not a metaphysical theory, nor is the absence of being in particular things, nor is *nirvāṇa* as the coming to repose of the manifold of named things. These resolutions of the crucial Buddhist concerns are not metaphysical theories, but elaborate expressions of the total posture of one on the Buddha's way.[12] We are today scarcely accustomed to this understanding of philosophy, but this is hardly an argument against it; in any case this is the attitude pervasively implicit and, at times, quite explicit (p. 238, 18) in the *Prasannapadā*, I believe.

Before taking up the crucial Mādhyamika concerns of the later chapters one further presupposition of their thought, so important as to be nowhere explicitly justified, must be singled out. According to Nāgārjuna and Candrakīrti, as I have just stated, reasoning is not ontologically bound; yet they proceed, unshakably assuming that what fails the tests of reason – what is less than utterly intelligible – cannot exist. They fault and reject as untenable, in a ruthless and perhaps intolerant manner, every proffered concept or viewpoint which can be shown to contain even the slightest ambiguity, unclarity or unintelligibility. The two expressions most frequently used throughout the *Prasannapadā* are 'this makes no sense' (*na yujyate*) and 'this is logically impossible', or, 'this is unintelligible' (*nopapadyate*); the former being, obviously, more general and less ontological, the latter being the final condemnation of a theory found to be, in rigour, unthinkable. For thinkers often held to be 'mystical', the Mādhyamika understanding of thinkability is surprisingly narrow and unyielding. Whatever attempts to own incompatible predicates is repudiated as unintelligible; unlike Hegel, Mādhyamike will not tolerate the synthesis of opposites. 'So, to "possess a characteristic" and "not to possess it" are contradictory. But what is contradictory cannot exist' (p. 105). The expression 'cannot exist' (*na saṁbhavati*) means either or both 'is not logically possible' or 'cannot come to be'; we might say it embraces both the possibilities of thought and of existence, though this distinction is not consistently maintained by Buddhists. The Mādhyamika is the most dogmatic rationalist of any tradition. It may seem that if Mādhyamika rejects the claim of what can*not* be clearly thought to be a description of the way things really are, it should hold that what can be clearly thought would be such a description. But Mādhyamika will not be committed to the opposite of what it repudiates; it will not, and cannot, agree that the utterly intelligible is the truth; and for a simple reason: there is nothing utterly intelligible. The mind (*buddhi*), is not, like Aristotle's *nous*, endowed with the ability to know being; far removed from that, its natural activity – conceptualization – is rather an obstruction, albeit a natural obstruction, which is to be calmed and clarified before the truth can be present (p. 172). The truth is not presented to the intellect alone, and, hence is not intelligible; it cannot be present until the intellect has clarified itself by surpassing the demands of intelligibility (p. 177, 7). If this can make sense, whether or not it is acceptable, then it becomes understandable how the Mādhyamika can be a rigorous rationalist in his negative destruction of all theories about existence, and yet not be bound to the complementary view that existence is rational.

The crucial concerns of Mādhyamika

The crucial concerns of Mādhyamika thought, the matters it cares about, for which it undertakes the serpentine tasks of philosophy, may now be mentioned against this background of presuppositions and general characteristics. Nāgārjuna, supported by Candrakīrti, first examined in the early chapters all known attempts to give an account of the world as it presents itself from day to day, and found that none of them made sense; that, consequently, the world, or 'life', as we ordinarily experience it, is without any meaning; and so, one might think, has worked himself into a nihilist or at least scepticist, *cul de sac*. But Nāgārjuna and Candrakīrti do not concede this. They are sure that the destruction of metaphysics is not the end of meaningful life but that it opens new possibilities of finding sense in human existence. It was Nāgārjuna's historical achievement to give the earliest coherent expression to Mahāyāna Buddhism, the new way of regarding human affairs in which the immediate awareness of the uncreated truth of all things allowed all things to serve as the occasion of human enlightenment. This non-mediated presence of the truth, a world removed from the personal intuition (*prajñā*) of early Buddhism, was known in the religious literature (*sūtras*) of Nāgārjuna's time as *prajñā pāramitā* – the surpassing or consummate *prajñā*. Though this expression is not used in the *Prasannapadā*, it, like the religious thought-world of Mahāyāna Buddhism in general, is held quietly in the background as a kind of invisible sounding board for the arguments being noisily worked over in the foreground.[13] The scepsis of the *Prasannapadā* does, I believe, stand firmly on its own feet as an adventure in rigorous thought; and yet its function is to make it possible to comprehend the *bodhisattva*, the enlightened man of Mahāyāna Buddhism. The *bodhisattva* is an enlightened being, and yet emhodied – transcendent *and* immanent – because, as the absence of being in things is their truth, the everyday world is the locus of *nirvāṇa*.

The thought of the *Prasannapadā*, understood in this way, presents us with the problem of grasping how it moves from a failed attempt to find a tenable account of experience in the conventional terms of causality, subject and attribute, motion, time, space, external objects, perception, passion, agent subject, and so on, as well as in the strictly Buddhist terms of suffering, bondage, freedom, and so on – a failure which could justify scepticism and even nihilism – to a hymneal affirmation of the surpassing worth of the human adventure. By what means does Mādhyamika restore meaning to a scene of analytical devastation?

To treat this problem adequately, assuming that one would dare to try, would be a major experiment in thought. At this juncture, with a view to easing the reading of what, for many, must be a strange book, nothing more will be attempted than a pointing up of the crucial turns in the Mādhyamika struggle to give an account of human experience commensurate both with its scepsis and the new Mahāyāna vision. I will suggest some preferred ways of understanding Mādhyamika, but will try to avoid closing off what must remain an open and continuing study. As crucial turns I count the following:

1 The enquiry into being, or 'self-existence'.
2 *Śūnyatā*, the truth of things.
3 The 'two truths'.
4 The encounter with the boundaries of language.
5 *Nirvāṇa.*
6 The middle way as resolution of the philosopher's conundrums.

Self-existence

Nāgārjuna's attack on the idea of self-existence, to which he devotes a separate enquiry (Chapter XIII) may be seen as the hinge of his reformation of Buddhist thinking. Earlier Buddhist metaphysicians had resolved the problem of permanence in seemingly universal flux by the notion of *dharma.*[14] There were thought to be limited numbers of ultimate, irreducible, simple constituents of existence which combined, in time, to produce the perishable mental states and things of the everyday world, without themselves perishing. *Dharmas* were not substances, nor qualities, nor relations, but self-characterizing, simple reals. Nāgārjuna, taking the idea of self-existence in full earnest, insists, in Parmenidean fashion, that what is self-existent must be uncreated, imperishable and not dependent on anything else: what *is* in and through itself. Parmenides' solution, however, could never have occurred to a Buddhist for whom the ceaseless arising and perishing of things is the primary given and who must have a world in which meaningful transformation of human existence is possible. Plato's imperishable substances, innocent of temporal and spatial qualification (*dharmas* as *eidoi*) were inconceivable to Nāgārjuna as they beg the question of permanence *in* time; and he would have quickly reduced Aristotle's *ousia* theory to mere nominalism. Nāgārjuna was committed to rejecting any solution which remained within the bounds of mere theory.[15]

Using the common example of the heat of fire, he argues that nothing in all of experience can meet the demands of the idea of self-existence: everything arises in time from causes. At this point Candrakīrti's answer to the question of an opponent constitutes one of the seminal passages in the *Prasannapadā*. Solely the unchanging nature of all things throughout all time is self-existent, he expounds (p. 156); this is nothing particular, nothing definable; it is what is common to all *dharmas*, namely, their lack (in the conventional sense) of both self-existence and non-self-existence; it is *śūnyatā*; and a synonym for *śūnyatā* is *tathatā* – the thus-it-isness, or thusness of things, a common way of speaking of the truth about things. So: the absence of being in things is their being, their self-existence, their truth. In this way Candrakīrti turns the problem around. He shows that the term self-existent is unthinkable within everyday experience and yet, far from discarding it, which he might have done, he elevates it to the realm of ultimate truth and *nirvāṇa*. Clearly its original sense must suffer some transformation in this process and not merely by becoming a metaphor.[16] It is more likely that an originally distorted, unintelligible expectation of finding self-existence in substantial form among ontic existents led, in spite of its falsity, to a search for something uncaused because outside the dimension of causality; to something approachable only as 'self-existent', yet beyond the dimensions of both conventional existence and conventional selfhood.

Despite the somewhat honorific use of the term self-existence to speak of what for Buddhists is ultimate, that is, enlightenment, it has become clear that nothing within the processes of the everyday can claim to be self-existent. The full weight of this turn of thought becomes evident when it is followed by the statement that if there is no self-existence in things neither can there be non-existence, as the two ideas are only reciprocally meaningful. Buddha's authority is drawn in to clinch the conclusion that both the notion of existence, or isness, and the notion of non-existence or is-notness are false dogmas and make it impossible to comprehend the truth of things in his sense. This sets the problem for the remaining excursions of Mādhyamika thought: how to carry on with meaningful talk about the central concerns of a philosophy which believes it can show that the idea of existence, of isness, of being, is empty? Language, without the force of the verb 'to be', would seem to be mere fantasy.[17] The simple sentence 'Enlightenment *is* neither existent nor non-existent' is unintelligible. How can Mādhyamika seriously hold such a position?

Śūnyatā

When we take up the term for which Mādhyamika is best known, *śūnyatā*,[18] the troubles become more interesting though not fewer. The term *śūnyatā*, which I translate throughout 'absence of being in things' snakes its way through all Mādhyamika thinking, arousing puzzlement, wonder, insight, and despair in those who try to follow its tortuous path. It has often been called the void, sometimes emptiness and at times, after its mathematical meaning, zero. It has been more recently understood as openness, and, in some usages at least, merits the translation 'the truth of things'. It is so utterly novel that we must exercise some patience in attempting to grasp its full significance for Nāgārjuna and Candrakīrti.

Tactically, Mādhyamika found itself attacking the realism of Buddhists who found being in the simple constituents of everyday things (*dharmas*) or of non-Buddhists, who found being in the everyday things themselves. In this sense, in denying that anything ontic has self-existence, or, has its being in and through itself, *śūnyatā* means simply *niḥ-svabhāva*, that is, absence of self-existence. This is by far the most frequent use of the term and, understandably, might be taken to be its definitive sense. Candrakīrti is, however, very careful to explain at every critical turn[19] (and this could be missed if one read only Nāgārjuna's verses) that though everyday things and their constituents are lacking in being, they would be falsely, indeed heretically, understood as non-existent in every sense; neither existence nor non-existence should be predicated of them. The full value of the term *śūnyatā* then should be given as 'the absence of both being and non-being in things'. That this simply must be so becomes clear when *śūnyatā* is related to the 'two truths', to the middle way, to Mādhyamika theory of language and to its understanding of enlightenment.

The hinge of Nāgārjuna's revolution is his re-thinking of the original root concept of Buddhism – dependent origination – as *śūnyatā*. Early Buddhism, after rejecting the theories of causation current at the time, gave an account of the everyday in terms of the dependence of one thing or event on a preceding: the sprout is not *caused* by the seed, but does *depend* on the previous existence of the seed for its own arising. This understanding makes sense only so long as its terms, 'seed' and 'sprout' are taken as real, as something between which the relation of dependence could be supposed. Nāgārjuna retains the expression dependent origination, but, having denied both seed and sprout self-existence, he must hold that the dependence of the one on the other can no longer be understood in the traditional realistic sense. It becomes rather the non-dependence of non-existents; there is no longer a real origination of anything in dependence on anything else. Candrakīrti comments bluntly, 'We interpret dependent origination as *śūnyatā*' (p. 235). If, in the world which each of us holds together for himself, the causal account is delusory, if, that is, all the things inner and outer which make up a world neither arise nor exist in the realistic, entitative way we naively suppose, then the events and sequences which compose life are analogous to a magician's deception: what truly goes on is made to appear like a series of causally dependent events, but is not.

The frequently recurring use of the analogy of magic (*māyā*) can be misleading. It does not mean that Nāgārjuna and Candrakīrti are hallucinationists, that a magic wand will serve to conjure up and to spirit away the everyday world. Their insistence, repeated impressively often,[20] that they are not nihilists, that the dogma of non-existence is as much a heresy as the dogma that everyday things as such are in being, should warn us to look for another understanding of the analogy of the magician's trick.[21] This is a subtle and difficult point. It may suffice at this juncture to remind that the indispensable factor in a magician's trick is the false interpretation placed on the evidence of the senses by the spectator. Coins, cigarettes and rabbits are manipulated by the magician strictly in accord with the laws of motion and gravity that govern all objects. It is the spectator who, due to the shallowness of his imagination, penetrates no deeper than his eyesight and sees these objects passing bewilderingly in and out of nostrils, pockets and top hats. The events making up the trick, the palming of the coin or cigarettes, the collapse of a false bottom in the hat, are not dream, not hallucination, but run of the mill space-time sequences onto which the spectator projects his false expectations.

Śūnyatā is not only the repudiation of a *causal* account of the everyday, it marks the repudiation of *any* account: it is not a theory about the space-time world. In the enquiry into *śūnyatā* and the 'two truths' (Chapter XVIII) the opponent's attempt to fix a metaphysics of nihilism on the notion *śūnyatā* is rejected by distinguishing between the delusive everyday (*saṁvṛti*), where metaphysical theories appear to have their proper locus, and a higher truth (*paramārtha*). The thought here is somewhat inexplicit but the way in which the distinction of the two truths is introduced at this point implies that *śūnyatā* is not one more theory among the many traditional theories offering an account of the factual world; it implies that such theories are delusive shadow boxing: accounts of what is not there, as if one set out to explain the delusive appearances of the magician's tricks strictly in terms of the delusive appearances themselves. Metaphysicians are, as it were, attempting to give a reasoned account of the emergence of rabbits from empty hats or of coins from nostrils. Mādhyamika is determined to expose the supposed world of fact as a magician's trick and in this way to render all metaphysics ridiculous. They attempt to show that theoretical explanation is founded on the delusive fiction of entities in being affecting each other causally. Nāgārjuna says this sweepingly, '*Śūnyatā* is the exhaustion of all views' (p. 150, 8) and adds 'Those for whom *śūnyatā* is itself a theory are incurable.'

The special status of *śūnyatā* – as not one more delusive view but something not of the nature of a view – is marked out in the chapter 'The Absence of Being in Things'. It is declared that all compound things are not what they pretend to be; that what is not what it pretends to be is unreal; that therefore all compound things are unreal (p. 144, 1). This can be taken as a restatement of the magician analogy; but in any case it provokes the natural rejoinder 'If all compound things are unreal, what is it in that case that pretends?' (p. 145, 2). That the answer is *śūnyatā* tells us much about the use of the term. There is no eternal being, no Absolute as Brahman, nor a real individual entity concealed behind the pretence; there is no pretender; there is simply, if unaccountably, a false imputation of being to particular things. Why *śūnyatā* is introduced at this point is not easy to comprehend, it is certainly not made explicit, but it may be because it is the preferred understanding of self-existence and hence the source of the pretence everyday things make of being self-existent entities. In any case *śūnyatā* extricates Mādhyamika from a situation very close to the liar's paradox and that can mark for our purposes the transition from *śūnyatā* as the preferred account of the everyday world to *śūnyatā* as the way into the Mādhyamika understanding of the world of the unborn. I will attempt to trace this often confusing way by considering what Nāgārjuna and Candrakīrti have to say about the 'two truths', the boundaries of language, *nirvāṇa* and the middle way.

The two truths

Though the notion of 'two truths' (*satyadvaya*) is implicit in Buddhism from the beginning, as it is in Vedānta and, indeed, in any philosophy or religion that holds to a norm distinct from the everyday, Mādhyamika alone makes the distinction into its *crucial* thought. The two truths elevate the distinction between the born – the temporal – and the unborn – the timeless – of the Buddha's own discourses to the reflective level. The problems which this distinction introduces into reflective thought become explicit and acute for Nāgārjuna under the terminology of *saṁvṛti* – the temporal, the everyday – and *paramārtha* – the timeless, the truth of enlightenment. Though these terms are used sparingly in the *Prasannapadā*, the distinction and its problems are implicit, just barely beneath the surface of discussion, throughout the entire course of the investigation. Candrakīrti takes up the problem explicitly in Chapter II. He argues (pp. 59-60) that neither is the idea of a characteristic apart from what it is a characteristic of intelligible, nor is the idea of what is characterized apart from its characteristics. This reciprocal dependence deprives each term of its claim to exist or to be intelligible in its own right, and that fact, Candrakīrti states, is the mark of *saṁvṛti*; it is unintelligibility which distinguishes it from *paramārtha* – the higher truth; it is the failure of the concepts 'characteristic' and 'thing' to make sense which tells us they cannot be true ultimately. Candrakīrti does not say that the truth of things *is* intelligible. It is the very main hinge of Mādhyamika that he does not feel committed to that conclusion. He is searching for an understanding of things without an explicit concept of what would count as the truth and yet confident he has a negative criterion adequate for the detection and rejection of what fails to be what he is searching for. How Mādhyamika resolves this conundrum, if it does, is perhaps the most interesting question it can raise for us.

Chapter XVIII, in spite of its title, is about the two truths and their relation to the absence of being in things. Nāgārjuna, replying to a critic who has accused him of being a nihilist, of holding the view that the putative entities of the everyday world do not exist in any sense, counters (p. 230, 8) that such a misguided critic is one who does not understand the two truths. It seems clear that he means to contrast the proper understanding of *śūnyatā*, namely that everyday things neither exist nor do not exist, with the naive view that things are self-existent entities. Candrakīrti explains (p. 238) that *śūnyatā*, properly understood is, itself, the higher truth of everyday things, and nothing else. The distinctions used in *kārikā* 10 between the transactional world (*saṁvṛti*), the higher truth (*paramārtha*) and *nirvāṇa* support the view that Mādhyamika worked with *three* truths, not two, distinguishing between the higher (more true) truth about everyday things (*paramārtha*), i.e. that things are *śūnya*, and the realization of that truth in enlightenment (*nirvāṇa*). But Nāgārjuna and Candrakīrti are not consistent on this point; more often *śūnyatā*, as the truth of things, is not separated from the incorrigible, trans-factual awareness of the way things really are, which is itself enlightenment. In this sense any theory of *śūnyatā*, however adequate, belongs, by definition, to the ordinary world, because it must perforce, in forming sentences with words, use the concepts of entity, characteristic, the verb to be and all the vocabulary of delusive *saṁvṛti* which Mādhyamika rejects as a vocabulary for philosophy. In so far as the higher truth is a theory, it falls, being *verbal* truth, within the lower truth. This ambiguity may be resolved on further study, but for the moment I am content to let it stand. The higher truth is *satya*, both a truth and a reality, both the explanation and the realization of enlightenment.

The limits of language

Such a seemingly clumsy *aporia* was not, of course, left unattended by Nāgārjuna and Candrakīrti. It is taken up further in terms of the limits of language. Chapter XIV, *kārikā* 7 makes it clear that language can *refer* only to perishable objects of thought (there are no other), not to the truth of things; and *kārikā* 9 says that the way things really are cannot be manifested as named things. In his commentary Candrakīrti explains that ordinary language ceases to be effective and valid (that is, no longer functions by reference to objects) in the realm of the higher truth. Nāgārjuna's scandalous aphorism (p. 262, 24) 'No truth has been taught by a Buddha for anyone, anywhere' appears to strengthen this view. This seems to be a dead end: only wordlessness is appropriate to the higher truth.[22] It is not, however, because Candrakīrti adds at once that there is a need to *point out* or to *teach* the higher truth and to do this one must fall back on ordinary language, as one who wants a drink of water makes use of a receptacle to fetch it, but drinks the water. It is clear that there is no special vocabulary or grammar reserved for discussion of the higher truth; in discussion it becomes an integral part of the everyday truth. But then how point to it or teach it at all? How understand the capacity of a wise man to use *words* when helping others toward enlightenment?

This is the crux, and the Mādhyamika answer turns on its denial of the cognitive function of language, whether in its ordinary use or in a putatively higher philosophical and religious use. There are, bluntly, no entities to which words *refer*. There is no entity 'person' distinct from an individual psycho-physical history, though we mistakenly think we refer to such; there is no entity corresponding to the word 'chariot' distinct from axles, wheels and so on. In all such cases the noun word functions not by naming, not by furthering cognition, but as a *prajñapti. Prajñapti* becomes, in Mādhyamika discussion, a technical term carrying a heavy burden of importance. This is widely recognized though it has not as yet been adequately studied.[23] I understand a *prajñapti* to be a non-cognitive, guiding term which serves to suggest appropriate ways of coping with the putative realities on which it rests for its meaning and to which it lends meaning. 'Person' rests on the putative reality of psycho-physical traits, and 'chariot' presupposes wheels, axle, and so on. There is, in truth, no entity 'person' and none 'chariot' named by these words and hence there is no entity to be cognized. This is a kind of nominalism and yet is much more.

Language is of one piece and does not function differently when used of the higher truth. *Kārikā* 18 (p. 238) is Nāgārjuna's great dictum in this matter. He says that dependent origination is *śūnyatā* and '*Śūnyatā* is a guiding, not a cognitive, notion presupposing the everyday.'

In this one sentence all of Mādhyamika metaphysics is converted to praxis; its two central terms, dependent origination and the absence of both being and non-being in things, are declared to be non-cognitive (*prajñapti*) as 'person' and 'chariot' are. They cannot be offered as descriptive words; to say of a person or a chariot that it neither is nor is not, cannot *describe* them because the refusal to use the verb 'to be' ontologically precludes the attribution of any descriptive predicates. What function remains to words then, but to suggest or prescribe appropriate ways of *behaving* toward 'things'? This is, of course, a crucial and a most difficult question, but, for my own part, the *Prasannapadā* makes sense in a total way only on some such interpretation of its key terms. A *prajñapti* is a guiding notion, a notion which a long tradition of successful teaching finds effective in helping students toward the clarity of mind that marks the wise man. Neither Nāgārjuna nor Candrakīrti anywhere says this explicitly, but, after the denial of the 'is' of predication, no other interpretation remains credible. When Nāgārjuna says that *śūnyatā* is a *prajñapti* presupposing a base (*upādāya*) as person presupposes psycho-physical traits and 'chariot' axle and wheels, he is saying, I believe, that his own philosophical vocabulary functions only presupposing ordinary, entitative language as its base of meaning; ordinary language is the receptacle that carries the water of wisdom. On this interpretation, the entire, august range of Buddhist notions, enlightenment (*nirvāṇa*), reality (*tattvam*), the truth of things (*tathatā*), the quintessence of all things (*dharmatā*), and Buddha himself become *prajñaptis*, serving to lead men toward freedom, but not claiming to describe any reality or convey any ultimate truth. Candrakīrti repeatedly avers that no Buddha used words except for the purpose of guiding beings to enlightenment (e.g., pp. 175–7).

That this seemingly heretical view is not a passing aberration is borne out in the chapter devoted to the inquiry into *nirvāṇa*, where, after Nāgārjuna's search through the traditional ways of understanding *nirvāṇa*, Candrakīrti concludes 'Therefore it has been established that even *nirvāṇa* does not exist' (p. 263). Any attempt to conceive *nirvāṇa* ontologically is undercut by the insistence that it is the utter dissipation of ontologizing thought (*kalpanā*) which is *nirvāṇa* (p. 249). To entertain concepts like personal afflictions (*kleśa*) or factors of personal existence (*skandha*) (which, Buddhists conventionally hold, must be removed in order to attain *nirvāṇa*) believing either that they are or are not is the very habit which ensures continued bondage. This is not merely an attack on academic theories; it is understood in the radical sense of withdrawing the affirmation of being from all things, inner and outer, without exception. This is formulated in the phrase 'the coming to rest of the manifold of named things' (p. 249) which is, throughout the investigation, among the many paraphrases and explanations of *nirvāṇa*, the most persistent.

Nirvāṇa

Mādhyamika may have, at this point, frustrated any attempt at conceiving *nirvāṇa* in terms of a reality, but one may still wonder if their position is anything more than Schopenhauerian negativism. One need not wonder for long. When the conventional conceptions of *nirvāṇa* have been repudiated, Nāgārjuna moves forward to a fresh understanding of Buddhism which radically influenced later developments and which retains a certain perennial appeal. *Nirvāṇa*, in Nāgārjuna's understanding, is not the end of life, nor the denial of life; it is a discovery of 'the way things are truly'; it is a return to the world following a radical purification of the 'being' who is to appreciate it; *nirvāṇa* lets the world become what it is.

This revolutionary understanding is developed in Chapter XIX, the culminating, if philosophically not the most intricate, investigation of the entire treatise. *Kārikā* 9 (p. 255) may be taken as the aphoristic quintessence of Mādhyamika thought: 'That which, taken as causal or dependent, is the process of being born and passing on, is, taken non-causally and beyond all dependence, declared to be *nirvāṇa*.' *Nirvāṇa* is a radically altered way of taking the process of being born and passing on, that is, the everyday. The everyday is the only 'locus' there is for *nirvāṇa* to realize itself in. This *kārikā* sets a conundrum for thought that cannot be brushed aside; and it makes the predominant Western interpretations of *nirvāṇa*, from Schopenhauer through Nietzsche and Max Müller to Albert Schweitzer seem inadequate, even distorted. Once and for all *nirvāṇa* is declared not to be realized in a locus other than the turmoil of birth and death; once and for all it is declared not to be extinction of life, nor an afterlife, nor a distant realm of being. *Kārikās* 19 and 20 (pp. 259–60) make this point even more provocatively; the one saying there is no specifiable difference whatever between *nirvāṇa* and the everyday world (*saṁsāra*), the other that *nirvāṇa* has no other ontic range than that of the everyday world. What a mind-splitting thunderclap this conception must have been to Nāgārjuna's contemporaries! At issue is the nature of Buddha, of the truth of Buddhism itself: how to grasp the embodiment of a sense of life that endures in all circumstances. Nāgārjuna's great insight is that *nirvāṇa* as an afterlife is unintelligible, because a limit to the illimitable. *Nirvāṇa* is wherever the Buddha-nature prevails: so, as ontic realms – and an afterlife is just as much an ontic realm as this life – there is no difference between *nirvāṇa* and *saṁsāra*. To say in English, as the translation does, that the 'ontic range' of *nirvāṇa* is the ontic range of *saṁsāra* is, on the face of it, a gross distortion: *nirvāṇa* can have no ontic limitations whatsoever as is self-evident. The difficulty is common to all efforts to bring the everyday into touch, by means of everyday language, with what surpasses it. Candrakīrti is quite clear about Nāgārjuna's meaning. He tells us that both the everyday and *nirvāṇa* are of the same basic nature, are of one essence (p. 260); dependent origination, which is to say non-dependent non-origination, the absence of being in things, the essentially peaceful nature of things, is the truth both of the everyday and of *nirvāṇa*. There is no other existence, no other world, of which *nirvāṇa* is the truth.

In the culminating pulse of the *nirvāṇa* chapter Candrakīrti's thought moves to its loftiest height and binds together the main threads of the entire treatise. He comments on Nāgārjuna's verse 'Beatitude is the coming to rest of all ways of taking things, the repose of named things' (p. 262, 24) by juxtaposing the crucial ideas of Mādhyamika. Beatitude – *nirvāṇa* – is understood in terms of two criteria: (1) the coming to rest of all ways of taking things (or of all ways of perceiving things); (2) the coming to rest of all named things (or of language as a naming activity). These two criteria are in Candrakīrti's application virtually one, though the second is the preferred formulation. He expounds by reviewing six essential aspects of the everyday world, the ceasing to function of each of which is an aspect of beatitude or *nirvāṇa*. These six aspects are: (1) assertive verbal statements; (2) discursive thought; (3) the basic afflictions; (4) innate modes of thought (*vāsanā*); (5) objects of knowledge; (6) knowing. *Nirvāṇa* is not produced by the cessation of these factors; their cessation *is nirvāṇa*; there can be no causal, or other, relationship between *saṁsāra* and *nirvāṇa*; *nirvāṇa* is not another something to which anything ontic can be related. The cessation of each of these six factors, is said to be the coming to rest, or the repose, of named things. Each cessation is somehow complete in itself, one way of elucidating what the repose of a world supposed to consist of entities with names, might be like. Such a world is not wiped out, or reduced to meaninglessness; the turmoil is drawn out of it so that it becomes transparent to the ever-present Buddha Truth. That is all. As assertions of knowledge have no place in *nirvāṇa* (being inseparable from some interest, however subtle) we need not ask for information about it, nor can we treat it as having being. Candrakīrti's final *coup* is 'Therefore it has been established that even *nirvāṇa* does not exist', and he quotes the verse '*Nirvāṇa* is no-*nirvāṇa* the lord of existence taught; a knot tied by infinitude and loosed even by the same' (p. 263).

Western interpretations of Mādhyamika

This understanding of *nirvāṇa* was difficult for the classical Indian critics of Mādhyamika to comprehend, and has been not less so for modern Western interpreters. Among the many conflicting interpretations, the French and Belgians, from Burnouf to Poussin, have tended to see a profound and unresolved scepticism, perhaps nihilism, in the final position of Mādhyamika. This has always been the frustration of those, whether Buddhist, Christian or atheist, who are wedded to realist attitudes, in the face of Mādhyamika's denial of being to persons and things. The thinking of the *Prasannapadā* is, of course, overwhelmingly critical and negative; but to overlook the way in which it explains enlightenment as hidden in the very obscuring misconceptions which critical thinking clears away is to miss the subtlety and main thrust of Mādhyamika thought. Still, the nihilistic interpretation forces us to recognize where the main hinge of Mādhyamika is located: namely, at the passage from critical thinking which, like a powerful acid, eats away our stock of everyday beliefs, to an affirmation of the faith which all along was struggling to express itself in the critical thinking.

The greatest Western Mādhyamika interpreters of the early twentieth century were Russian and Polish under the strong philosophical influence of Hegel and Kant. Of the many scholars who devoted themselves to Buddhism the writings of Stanislaw Schayer and T. Stcherbatsky are most easily accessible to us. Schayer translates *svabhāva*, which I render 'self-existence' as *das absolute Sein*, although 'absolute being' is not an idea likely to be at home in Buddhist thinking. He speaks of the 'ultimate totality of existence – the one reality'; thinks Mādhyamika is a 'radical monism'; and holds that the 'presence of the Absolute' is intuited in a mystical act. As a countervailing emphasis to the early nihilist interpretation this had great value, though Schayer continues to use the language of ontology past the point where Mādhyamika enjoins us to put it aside.[24] Stcherbatsky was more Kantian than Hegelian and read the *Prasannapadā*, which he entitles 'A Treatise on Relativity' in terms of phenomena and the thing in itself which underlay them.[25] He thinks *śūnyatā* is the relativity of things but that the universe viewed as a whole is the Absolute; Mādhyamika is an assertion of the absolute whole, it is a radical monism. Stcherbatsky's translation of two chapters of the *Prasannapadā*[26] was an indispensable step in the modern recovery of this ancient school of thought. If one wishes to criticize his interpretation one can point out that it contributes little to our understanding of the relation of a *śūnyatā* philosophy to the Buddhist faith; he does not make clear how 'universal relativism' supports the middle way.

T. R. V. Murti's book *The Central Philosophy of Buddhism* brought Mādhyamika thought squarely into the English-speaking world. Though still somewhat under Hegelian and Kantian influence (and of firm Vedantist conviction) Murti avoids both the nihilist interpretations of Burnouf and Poussin and the ontologizing interpretations of Schayer and Stcherbatsky. He treats the work, focussing more on Nāgārjuna's verses than on Candrakīrti's commentary, as an opus in philosophical dialectics, that is, as a demonstration how each and every philosophical dogma must disintegrate from internal contradiction. Grasping the full implications of this, 'the reflective awareness of the dialectical play of reason', is the fruit of philosophy and leads to an utter clarity of the mind which, as an intuition of the Real, is, though without an object juxtaposed to it, still the Mādhyamika Absolute. Murti repeatedly repudiates a nihilistic interpretation of Nāgārjuna. His work, emphasizing the critical, analytical, sceptical method of Mādhyamika, frees it from the metaphysical interpretations of Schayer and Stcherbatsky and opens the way to an interpretation more in keeping with the problems of Indian philosophy. If there is to be a comment on Murti's book it is that he works from an epistemological model of enlightenment which still leaves the existential grounding of the Buddhist middle way something of a question mark.

A fresh attempt to convert Nāgārjuna into contemporary terms has been made by F. J. Streng,[27] who works with unmistakably religious questions in mind. Streng insists that there is no Absolute in Mādhyamika; *śūnyatā*, which he takes as 'emptiness', stands rather for the openness of the world to personal transformation. *Śūnyatā* is not metaphysics, nor an object of cognition, it is an aid to the removal of human afflictions. The higher truth is not an absolute, it is a power aiding release from the need of an absolute. This emphasis on the soteriological purpose of Mādhyamika thought is, it seems to me, a move in the right direction; I can understand its purpose in no other way. Streng's emphasis, however, does, at times, seem to draw the higher truth down into the ceaseless flux of existence in a way that endangers its status as 'the' Buddhist truth. Dependent origination, understood as the 'flux of existence', becomes, in Streng's account, the primary datum. It is here that my own understanding diverges. Dependent origination is itself *śūnya*, neither in being nor not in being, is, indeed, synonymous with *śūnyatā*, as both Nāgārjuna and Candrakīrti are careful to explain, and so could not serve as a primary datum against which beliefs must test themselves: in Mādhyamika there is and can be no primary datum available to us through concepts.

The middle way

When one feels the full weight of the *Prasannapadā* as a whole, neither singling out Nāgārjuna's pronouncements nor isolating Candrakīrti's comments from them, the impact, so it seems to me, is squarely and crushingly on the idea of being. More times than anyone has counted, the text insists, sometimes quoting early *sūtras*, sometimes later ones, sometimes arguing from the unacceptability of pairs of opposites, sometimes demonstrating the unintelligibility of self-existence, that there is no way of thinking the notion 'is'; and if not 'is' then not 'non-is' either, nor any combination of the two. Being is unintelligible and hence a misguided attempt to grasp the sense of the human predicament (pp. 154–5, 7). Buddha is singled out for praise because he understood this fully. What follows from this is nothing less than the invalidation of all metaphysics or, more sweepingly, of any understanding of life which is based on the notion being. This, nothing less, is the implication of *śūnyatā*. If it is delusive to think being, then it is delusive to believe that one can make cognitive assertions about anything.

How are we then to think the things and ideas and people of the everyday world, if not as existing or not existing? Any suggestion involving cognitive claims has already been ruled out; how then to *say* what the true way of things is? The Mādhyamika answer, and this is one way of stating the heart of their thinking, would, I believe, go like this: The way the enlightened man deals with things, is the way they are, is their truth. If one adheres strictly to the Mādhyamika repudiation of being and so does not attempt to determine the status of chariots and all other nominal entities, either by asserting that a chariot exists (Plato) or that it is merely a name, i.e. does not exist (Berkeley) or that it exists only as an ineffable union of matter and form (Aristotle), what other means of saying anything about things conceivably remain to us? Mādhyamika avoids making cognitive assertions about things by holding[28] that the truth of things is what they mean to the enlightened man; this makes no use of the notion of being; it implies that things become themselves only as they become integral to the way of an enlightened being: the middle way.

The middle way is, in my understanding, the beginning and ending of Mādhyamika thought. It overcomes the finality of being and the meaninglessness of non-being, not by discovering a third mode of 'to be', somehow suspended between being and non-being, but by moving away from this thought wholly. 'Middle' means a way that, although it can be pointed out only by repudiating the pair of opposites, being and non-being, is itself to be understood in a quite other dimension of thought. A way is neither in being nor is it nothing, even though the verb to be is used in talking about it. Language that is not, even implicitly, ontological (and Mādhyamika holds that even ordinary language is only delusively ontological), must be understood in some other way, as exclamatory, or exhortative, or persuasive, or prescriptive, or pragmatic, or some combination of these. In the *Prasannapadā* ordinary language is assumed to be all these things, and enlightened language, whose function is to guide beings to enlightenement, is no less so; in neither use is it cognitive or ontological.

What kind of world do we find ourselves in, if words do not name things in being? Certainly it would be as far from Aristotle's world as is conceivable. One could not know anything in the traditional sense of possessing true beliefs about things in being; nothing could, in honesty, be held to exist as conceived. Such a world, if I grasp Mādhyamika at all, would consist of *seeming* things which in *truth* are not there, though they are most certainly not mere fantasies either. At this point we are very close to the useful limits of language, and indeed Candrakīrti often introduces the analogy of the magician's trick when he must say what takes the place of a world based on things in being. No account can be given of such a world because accounts presuppose things in being. No human can do more than commend a *way* of dealing with seeming things and that is just what the middle way is and what Mādhyamika does. On the middle way, seeming things, while not accepted, are not scorned; delusion is not replaced by a delusion-proof reality. The middle way is possible only in the face of the untiring insistence of seeming things to be taken as real things and is the sovereign, unruffled capacity to see them, respectfully, as doing just that.

Underlying and supporting this middle way of coping with the human predicament is of course the historical fact that Nāgārjuna and Candrakīrti, as Buddhists, were in no doubt that Buddha had lived in the middle way. Buddha's life was all the evidence needed that the middle way of coming to grips with the magician's trick unloosed a universal compassion for all beings suffering in delusion; that, in the middle way, there was freedom from false belief and the promise of human dignity.

So deep and so unaware was this conviction that it takes the place of much explicit argument. Nowhere do Nāgārjuna and Candrakīrti analyse the middle way as I have attempted to do in these few paragraphs.[29] It was not, for them, a *problem*: after all they could *live* it. For us, who are attempting to understand, in twentieth-century terms, what they lived, it must remain a problem of interpretation. That the middle way supersedes philosophical theory and moral exhortation, fusing in itself feeling and will and intellect, is offered here as a contribution to that understanding. This interpretation of Mādhyamika must, I presume, lean a little to one side or the other yet it does so as little as I can make it. The text which follows is the touchstone.

Notes

1 The dates of Candrakīrti and Nāgārjuna are as uncertain as most other dates in earlier Indian history. The specialists are actively debating these matters but we must know much more about the history of Buddhist ideas and their spokesmen before temporal relationships can be clarified closely. I have accepted current estimates without hesitation as details do not affect the philosophic picture. R. Robinson, *Early Mādhyamika in India and China* gives a balanced picture and Karl Potter, *Encyclopedia of Indian Philosophies*, vol. 1, brings together the most plausible estimates. E. Frauwallner, *Die Philosophie*

des Buddhismus is sound and stimulating. The important point is that Nāgārjuna lived in a classical time of philosophical creativity, whereas Candrakīrti, separated from him by four or five centuries of logical and epistemological discovery, belongs to an age of sophisticated commentary.

2 This designation derives from *madhyama* which is the superlative form of *madhya*, 'middle'. Strictly, the philosophy we are dealing with – the 'ism' – is the *madhyamaka*, i.e. 'middlemostism', and a member of the school would be a *mādhyamika*. By commonest (but not universal) usage, however, one refers to the philosophy, the school, and its exponent as *mādhyamika.*

3 Most scholars agree. Winternitz, *Geschichte der Indischen Literatur*, vol. 2, p. 250 thinks the earliest of the great Mahāyāna *sūtras* – the *prajñāpāramitā sūtras* – were composed in the school of Nāgārjuna; and Conze, *Buddhist Thought in India*, p. 203 says that the Mahāyāna phase of Buddhism was in effect almost a new religion. A. K. Warder, on the other hand, has argued that Nāgārjuna was not of this order of importance; cf. 'Was Nāgārjuna a Mahayanist?' in Sprung, ed., *The Problem of Two Truths in Buddhism and Vedānta*.

How Mahāyāna Buddhism *is* related to the earlier movements – the Hīnayāna – is complex and, historically, obscure. For present purposes it is important to remember that early Buddhism spread its wings in the age of the classical Upaniṣads; the *prajñāpāramitā sūtras* and Nāgārjuna had to flourish in the India of the Baghavad Gītā. This might be comparable to the difference between the worlds of Socrates and Augustine. Cf. N. K. Dutt, *Mahayana Buddhism*, Chapter 3; E. Conze, *Buddhist Thought in India*, Part III, Chapter 1. For a different view cf. A. K. Warder, *Indian Buddhism*, pp. 352–72.

4 The history and fate of Mādhyamika is a story in itself. Its influence became felt, in time, from south India through Tibet and Mongolia to China, Korea and Japan. In India two tendencies arose: (1) to present and defend Nāgārjuna's thought through the logical means elaborated in the centuries after his death; the best known spokesman for this tendency – designated the *svātantrika* – was Bhāvaviveka; cf. S. Iida, 'The Nature of Saṁvṛti and the Relationship of Paramārtha to it in Svātantrika-Mādhyamika', in *The Doctrine of Two Truths in Buddhism and Vedānta*, pp. 64–77, and Y. Kajiyama, 'Bhāvaviveka's Prajñāpradīpa' (I. Kapitel) in *Wiener Zeitschrift fur die Kunde Sud und Ostasiens*, Band VII, 1963 and VIII, 1964. (2) Another, and probably dominant, tendency presented Nāgārjuna as the destroyer of metaphysics and epistemology and as the true interpreter of the Buddha's transcendent insight; this tendency acquired the name *prāsaṅgika* and its most uncompromising spokesman was Candrakīrti, the author of the *Prasannapadā*. The swiftest and most interesting summary of the history of Mādhyamika in India is given in T. R. V. Murti, *The Central Philosophy of Buddhism*, pp. 83–103.

5 The assumptions and methods of comparative thought are discussed more fully in 'The Question of Being in Comparative Philosophy' in Mervyn Sprung, ed., *The Question of Being*.

6 Eugène Burnouf, *Introduction à l'histoire du Bouddhisme*, 2nd ed., Maisonneuve, Paris, 1876 (1st edn, 1844).

7 An often, if sometimes loosely, used expression. T. R. V. Murti adopts it as the central notion of his exposition of Mādhyamika (cf. especially *The Central Philosophy of Buddhism*, pp. 121–43); R. Robinson, *Early Mādhyamika in India and China*, pp. 50–8 makes some sober observations.

8 Cf. P. T. Raju, 'The Principle of Four-Cornered Negation in Indian Philosophy', *Review of Metaphysics*, vol. 7, no. 4, June 1954, pp. 694–713; A. Kunst, 'The Concept of the Principle of Excluded Middle in Buddhism', *Rocznik Orientalistyczny*, vol. 21 (1957), pp. 141–7; R. Robinson, 'Some Logical Aspects of

Nagarjuna's System', *Philosophy East and West*, vol. 6, no. 4, January 1957, pp. 291-308.

9 The controversy between the two branches is still being studied by Tibetan (Bhāvaviveka is preserved only in Tibetan) and Sanskrit scholars. Cf. note 4.

10 Cf. B. K. Matilal, 'Negation and the Mādhyamika Dialectic', in *Epistemology, Logic and Grammar in Indian Philosophical Analysis*, pp. 146–67.

11 Cf. p. 160, 'Discerning that the cycle of birth and death springs from holding the view that the person is real, and discerning that the self is the basis of this view that the person is real, the *yogī*, through not taking the self as real, abandons the view that the person is real, and having abandoned this view, discerning that all the basic afflictions come to an end.'

12 Cf. the notion of *prajñapti*, p. 17.

13 R. Robinson examines the relation of Nāgārjuna's *kārikās* and the *prajñāpāramitā sūtras* in *Early Mādhyamika in India and China*, pp. 61–5. An opposite view is A. K. Warder, 'Was Nāgārjuna a Mahayanist?' in Mervyn Sprung, ed., *The Problem of Two Truths in Buddhism and Vedānta.* E. Conze, N. Dutt, M. Winternitz, E. Frauwallner *et al.* agree that there is the most intimate creative relationship between Nāgārjuna's thought and the Buddhism of the *prajñāpāramitā sūtras*. What that relationship is, is a question probing the most difficult areas of philosophical belief and religious thinking – and it remains a question.

14 The standard work on the buddhist concept of *dharma* is T. Stcherbatsky, *The Central Conception of Buddhism.* Legion are the comments on the subject. Cf. A. K. Warder, 'Dharmas and Data', *Journal of Indian Philosophy*, vol. 1, no. 3, November 1971, pp. 272-95.

15 The impossibility of metaphysical theory in Mādhyamika is dealt with in Mervyn Sprung, 'Nietzsche and Nāgārjuna. The Origins and Issue of Scepticism', in *T. R. V. Murti Festschrift*, Dharma Press, Emeryville, Ca., 1977.

16 Self-existence as metaphor or analogy is more fully discussed in Mervyn Sprung, 'The Problem of Being in Mādhyamika Buddhism', in D. Amore, ed., *Modern Studies in Buddhism*, 1977.

17 Cf. M. Heidegger, 'Der Weg zur Sprache' in *Unterwegs zur Sprache*, Neske, Pfullingen, 1960, p. 241. 'Man would not be man if he could not speak "It is".

18 A note on this term would have to become an essay; it is better that the text speak for itself. For some views cf. (1) E. Obermiller, 'A Study of the Twenty Aspects of Śūnyatā', *Indian Historical Quarterly*, vol. 9 (1933), pp. 171–87. (2) E. Obermiller, 'The Term Śūnyatā and its different interpretations', *Greater India Society Journal*, vol. 1 (1934), pp. 123–317. (3) J. May, 'La philosophie bouddhique de la vacuité', *Studia Philosophia*, vol. 18 (1959), pp. 123–317. (4) F. Streng, *Emptiness.* (5) D. T. Suzuki, *On Indian Mahayana Buddhism.*

19 E.g. p. 150; p. 153b; p. 155; p. 201, 18; p. 228–9.

20 E.g. pp. 223–8; pp. 179–80; pp. 232, 11 and commentary.

21 Close to the analogy of magic is that of the reflection in a mirror. Candrakīrti quotes *sūtra* passages in which the reflection analogy is used, but never analyses it further, perhaps for the good reason that it has strong contra-mādhyamika implications. The self and the *tathāgata* are both as insubstantial and delusive as reflections in a mirror; this half of the analogy is acceptable, but not the other half which must account for the source of the reflection. According to Mādhyamika this source cannot have being, but must be mere ignorance. There is more to be drawn out of this analogy than Candrakīrti does.

22 L. Wittgenstein must come to mind here. The striking similarity between some of Wittgenstein's convictions and some of Mādhyamika's has been noted, though usually with reference to Japanese Zen Buddhism. Without doubt a study of Nāgārjuna and Wittgenstein will throw further light on the thought of both.

23 Cf. J. May, *Candrakīrti Prasannapadā Madhyamakavṛtti*, notes 489 and 494; Douglas D. Daye, 'Mādhyamika', in C. S. Prebish, ed., *Buddhism: a Modern Perspective*, pp. 89–93; Mervyn Sprung, 'Non-Cognitive Language in Madhyamika Buddhism', in *Buddhist Thought and Asian Civilization* (Herbert Guenther Festschrift), 1977. Cf. p. 201, 11; p. 168; p. 247, etc.

24 None the less Schayer's 'Einleitung' to his *Ausgewählte Kapitel aus der Prasannapadā*, Krakow, 1931 is one of the most sensitive comments on Mādhyamika we have as yet.

25 Cf. a useful review of recent interpretations by J. W. de Jong, 'Le problème de l'absolu dans l'école Madhyamaka' in *Revue philosophique de la France et de l'etranger*, vol. 140 (1950), pp. 322–7. This paper has been published in English in the *Journal of Indian Philosophy*, vol. 2, no. 1, December 1972, pp. 1–6.

26 *The Conception of Buddhist Nirvāṇa.*

27 *Emptiness.* Cf. the comments of J. W. de Jong on Streng's book in the *Journal of Indian Philosophy*, vol. 2, no. 1, December 1972, pp. 7–15.

28 As I believe. Cf. the last paragraph of this Introduction.

29 This is dealt with at greater length in 'Being and the Middle Way' in Mervyn Sprung, ed., *The Question of Being*, State University of Pennsylvania Press, 1977.

Lucid Exposition of the Middle Way

The Essential Chapters from the *Prasannapadā*

Candrakīrti's Salutation to Nāgārjuna

After making my obeisance to Nāgārjuna,

who was born of the ocean of wisdom of the perfectly enlightened one and who rose above the realm of dualities;

who compassionately brought to light the hidden truth of the treasury of Buddhism in Buddha's sense;

who, by the intensity of his insight, consumes the views of his opponents as though they were fuel, and burns up the darkness in the minds of men;

whose utterances of incomparable wisdom, like a shower of arrows, disperse utterly the adversaries of life;

whose words reign majestically over the three realms of the world and over Buddhists and gods as well;

After making obeisance

I shall expound the verses of his treatise in correct, comprehensible statements, which will be free of vain argument, and lucid.

I

Concern, Method and Assumptions of the Middle Way Philosophy

Origin, subject-matter and ultimate concern of Nāgārjuna's treatise

2.5 The great treatise we are to discuss is the one beginning 'Not of themselves, nor from another, nor from both. . . .'[1]

We have to ask what is the origin, what the subject-matter and what the ultimate concern of this great treatise. In the *Madhyamakāvatāra*[2] it was stated that the wisdom of a perfectly realized one has its origin in an initial vow of dedication issuing from universal compassion and graced with compre-
3 hension going beyond all duality. In this sense Nāgārjuna, knowing unerringly how to teach transcendent insight,[3] developed this treatise out of compassion and for the enlightenment of others. So much can be said about its origin. 'To command the hostile afflictions and to inure against the vicissitudes of life: a genuine treatise has a teaching that is a stronghold. These two qualities are not found in any other treatises.'

Nāgārjuna himself gives us a glimpse of the subject-matter and ultimate concern of the exhaustive treatise we are to discuss. With perfect and unerring clarity, having risen to a lofty height of mind, and desiring to honour, by a treatise, the supreme teacher, the perfectly realized one who is inseparable from the existence and truth of such a lofty height of mind, he says

> Neither perishing nor arising in time, neither terminable nor eternal,
> Neither self-identical nor variant in form, neither coming[4] nor going;

[1] Commencement of the first *kārikā* of Nāgārjuna's treatise. See p. 36.

[2] Another work of Candrakīrti.

[3] *Prajñāpāramitā*, the consummate awareness of the truth of things.

[4] Movement (*gam*) may have two other meanings: (a) attainment, (b) coming to know.

Such is the true way of things,[1] the serene coming to rest of the manifold of named things,
As taught by the perfectly enlightened one whom I honour as the best of all teachers.

The true way of things, as characterized by the eight terms, 'neither perishing nor arising' and so on, is the subject-matter of this treatise.

4 The ultimate concern of the treatise is clearly stated to be *nirvāṇa*: the serene coming to rest of the manifold of all named things (*sarvaprapañcopaśama*).

The salutation is given in the words 'I honour the best of all teachers.'

So much for the meaning of these two verses as a whole. The meaning of each term will now be analysed. 'Perishing' means annihilation, the utter perishing of every moment. 'Arising' means origination, the emergence of self-existent things. 'Terminable' means terminating, the disruption of a series. 'Eternal' means permanent, endurance through all time. 'Self-identical' means to be one thing, to be unspecifiable, to be undifferentiable. 'Variant in form' means to be specifiable, to be differentiable. 'Coming' means the very moving toward, it is the arriving at a proximate place of what was in a remote place. 'Going' is the very moving from, it is the movement to a remote place of what is in a proximate place.

The term pratītyasamutpāda

5 The root *i* means motion; the preposition *prati* means arrival or attainment. But the addition of a preposition alters the meaning of the root. 'A verbal root is forced, by the addition of a preposition, to alter its meaning even as the sweet waters of the Ganges on emptying into the ocean.' So, in this case, the word *pratītya*, as gerund, means 'attained' in the sense of 'dependent' or 'relative'. Again, the verbal root *pad* [to go, to fall] preceded by the preposition *samut* [out of] means to arise or to become manifest. *Samutpāda*, then, has the meaning 'to arise' or 'to become manifest'. The full meaning of the term *pratītyasamutpāda* is therefore the arising, or becoming manifest of things (*bhāva*) in relation to or dependent on causal conditions.

[1] *pratītyasamutpāda.* Traditionally 'dependent origination'. In Nāgārjuna's hands this term comes to mean non-dependent non-origination, that is, the absence of being in things. This verse, which is given again on p. 35, appears to be the dedication of Nāgārjuna's treatise.

5.7 There are others who hold that the term means the arising of things which vanish in the moment. This is bad etymology and cannot explain *all* uses of the term in the *sūtras*[1] and in the *Abhidharma.*[2] Bhāvaviveka[3] attacks both this interpretation and our own. If, he says, 'to be dependent on' or 'to be relative to' means there are two separate things, then there can be no origination, because the one thing must already have arisen before it can be dependent on, or relative to, the second. This, however, is agreed to, and so is no objection to our view. Bhāvaviveka adds that the term *pratītyasamutpāda* consists of two parts because it refers to the conditional statement 'if this exists, that will arise'.[4] This is erroneous: the term has merely two etymological parts. Again, he says the term is a mere conventional expression, a metaphor. But Nāgārjuna insists that the meaning of the entire term 'dependent origination' derives from its parts: 'whatever arises in dependence on something else does not arise in truth'. Bhāvaviveka, however, gives an account which is the same as our own, in saying 'the long exists in dependence on the short, so far as there is the short, relative to the long'. Thus he accepts what he had criticized as false, which does not make sense. But enough of this disputation.

10.11 The illustrious one showed so clearly that things arise in dependence on causal conditions and he rejected the idea that origination could be without cause or from one cause or from a variety of causes, or that things could be produced of themselves, from what is other than themselves or from both. By this rejection the true delusive everyday nature (*sāṁvṛtam svarūpam*) of delusive everyday things (*sāṁvṛtānām padārthānām*) is revealed as it really is. Dependent origination[5] is
11 thus itself delusive because, in the comprehension of the wise man, nothing self-existent arises in it nor is there actual destruction, and by the same token, no actual movement.[6] It is distinguished by the eight characteristics, 'non-perishing' and the others. That the characteristics 'perishing' and so on do not hold for dependent origination, as the way things are

[1] Putatively the discourses of Buddha.

[2] Commentaries and expositions of the early *sūtras.*

[3] An earlier (c. 550 AD?) commentator of Nāgārjuna's treatise. He represents a rival and relentlessly attacked sub-school of Mādhyamika, the *svātantrika* school.

[4] Putative formulation of Buddha. Cf. Kindred Sayings, vol. 2, p. 23, Pali Text Society, Translation Series, Luzac, London, 1952.

[5] In its traditional, causal sense.

[6] Change, attainment.

truly, Nāgārjuna will expound throughout the whole of this treatise.

Though the characteristics of dependent origination, as the way things are truly, are endless, these eight have been chosen primarily for purposes of argumentation. When dependent origination is seen by the wise (*ārya*) as it truly is because the manifold of named things (*prapañca*) – the duality of name and what is named, and so on – has ceased utterly, the manifold of named things comes to rest in it. Nāgārjuna holds that dependent origination is nothing else but the coming to rest of the manifold of named things. When the everyday mind and its contents are no longer active, the subject and object of everyday transactions (*vyavahāra*) having faded out because the turmoil of origination, decay, and death has been left behind completely, that is final beatitude.[1]

That Nāgārjuna's primary intention is to expound the nature of dependent origination as we have characterized it, is indicated by the dedication.

> Neither perishing nor arising in time, neither terminable nor eternal,
> Neither self-identical nor variant in form, neither coming nor going;
> Such is the true way of things, the serene coming to rest of the manifold of named things,
> As taught by the perfectly enlightened one whom I honour as the best of all teachers.

12 Nāgārjuna, through his understanding of dependent origination as we have described it, that is, as the way things are truly, discerned the unerring teaching of the only perfectly realized one; he looked upon all false doctrines as the idle chatter of foolish people and expressed his surpassing reverence by calling the illustrious one 'the best of all teachers'.

In the dedication 'perishing' is repudiated first. This makes it clear that there is no basis for a fixed order of succession between origination and perishing. Nāgārjuna will say later[2] 'If birth came first and old age and death later then birth would be free of old age and death and the deathless would be born.' So it is not a fixed rule that what arises is prior and what perishes is subsequent.

[1] This paragraph anticipates the conclusions reached in the '*Nirvāṇa*' chapter.

[2] XI, 3. Not included in this translation.

The first kārikā

Nāgārjuna will now undertake to expound that dependent origination which is characterized as 'non-perishing' and so on. He takes up, first of all, the repudiation (*pratiṣedha*) of 'arising' knowing that, if it is repudiated, 'perishing' and the other characteristics are more readily repudiated.

When other schools reflect on arising they think of it either as spontaneous, or as from another, or from both, or at random. Nāgārjuna says that all these conceptions are, on reflection, unintelligible (*nopapadyate*).

> 1 No things whatsoever exist, at any time, in any place, having arisen of themselves, from another, from both or without cause.[1]

13 In this *kārikā* 'at any time' means 'ever', the expression 'in any place' means 'anywhere at all', the expression 'whatsoever' is equivalent to 'at all'. The formulation therefore is, 'Not as arisen of themselves do any things at all exist, ever, anywhere at all.' The other three assertions make sense in the same way.

Controversy concerning Mādhyamika method

Someone may object that one asserting 'Things do not arise of themselves (*svataḥ*)' is committed, against his will, to the conclusion 'Things arise from what is other than themselves (*parataḥ*).' One is not so committed, however, because this negation is not intended to imply an affirmation. We will repudiate equally the view that origination is from what is other, and for the same reason for which origination from self is not possible. What that reason is can be ascertained from the *Madhyamakāvatāra*: 'Therefore, if something, of whatever kind, has arisen there can be no point at all in a subsequent birth of this birth: it would be nonsense.'[2]

14 Indeed, Buddhapālita[3] says: 'Things do not arise of themselves because such spontaneous origination would be purposeless and because it entails an absurdity. There would be no purpose in the repeated origination of things which are in

[1] In paraphrase: 'No things whatsoever exist, having arisen spontaneously from self-generation, or from what is other than themselves, from both these sources or at random, from no cause at all.'

[2] VI, 8.

[3] An earlier (c. 500 AD?) commentator on Nāgārjuna's treatise whom Candrakīrti attempts to follow.

existence already. That is, if something exists it would not arise again and yet there would never be a time when it was not arising.'

14.4 Bhāvaviveka has pointed out syllogistic faults in Buddhapālita's statement and demands from him more than an exposure of the untenability of the opponent's argument. But Buddhapālita, in arguing against the Sāṁkhya[1] in this matter is not obliged, as a Mādhyamika, to do this. It is meaningless
16.2 for a Mādhyamika, because he cannot accept his opponent's premises, to propound a self-contained argument (*svatantra anumāna*) from his own point of view (*svataḥ*). As Āryadeva[2] expresses it, 'If one makes no claim that something is, or is not, or is not both, it will take a very long time to refute him.'

And Nāgārjuna says in the *Vigrahavyāvartanī*,[3] 'If I were to advance any thesis whatsoever, that in itself would be a fault; but I advance no thesis and so cannot be faulted.' 'If, through the means of valid knowledge I cognized any object at all, I would affirm or deny its existence; but as I do not do this I
16.10 am not culpable.'

Bhāvaviveka should not, therefore, require Buddhapālita to establish his own argument against the Sāṁkhya claim that the effect pre-existed in the cause and is therefore self-generated.

18.5 But Bhāvaviveka may be saying that though the Mādhyamikas do not establish any thesis by examples and reasons and adduce no self-contained arguments and so are unable to prove the repudiation of spontaneous generation and to show that the adversary's argument is inconclusive on grounds acceptable to both; none the less, in being obliged to show up the internal contradiction in the adversary's argument, they must do this by means of arguments which are themselves free from all faults pertaining to examples, reasons and so on. Buddhapālita, not having adduced arguments free of such errors, stands faulted.

19 This is not the way things are, we reply. Of course anyone making a positive assertion must establish his argument with his adversary and the latter should be persuaded to accept it. But the Mādhyamika brings no reason *against* his adversary; he makes no use of reasons and examples but pursues his own

[1] The oldest of the Indian schools of philosophy; the proponent of the theory of spontaneous generation, i.e. that the effect is contained in the cause.

[2] *Catuḥśataka*, XVI, 24. Āryadeva was an immediate follower of Nāgārjuna.

[3] *The Refutation of Objections*, a logical work of Nāgārjuna, written later than the present treatise. These verses are 29 and 30.

thesis only until the adversary gives up his. He proceeds on assumptions which are not provable claims; he goes so far as to contradict himself and is not capable of convincing his opponent. This is, surely, a clearer refutation that the opponent's own thesis is not adequately established. In such a situation, what would be the purpose of attempting a refuta-
19.7 tion by superior counter-argument?

Even so Buddhapālita's comment could be expressed in a formal argument as, by implication, he gives both an example of self-origination and a reason against it. Whether we take the example of the clay and the pot or the threads and the cloth, he has shown clearly and with good reasons, that the Sāṁkhya position, according to which the effect [pot and cloth] pre-exists in the cause [clay and threads] does not make sense, namely, because, if they really pre-*exist*, there is no sense in their arising a second time.

23.3 The adversary is bound to a conclusion which is perverse by logical necessity (*prasaṅgaviparītena*). We are not so bound because we advance no thesis of our own. It is therefore impossible to invalidate any argument of ours. Our intention is fully satisfied so long as a multitude of logical faults, due to internal contradictions (*prasaṅgaviparīta*), descend on our adversary.

24 How can Buddhapālita, an unerring adherent of Nāgārjuna's thought, possibly conclude anything inadvertently which would give his adversary an opening against him? If one who holds that particular things do not have self-existence exposes the logical faults in the view that they have, how can there be logical inconsequence in an argument which merely exposed logical inconsequence? Words are not like policemen on the prowl: we are not subject to their independence. On the contrary, their truth lies in their efficacy (*śakti*); they take their meaning from the intention of the one using them. It follows that we have merely invalidated our adversary's thesis. We need not accept the antithesis of the logical fault we have exposed.

Nāgārjuna, very especially, merely pointed out logical faults when he was demolishing the thesis of an opponent. For example: 'There is no infinite space prior to the nature of infinite space: if it were prior to its nature it would be, illogically, without a nature.'[1] 'Objects are not perceived apart from matter as their cause; matter as cause is not perceived apart

[1] P. 103, 1.

from objects.'[1] Again, '*Nirvāṇa* is not ontic, for then it would
25 follow that it was characterized by decay and dissolution. For there is no ontic existent not subject to decay and dissolution.'[2]

Bhāvaviveka would say 'Of course these are terse sayings. One must develop the various reasons and consequences of the profound sayings of Nāgārjuna. Why does Budhapālita not develop his formulations in this manner? For it should be the endeavour of commentators to give syllogistic arguments.'

It is not so. Nāgārjuna commented on his own *Vigrahavyāvartanī* without employing syllogistic arguments (*prayogavākya*). Bhāvaviveka is merely exhibiting his skill in the art of dialectics. Though he claims to be a follower of the Mādhyamika school he none the less advances syllogistic arguments which aim to be conclusive (*svatantra*). Mādhyamika is a great impediment for a logician such as he would be. He accumulates fault after fault.

How is that? He has advanced the following syllogistic argu-
26 ment: The contents of the mind (*ādhyātmikāny āyatanāni*) do not, *in higher truth* (*paramārthataḥ*) arise out of themselves, because they exist already, even as pure consciousness does.

But what is the purpose of the qualification 'in higher truth', which he introduces? If he says it is because origination as it is understood in the everyday world cannot be denied, because, if it is, then its transcendence will not be required, as we believe it is, this does not make sense. Even in the everyday world spontaneous origination is not accepted. The *sūtra* says 'A sprout arising from a seed as its cause is not generated from itself nor from what is not itself, nor from both, nor at random; and it does not arise from god, from time, from atoms, from matter nor spontaneously.'[4] And again, 'The sprout of a seed is not the seed itself, being the sprout; nor is it other than the seed; yet it is not the same; it is neither perishable nor eternal, but is of the essence of things.'

And Nāgārjuna will say in this treatise, 'Whatever comes into existence dependent on something else cannot be that very thing; nor can it be wholly other either; therefore it neither perishes completely nor is it eternal.'[5] If Bhāvaviveka says that the qualification 'in higher truth' holds only for the opponent, that does not make sense. We do not accept an opponent's concepts even for the everyday world. As non-

[1] P. 98, 1.
[2] P. 251, 4.
[3] An argument directed against the Sāṁkhya for whom pure consciousness (*puruṣa*) is ever-existing.
[4] Cf. Śíkṣāsamucaya, p. 213.
[5] P. 184, 10.

27 Buddhists lack unerring insight into the nature of the two truths,[1] both should be excluded if the discussion is to proceed successfully. Thus it does not make sense to introduce this qualification when referring to the argument of an opponent.

Nor does the ordinary man understand causality as spontaneous generation and therefore the qualification is useless in his case as well. He does not penetrate into the problems of origination from self or from another, that an effect is produced from a cause, and so on; he understands it simply as it appears to be. Nāgārjuna himself settled the matter in this way. It is clear that this qualification is in every sense utterly pointless.

However, if Bhāvaviveka introduced this distinction so that he would not repudiate origination in the everyday sense, then this would involve two fallacies, that of an argument invalid because its substance is untrue for its proponent, and that of an invalid reason (*hetu*)[2] as the basis of the argument: he does not himself accept the existence of visual perception and the other mental faculties in higher truth. If he objects that there is no fallacy because vision and the other mental faculties are facts in the everyday sense, then for whom is the qualification 'in higher truth' binding. Perhaps he will say that the origination of delusive everyday vision and the other mental faculties is repudiated 'in higher truth' as a way of specifying the kind of repudiation. If that is so he should have expressed himself
28 in this way: 'Visual perceptions and the other contents of the mind do not arise in higher truth.' He did not, however. But even had he, he would still have had an invalid argument because its basis is unacceptable to the opponent: for he accepts vision and the other mental faculties as real entities but does not take them to be pragmatic terms serving everyday purposes (*prajñaptisatā*).[3] So this does not make sense.

28.4 If Bhāvaviveka would reply that all philosophical dispute proceeds in spite of the parties not accepting each other's presuppositions, this will not do. He cannot advance an independent argument about the cause of the faculties of consciousness because just these, he, as a Mādhyamika, knows do not exist.

30 In so far as the explicit intention is to repudiate origination utterly, one must repudiate both entities and their causes whose supposed reality is rooted in mere misbelief (*viparyāsa*).[4]

[1] On the two truths cf. pp. 230 f.
[2] Cf. p. 38, 'because they exist already'.
[3] This is the Mādhyamika view.
[4] i.e. false belief; cf. Chapter XVII.

This repudiation must be unconditional. Misbelief and the absence of misbelief (*aviparyāsa*) are incompatible (*bhinna*). So long as, because of misbelief, one seizes on the unreal as real, even as the victim of an eye defect falsely perceives hairs and other things in front of the eye, how will one in the least way grasp the way things really are? However, so long as, because of the absence of misbelief, the unreal is not reified into the real, even as those with healthy eyes do not see hairs and other things in front of the eye, then how could one in the slightest perceive as real what is non-existent? To do that constitutes the delusive everyday world. Precisely this is the intention of Nāgārjuna's verse: 'If through the means of valid knowledge I cognized any object at all I would affirm or deny its existence; but as I do not do this I am not culpable.'

In this sense, therefore, misbelief and its absence are incompatible. Therefore, as for the wise there can be no misbelief where the absence of misbelief has been established, how could the mental faculties be real entities in the false everyday world? Bhāvaviveka's argument is, thus, faulty because it uses unacceptable assumptions; further, its reason is faulty as it lacks any ground. It does not therefore confute us.

There is no analogy between the existence of the mental faculties and the impermanence of sound. Whereas there is agreement about the general nature of sound and impermanence there is no agreement about the mental faculties between those who hold them to be devoid of self-existence and those who hold them not to be so devoid, either in the everyday sense or in the higher sense. So the two instances are not the same. What has been said about the fallacy of a thesis without substance for its proponent applies equally to the fallacy of adducing 'existence' as the reason in an argument.

31 At times Bhāvaviveka himself falls back on the unfoundedness of all reasons as when he repudiates causality in the ultimate sense. But if reasons are unfounded proof is impossible. It may then be objected that our own arguments are as invalid as those we attack. This is true only if one, like Bhāvaviveka, advances *independent* arguments (*svatantra anumāna*). But we do not construct independent arguments. Our arguments effect the refutation of the claims of our opponents.

34.6 For example, someone claims 'The eye sees what is other than itself.' That will be invalidated solely by an argument which such a one accepts himself. 'You think that the eye does not have the capacity to see itself and it is agreed that this capacity is never separated from the capacity to see what is

not itself', we will urge.[1] 'Therefore whenever there is no seeing of self, there is no seeing of what is not self either, as in the case of a jar. But the eye does not see itself, and therefore it cannot see what is not itself either.' So there is a contradiction between not being able to see itself and seeing what is not itself, like the colour blue and such things. This contradiction is exposed by an argument based solely on the opponent's own presuppositions. Only that much is achieved by our arguments. How can the fault referred to above be turned against our
34.12 thesis? How could it have the same fault?

36 In short, to apply the technicalities of discursive disputation is purposeless. The Buddhas themselves, out of concern for those they were guiding, who were ignorant of logic, made their points in terms of the conventional ideas of these people themselves.

The commentary resumed

Enough of all this. Let us resume our commentary on the main work.[2]

Nor do things arise out of what is other than themselves (*parataḥ*) because such 'other' does not exist. As Nāgārjuna will express it later on, 'The self-existence of things cannot be found in their causes and conditions.'[3] It follows that, because the 'other' does not exist, things cannot arise from what is other than themselves. Further, some passages from the *Madhyamakāvatāra* make it clear that origination from the 'other' has to be repudiated. 'If what is other is entirely dependent on what is other, then fire could give rise to great darkness. Indeed, anything could arise from anything, and perfect otherness amounts to no cause at all.' Buddhapālita elucidates: 'Things do not arise from what is other than themselves, because it would follow that anything would be possible from
36.12 anything.'

Bhāvaviveka attacks this as being a statement which merely exposes the inner contradictions of an opponent's argument, without advancing an independent counter-argument.[4] But we have shown that such a statement is valid and that one does not affirm the opposite of what one denies.

38 Nor are things born from both[5] taken together. The illogicality will apply to both theses taken together, as origination is

[1] Cf. p. 91.
[2] Commenced on p. 36.
[3] Perhaps p. 66, 3d.
[4] i.e. a *prasaṅga* statement; cf. p. 38.
[5] i.e. 'self' and 'other'.

incomprehensible in terms of either. Nāgārjuna will say later on[1] 'Afflicted existence (*duḥkha*) could arise from two causes if it could arise from one cause.'

But things cannot arise without any cause at all. 'If there is no cause, there will be no means nor effect either.'[2] The illogicality of this will be discussed later. The illogicality is further pointed out in such verses as 'If the entire world were devoid of causes nothing at all could be comprehended, it would be precisely like the scent and colour of a lotus in the sky.'[3] Buddhapālita observes, 'Things cannot arise without cause, because that would entail that anything could arise at any time, anywhere.'

38.12 Bhāvaviveka attacks this statement as well for being mere dialectics and because it implies the truth of its opposite. But
39.4 these objections have been dealt with.

39.5 Further, any espousal of God and such ideas is equally unintelligible, because they cannot exist apart from the agreed conceptions used in the theses given by ourselves and our opponents. And so it has been established that there is no origination because it is not possible (*asaṁbhavāt*).[4] The way things are in truth, however, characterized as neither perishing nor arising and so on, has been established.

Some may object: If, in this way, you characterize dependent origination as neither perishing nor arising and so on, what then of the words of Buddha, 'Personal dispositions are dependent on ignorance; if ignorance comes to an end, dispositions come to an end.' Or, 'Personal dispositions are impermanent and belong to something which itself arises and perishes. Having come into being, they cease again; bliss is their qui-
40 escence.' Again, 'Whether perfectly realized ones arise or do not arise, there is one essential truth established for all things. There is one practical rule for the sustenance of beings: the fourfold nourishment. There are two factors which protect the individual: humility and justice.' Again: 'One attains this life (*loka*) coming from another: one attains another life departing from this.' It is clear that Buddha taught dependent origination as characterized by perishability and so on. Does this not contradict your interpretation?

From such passages the characteristics of dependent origination are taken to be 'perishing' and so on.[5]

[1] XII, 9. Not included in this translation.
[2] Cf. pp. 117–18, 4. [3] *Madhyamakāvatara*, VI, 99.
[4] Impossible to conceive.
[5] i.e. the opposite of Nāgārjuna's characterization.

Sūtras *for mankind at large and* sūtras *for the initiates*

41 This is precisely why Nāgārjuna composed this treatise on the middle way; he wanted to demonstrate the proper distinction[1] between those *sūtras* which are for mankind at large (*neyārtha*) and those which are for the initiates (*nītārtha*). The former speak of arising, perishing, and so on, as characteristics of dependent origination; they have no reference to things as they are in themselves (*viṣayasvabhāva*), unsullied because the defect of primal ignorance has been dispelled. They relate, on the contrary, to the knowledge of things as bound by convention and accept the limitations of primal ignorance.

But the illustrious one has spoken of seeing the way things truly are (*tattvadarśana*). 'That, o monks, is the higher truth, it does not pretend to be what it is not, it is *nirvāṇa*. The realm of the compounded is not what it pretends to be and so is unreal' and so on. Again: 'In this world there is neither truth nor absence of untruth. Everything pretends to be what it is not; it is essentially a swindle; it is unreal; it is a conjuring display (*māyā*); it is the babbling of a child.'

A further quotation: 'Things are but a ball of foam; feelings but a bubble; ideas are like a mirage; personal dispositions are the stem of a banana tree; consciousness is but a conjuring display; thus has spoken the sunlike Buddha.'[2]

42 'A monk, seized with vigour, analysing the elements of things day and night, mindful, perfectly gathered and aware, should make his entry into the realm of peace, the realm of bliss where all personal forces are at rest.' 'Because all elements of existence lack an inherent self.' And so on.

For the one who, due to ignorance of the real meaning of Buddha's teaching, is in doubt whether certain passages are mere teaching devices, or speak of the way things really are, as well as for the one who, due to a feeble mind, mistakes a teaching utterance intended for mankind at large for a teaching aimed at wise initiates, for both of these persons who need guidance, Nāgārjuna undertook this treatise. Its purpose is to dispell false opinion and doubt by the use of both reasoning and authority.

[1] The distinction between *neya* and *nīta* is indispensable to Mādhyamika's interpretation of the mass of Buddha statements accepted as canonical. The widespread translation 'provisional' (*neya*) and 'final' (*nīta*) truth cannot hold for Mādhyamika which dispenses with the notion of propositional truth.

[2] 'Saṁyutta Nikaya', *Kindred Sayings*, vol. 3, pp. 120–1.

The reasoning was given in discussing the verse 'Not of themselves, nor from another . . .' and so on. Authority is adduced in verses like these: 'Whatever is not what it pretends to be, that is unreal declared the illustrious one. All things are not what they pretend to be and are therefore unreal.'[1] 'The great sage declared that an absolute beginning is incomprehensible; afflicted existence is without beginning and end: there is
43 no first, no last.'[2] 'In the *Kātyāyanāvavāda Sūtra*, the illustrious one, who comprehends existence and non-existence, repudiated the thoughts "what is, is imperishable", "what is is perishable", or "what is, is both imperishable and perishable".'[3]

And in the *Akṣayamati Sūtra* it is said: 'Which are the *sūtras* for mankind at large and which are for initiates? Those spoken for the sake of entering the path are said to be for mankind at large; those spoken for the sake of attaining the final goal are said to be for initiates. Whichever *sūtras* are concerned primarily with liberation characterized by the absence of being in particular things, by the absence of external objects and bigoted views, of willed action, of birth, origination, existent things, inherent natures, by the absence of individual beings, of personal spirits, of the person and of the self – such *sūtras* are for wise initiates. This, venerable Śāriputra, is called cleaving to the *sūtras* which are for initiates, not to those for mankind at large.'

44 And as the *Samādhirāja Sūtra* has it: 'The one who can single out those *sūtras* which are for the initiates knows the truth of the absence of being as taught by the perfect one; where, however, person, individual, and soul are spoken of, he knows all such terms are for mankind at large.' In this sense Nāgārjuna undertook to demonstrate the falseness of the understanding of dependent origination as arising, perishing, and so on.

Someone may object: 'If the attributes "arising", "perishing" and the others do not hold, and if Nāgārjuna undertook this work with the purpose of demonstrating the falsity of all possible assertions (*sarvadharmānām mṛṣātva*) – whatever is false being non-existent – it follows that there are no bad deeds and, in their absence, no miserable lives. Nor can there be good deeds, and, in their absence, no good lives. But if there is no possibility of differentiating a good life from a bad, there can be no birth-death cycle in the Buddhist sense. And

[1] P. 144, 1.
[2] XI, 1. Not included in this translation.
[3] P. 158, 7.

then there would be no purpose at all in undertaking any deed whatsoever.'

The delusive everyday as the basis of freedom

In reply we urge the essential falsity of things in order to counteract the inveterate commitment of the ordinary man to the reality of his everyday world as 'the' reality. It is definitely not so for the realized wise ones who take nothing at all as either false (*mṛṣā*) or not false (*amṛṣā*). Furthermore, how could there still be soterically relevant deeds or a birth–death cycle for one who has comprehended the falseness of all the putative elements of existence (*dharma*)? Such a one does not seize on any putative element whatsoever either as existing or as not existing.

45 As the illustrious one says in the *Ratnakūta Sūtra*: 'If one searches for the mind, Kāśyapa, one cannot perceive it; what one does not perceive that one cannot take as real; what one does not take as real, that is neither past, future nor present; what is neither past, future nor present, that is not self-existent; what is not self-existent does not arise; what does not arise does not perish', and so on.

Now anyone who is in the grip of misbelief will never comprehend the essential falseness of all putative elements of existence: he persists incorrigibly in the belief that dependent things are self-existent. Being thus incorrigible and being committed to the belief that what is directly given in the form of the putative elements of existence is reality, he carries out actions and he cycles in the birth–death cycle; being rooted in misbelief he will not attain *nirvāṇa*.

How can there be an adequate basis for affliction and freedom therefrom if things are false by their very nature? Just as it is in the case of an apparitional young beauty for those ignorant of her illusory nature, or in the case of a vision evoked by the realized one for those of favourable character.

46 The *sūtra* on the *Discourse with Dṛḍhādhyāśaya* says: 'It is, o son of a noble family, as when one is present at a magical show: one's mind fills with desire on seeing a woman created by the magician; but, embarrassed, one leaves, and, having left, one tries to convince oneself that this magical woman was ugly, perishable, void and without reality', and so on.

And in the *Vinaya*[1] it is told: 'An artisan created a doll in

[1] *Vinaya piṭaka*, a major component of the *tripiṭaka*, the Buddhist canon. It is concerned with the discipline of the community of monks.

the form of a young woman. Though not in reality a young woman it was just like one in appearance. It became the object of true love and desire for a certain painter. Similarly even things which are wholly false can provide, for the unenlightened, an adequate basis for affliction and freedom therefrom.'

47 And in the *Ratnakūta Sūtra* there is a story of the five hundred apostate monks who withdrew from the Buddha's presence. They were taught by two apparitional monks created by the Buddha that their chosen realities – meditational trance, ultimate insight, freedom, and the intuitive vision of freedom – merely hint metaphorically at *nirvāṇa* but are devoid of self-existence and any inherent nature. The two apparitional monks taught them to reject even the idea of ultimate *nirvāṇa*; taught them that one should not brood on ideas about ideas, nor seek knowledge through mere ideas; for one who does becomes enslaved to his ideas. They taught the five hundred that they should attain that state where all knowing by means of ideas has come to an end; that there is nothing beyond the cessation of knowing by means of ideas for a monk to achieve.

49 The apostate monks then returned to the Buddha's presence and the Bodhisattva Subhūti questioned them: 'Wither did you go and whence are you coming?' 'The Buddha's teaching knows no going thither nor coming hither, Subhūti.' 'Who is your teacher?' 'One who was neither born nor will vanish into *nirvāṇa*.' 'And what teaching have you heard?' 'It was neither of bondage nor freedom.' 'Who gave you your discipline?' Subhūti then asked. 'One who has neither body nor mind.' 'What was the course of your discipline?' 'It was neither in the sense of removing ignorance nor of acquiring knowledge.' 'Whose followers are you?' 'His, who did not rest in a personal *nirvāṇa* nor personal enlightenment.' 'Who are your fellow wayfarers?' 'Those who do not course about in all the three worlds.' 'How long must you wait for your final emancipation?' 'Until all creatures of the perfectly realized one are finally emancipated.' 'How do you achieve your goal?' 'By fully comprehending the "I" sense and the "mine" sense.' 'Have, for you, the basic afflictions vanished?' 'Because of the utter dissolution of all the putative elements of existence whatsoever.' 'Have you overpowered Māra, the tempter?' 'By not taking as real the temptation of the factors of personal existence.' 'How do you revere your teacher?' 'Not by overt deed, nor by words, nor by thought.' 'How do you solve the problem of giving?' 'By not taking anything and by not

accepting anything.' 'Have you transcended the birth-death cycle?' 'By holding neither to the naturalist, nor the eternalist view.' 'How do you practice giving?' 'By being utterly free from all grasping.' 'What is the purpose of your faring?' 'The
49.15 purpose of all the creatures of the perfectly realized one.'

50.4 to So it was that the two unreal apparitional monks which
50.5 Buddha created provided the basis for the liberation of five hundred monks.

50.6 And the *Vajramaṇḍadhāraṇī* has it: 'Just as smoke, Mañjuśrī, dependent on a piece of wood, the friction of rubbing and the action of someone's hand, begins to appear and then fire follows, the actual flame however not being based solely in the wood or the rubbing or in the action of the hand; precisely so, Mañjuśrī, do the flames of desire, aversion and illusion arise for the person who is deluded by illusory false beliefs; for these flames are based neither in himself, nor outside of himself, not between the two.

'Again, Mañjuśrī, for what reason is being deluded known as delusion (*moha*)? It is known as delusion because it is de-
50.12 fined as being utterly deluded about all the putative elements of existence whatsoever.'

Then Mañjuśrī explained to the Buddha that he believed the dreams and imaginings of hellish tortures were equally
52.12 illusory. 'And precisely in this sense, illustrious one, did the illustrious Buddhas proclaim their doctrine for beings deluded by the four misbeliefs.[1] In this world there are no women, men, individuals, eternal souls or persons. All such putative realities are erroneous, unreal and confusing; they resemble a
53 conjuring trick or a dream or an apparition or a reflection of the moon in water. Those who have listened to this teaching of the perfectly realized one look on all things as purged of desire and delusion, that is, as without self-existence and free of false appearance. Such meet their death with their spirits
53.5 at home in the infinite; after death they will all enter the realm of perfect *nirvāṇa*.'

54.5 By all this we have established that everyday things, lacking in self-existence and distorted by self-imposed misbeliefs of the unenlightened, are the cause of the basic afflictions. This is the birth-death cycle. How things whose nature it is to be unreal can bring about a purging of the afflictions is explained in the *Madhyamakāvatāra.*

Someone may object: But if things arise neither of them-

[1] Cf. Chapter XVII.

selves nor from another nor from both nor without cause, how can the Buddha's words be understood: 'Personal dispositions are dependent on primal ignorance'? The answer is: That holds for the everyday personal world but not for the way things are in truth.

How is the nature of this everyday world defined? We hold that the everyday world is determined by pure conditionedness, by being utterly conditioned (*pratyayatā matreṇa*). It cannot be established by the four theories of causality because they entail the self-existence of particular things, which is unintelligible.

55 If one accepts everything as utterly conditioned, that is, the reciprocal dependence of cause and effect, then neither of these exists in its own right and the theory of self-existence fails. That is why it is said, 'People argue that afflicted existence arises of itself or from another, or from both or without a cause; but you[1] proclaimed it born of dependence.'

And Nāgārjuna will say,[2] 'An agent subject can be held to exist only on the presupposition of a product, and a product can be held to exist only on the presupposition of an agent subject. We discern no other basis for establishing their existence.' Buddha himself has said precisely the same thing. 'The theory of the elements of existence implies: "if this is, that will arise; because this has arisen, that will arise". Personal dispositions are dependent on primal ignorance, personal consciousness is dependent on personal dispositions and so on.'

The wise are not dependent on the means of cognition

55.11 There are those who will protest: You say that things do not arise from causes. Is this cognitive assertion (*niścaya*) based on some means of knowledge or is it not? If you consider that it is based on knowledge (*pramāṇaja*) you must speak to these points: How many means of knowledge are there? What are their characteristics? What are their distinctive objects? Do they arise spontaneously or from another, from both or without cause? If your cognitive assertion is not based on some means of knowledge this is unintelligible, because knowing something depends on a means of knowledge. Something that is unknown cannot become known except by some means of knowledge. In the absence of any means of knowledge nothing can be known. How then is your own cognitive assertion

[1] Buddha.

[2] P. 123, 12.

possible? It can make no sense to claim 'things do not arise
from causes'. With the same right with which there is the
assertion that things do not truly arise I will maintain that all
56 things do come into existence. Should you, however, *not* hold
the view that all things do not truly arise, then, as there is no
conviction on your own part, your opponent cannot possibly
be persuaded and the composition of this treatise will have
been entirely futile. That all things do exist will not be refuted.

In reply we say that if we Mādhyamikas made any cognitive
assertion at all it would either be based on a means of knowledge or it would not be. But we make no such assertions. How
is that to be understood? In your thinking, where there is a
negative assertion (*aniścaya*) there would have to be a counter
assertion which, with reference to the first, would be positive.
But as we make no negative assertion whatsoever how could
there be a positive thesis which would either contradict or not
contradict it? Because the opposing terms would be meaningless, as are the length and shortness of a donkey's horns. So
57 long as, thus, no cognitive assertion is made, what would the
means of knowledge, which we speculated about so much,
serve to establish? How can they have a correct number, definition and object? How can they arise spontaneously, from
another, from both self and other, or at random? It is not for
us to answer such questions.

If a Mādhyamika does not, in any sense at all, advance cognitive claims, how is your assertion 'things do not arise spontaneously or because of another, or because of both or from no cause at all' to be understood? It has the form of a cognitive claim.

Our reply is that this pronouncement is an assertion for the ordinary man because it is argued solely on a basis which he accepts. But it is not a cognitive assertion for those wise in the Buddhist way.

Is there then no reasoned argument (*upapatti*) for the wise?

How could we say whether there is or there is not? The higher truth, for the wise, is a matter of silence (*tuṣṇīṁbhāva*). How then would everyday language, reasoned or unreasoned, be possible in that realm?

But if the wise ones do not give a reasoned account how will they convey the idea of a higher truth to the ordinary man? The wise do not give a reasoned account of the everyday experience of the ordinary man. Rather, adopting for the sake of enlightening others, and as a means only, what passes for reasoning in the everyday world, they work for the enlighten-

ment of the ordinary man. It is precisely as with impassioned men who, in the grip of misbelief erroneously impute an unreal quality of goodness to the body because they do not perceive that it is in fact impure, and who so suffer torments. In order to dispel their passions, a god, or someone created by a Buddha would disclose the imperfections of the body previously concealed by the idea that it was good saying 'There are hairs on this body and other imperfections.' And they will
58 become free from this erroneously imputed idea of goodness and achieve freedom from the passions.

And so it is in this case. The wise ones do not, in any way, take particular things as having essential natures. But ordinary men, whose thought, because of weak vision, has succumbed to the defect of ignorance, impute an erroneous self-existence to any and all particular things and suffer excessively. The wise ones then discourse with them using only such arguments as ordinary men accept. For example, if someone[1] argues: 'A pot that exists does not arise from clay and the other factors' this is accepted as a basis for argument. Then it can be concluded: 'If a pot exists before it originates, it cannot originate because it is already in existence.' Or if someone[2] argues: 'A sprout cannot be produced from what is totally other, for example, from glowing coals' this is accepted as a basis for argument. But then it can be concluded: 'Neither can it arise from seeds, earth and so on which are usually given as its causes.'[3]

Should someone[4] now say: 'But such origination is immediately given to us in experience', this would not make sense either. The reason is that what is immediately given in experience (*anubhava*) is false, just because it is immediately given in experience (*anubhavatvāt*). It is like the givenness of two moons for one with an optical defect. Consequently it does not make sense to set aside our objection, because 'what is immediately given in experience' must first be justified.[5]

Conclusion

And so the endeavour of this first chapter[6] is to establish that

[1] The Sāṁkhya school. [2] The Vaiśeṣika school.

[3] Because these too are other.

[4] Possibly the Buddhist epistemologist Dignāga.

[5] I.e. presumes what must first be proved; a *petitio principii.*

[6] The first chapter of the *Prasannapadā* probably ended at this point originally, though in its present form it includes Chapters II and III of this translation. Cf. Preface, pp. xiii–xiv.

things do not really arise by opposing the perverse foisting (*adhyāropa*) of an essential nature on things. It will be the endeavour of the remaining chapters to invalidate and reject any and all reifying distinctions (*viśeṣa*) which are foisted on things. All reifying distinctions such as, 'the one in motion', 'space to be traversed' and 'movement' do not obtain and it is the pur-
58.13 pose of the doctrine of 'dependent origination', i.e. the true way of things, to establish this.

II

Attack on the Possibility of Knowledge: Controversy with a Buddhist Epistemologist

58.14 Should someone[1] say 'It is the ordinary man's experience of cognition and its objects which is described in our treatise', we would counter 'But what is the purpose and worth of this description?' If it is rejoined 'Incompetent logicians[2] have ruined the subject by setting up faulty definitions; we have given the correct definitions' this makes no sense either. If
59 incompetent logicians have developed an erroneous description of cognition, clearly this would contradict the experience of the ordinary man and there would be no good purpose in undertaking to correct it. But this is not the case and your undertaking is quite pointless.

Furthermore, Nāgārjuna, in the *Vigrahavyāvartanī* pointed out the following logical difficulty, among others, 'If the attainment of knowledge rests on the valid means of knowledge, by what are these guaranteed?' As you do not refute this objection your 'correct' definitions have no true explanatory power.

In any case, if you assert that there are but two valid means of knowledge (*pramāṇa*),[3] conforming to a self-characterizing particular (*svalakṣaṇa*) and a universal (*sāmānyalakṣaṇa*) respectively, what is the subject which these two characterize? Or does it not exist? If it does, then it is an object of knowledge different from them. What becomes then of the mere duality of the means of knowledge? Again, such a subject might not exist. In that case even the characteristics, lacking a subject

[1] Probably a representative of the school of the Buddhist epistemologist Dignāga (480–540 AD), though the counter-arguments cited could also be those of Bhāvaviveka.

[2] Non-Buddhist logicians of the Nyāya school.

[3] These are in the Dignāga school: (a) *pratyakṣa*: intuitive, unmediated knowledge; (b) *anumāna*: knowledge mediated through concepts, i.e. inference. The first gives access to ultimate reality, *paramātha sat*; the second to the everyday reality, *saṁvṛtisat*: Mādhyamika must fight this view because it makes enlightenment ontological, not the realization of a way.

to characterize, would not exist. What then of the mere duality of the means of knowledge?

The self-characterizing particular

As Nāgārjuna will say: 'A subject of characterization is unintelligible without actual characteristics. If the subject of characterization is not established, characteristics become impossible as well.'[1]

60 It may be rejoined: 'But the characteristic does not characterize something other than itself; rather, if we take the suffix "istic" as the subject of "character" according to the common grammatical rule, then the characteristic characterizes itself.'[2]

Even so it is logically impossible for something to be characterized by itself, because of the difference in meaning between what characterizes and what is characterized, as between means and end. And this is precisely the flaw.

It may be rejoined: 'There is no logical flaw here, because knowledge is itself instrumental and the self-characterizing particular is an integral part of this.' We reply. It is commonly accepted that a self-characterizing particular is the exclusive (*ātmīyam*), unique nature of a thing (*svarūpam*), which it does not have in common with anything else. For example, of earth it is impenetrability, of feeling the immediate experience of an object, of consciousness (*vijñāna*) it is the reflected awareness of objects. It is agreed that by such characteristics these things are characterized. But you, having cast aside the usually accepted meaning of the term, suppose that the subject is itself the means of characterization. Further, if you argue that perceptual consciousness (*vijñāna*) is instrumental, this is saying that the self-characterizing particular is alone object[3] whilst
61 the instrumentality of consciousness is another such self-characterizing particular. In this case, if the unique nature of consciousness is to be instrumental there will have to be an object (*karma*) different from consciousness. And precisely this is the flaw.

The logician may rejoin: 'The impenetrability of earth and the other characteristics – i.e. what consciousness cognizes – are precisely the objects of consciousness and they are not different from the self-characterizing particular.'

This implies that as the self-characterizing particular,

[1] P. 105, 4.
[2] This makes readier sense in Sanskrit than in English.
[3] I.e. subject of characterization.

consciousness, is not an object, there is no object to be cognized. But a self-characterizing particular can be known only as object. The following distinction should therefore be made concerning the double nature of the object of knowledge – the self-characterizing particular and the universal: there is a self-characterizing particular which is an object of knowledge and that is what we call the thing characterized; there is something which is not an object of knowledge[1] and it is said to be characterized by something else. If then this latter is, in turn, to be an object, it will have to be by some means other than itself.[2] So, vainly theorizing that a further act of knowledge will be this means, you incur the fault of an argument lacking a ground.[3]

Unmediated self-awareness

Furthermore, you hold the theory of unmediated self-awareness (*svasaṁvitti*), that is, that objectivity is assured of being integral to the object cognized because cognition is by means of unmediated self-awareness.

The refutation of unmediated self-awareness is given in
62 detail in the *Madhyamakāvatāra*. It does not make sense that one self-characterizing particular should be characterized by another[4] and that in turn be known through unmediated self-awareness. What is more, this last act of consciousness can in no way exist; it cannot be real except as a self-characterizing particular, there being no subject to be characterized; and because characteristics without a subject are unreal. What now of unmediated self-awareness?

To quote from the *Questions of Ratnacūḍa*: 'The Bodhisattva[5] contemplates the mind and enquires into the stream of consciousness asking "whence does consciousness arise". And he thinks: "consciousness arises given an object". Does that mean that the object is one thing and consciousness another? Or are they identical? If the object is one thing and consciousness another there will be a duplication of consciousness. If they are identical how can one perceive consciousness by means of consciousness? But consciousness does not perceive
63 consciousness. The edge of a sword cannot cut its own edge nor can the tip of a finger touch that very tip. In the same way one act of consciousness cannot directly perceive the same act

[1] Consciousness. [2] I.e. by a subsequent act of consciousness.
[3] An argument of infinite regress.
[4] Consciousness as means. [5] An enlightened one.

of consciousness. So it is that for such a one, concerned with what arises in the mind, the mind is impossible to ground, is without beginning or end, is not unchanging, is not uncaused nor unconditioned, is neither identical with itself nor different. He knows and sees the stream of consciousness like a twining creeper, he knows and sees the essential nature of consciousness, the groundlessness of consciousness, the hiddenness of consciousness, the imperceptibleness of consciousness, the absolute uniqueness of consciousness. As he knows and sees it thus, so he knows and sees it as it really is and he does not suppress it. This is the analysis of consciousness as he truly knows it and sees it. This, noble son, is the Bodhisattva's contemplation of consciousness, this is his penetration into thought.'

There is thus no unmediated self-awareness.[1] As there is not, what will be characterized by what?

Character and characteristic

Further, something which is a characteristic (*lakṣaṇam*) must be either different from what it characterizes (*lakṣyam*), or not different. In the first case, as the characteristic is distinct from what is characterized it does not characterize it and is not a characteristic. And as the subject, what is to be characterized,
64 is distinct from the characteristic it will not be characterized and will not be its subject. That is, because the characteristic is distinct from the subject, the subject would be without relation to its characteristics and so, lacking any relation to the characteristics, like a lotus in the sky – would not be their subject.

In the second case the subject and its characteristics are not distinct. Not being separate from its characteristics, as these have become one with it, the subject loses its character of being a subject. The characteristics, not being separate from the subject, as this has become one with them, are not truly characteristics.

It has been put this way: 'If the characteristic is other than the subject, then the subject is without characteristic; but if there is no difference between the two you have obviously declared that neither is real.'[2] And there is no other way of establishing the reality of subject and characteristic except through their essential difference.

[1] If there were, Mādhyamika would have to give up its view that nowhere is an absolute fact vouchsafed us.

[2] One of Nāgārjuna's religious verses, Lokātīta Stava 11.

Nāgārjuna will put it this way:[1] 'How can a pair of things exist at all if they cannot be proved to exist either as identical or as different?'

If, further, one suggests that their reality is inexpressible (*avācyatā*) it cannot be so. What is called the inexpressible exists only where there is no clear knowledge of the difference between reciprocally dependent concepts. Where there is no clear knowledge of the difference it is not possible to define the difference as 'such is a subject', and 'such is a characteristic', and so it is impossible for either of them to exist separately.[2] Therefore the reality of subject and characteristic cannot be established as inexpressible either.

The agent of perception

There is another question. If an act of perception (*jñānam*) is a means, and the object (*viṣaya*) is separate from it, who is the
65 agent? A means and an object are not possible apart from an agent as in the case of an axe used for cutting. If it is supposed that agency resides in consciousness itself (*citta*), that too fails to make sense. Because the intuition of the bare object is due to consciousness whereas the perception of an object with qualities is due to the contents of consciousness (*caitasa*). It is generally accepted that 'the intuition of the object is consciousness; the object's qualities, however, are mental content.'

Where there is one principal function at work then means, agent, and action, each in its own right, are taken as component members according to the actual nature of the function. But in this case there is not one principal function for both pure intuition and perception. Rather, the principal function of pure intuition is singling out the bare object whereas in perception the object is determined by its qualities. Perception cannot be the means nor can consciousness be the agent. This is precisely the logical flaw.

You might argue that, according to scripture, all putative elements of existence are without inherent natures because in no sense is there an agent in them; and yet, though lacking an agent, the transactions of the everyday are quite real. But neither is this so; it does not penetrate the true meaning of the scriptures. This has been explained in the *Madhyamakāvatāra*.

[1] P. 87, 21.
[2] One of the deepest of all Mādhyamika presuppositions.

Everyday predication

66 Again, you might argue that a self-characterizing particular is analogous to 'the body of the statue' or 'the head of Rāhu',[1] where, though there is no attribute that is not of 'body' or of 'head' there is none the less subject and attribute. Even as one says 'the self-characterizing nature of earth' though earth is impossible apart from that nature.[2]

It is not so because the cases are not analogous. A thoughtful man, because of the factual relationship of the words 'body' or 'head' to other existing things, like the words 'mind' or 'hands' will, having in mind their connection, enquire into the object of the words 'body' and 'head' and will ask 'whose body?' 'whose head?' Another man, not concerned with their relationship to other things, using merely verbal qualifications of the statue and Rāhu following common practice, will ignore the concern of the first. This much is understandable. But, as earth and the other elements cannot exist apart from 'impenetrability' and so on, the relationship of a subject and its characteristics does not make sense. If you think that it is not reprehensible to employ qualifying terms as the non-Buddhists do on the assumption of a separate subject, this would not be
67 right. One should not accept for oneself concepts which the non-Buddhists have imagined and which are devoid of sense, because then one is committed as well to accepting their view of the valid means of knowledge and other such ideas.

Perhaps it is like pragmatically useful and tenable ideas (*prajñaptivat*) such as the individual person (*pudgala*)? This analogy is not apposite. It is true that, as part of ordinary discourse, one makes the uncritical attribution, namely that the statue is the possessor of its own possessed body or that Rāhu is the possessor of a possessed head. If you say this comparison does hold because no other thing exists apart from the head and the body, none being directly perceived, it is not so. In ordinary discourse, everyday terms, which on being critically examined cease to be effective, function uncritically. A personal self (*ātman*), for example, cannot, critically speaking, possibly exist separate from a body and the other factors of personal existence, even though in the world of the ordinary man it exists unrelated to such factors. But this case is not apposite to Rāhu and the statue.

[1] A legendary Indian demon who consists only of a head.

[2] I.e. the difficulty with the expression 'self-characterizing' is merely an awkward verbal habit.

Definition of the everyday

Thus, if, after critical analysis, there is no subject separate from impenetrability and the other characteristics of earth and from the characteristics of the other elements as well, and equally no characteristic without a basis and separate from a subject, this is then precisely what we call the 'false everyday world' (*saṁvṛti*). By virtue of the reciprocal dependence (*parasparāpekṣā*) of these two concepts[1] Nāgārjuna has rigorously established the nature of the false everyday world. And
68 it is essential to understand it in this way; because otherwise the false everyday world could not be distinguished from what makes sense (*upapatti*); and it itself would be the way things really are (*tattvam*) and not the false everyday world. It is not only the bodies of statues and such things which, on being critically examined are not in reason possible; rather, it will be argued later on, body, feelings and the other factors of personal existence are not, in reason, possible either. Then is it to be accepted that they, like the body of a statue and so on, are non-existent in the false everyday world? Not at all; that would be wholly false.

You may interject: Are we not just splitting hairs? We are certainly not declaring the entirety of transactional experience based on knowing and objects of knowledge to be true; it is rather that our argument establishes what the ordinary man accepts as true.

We reply that we too would say: Why this hairsplitting? The investigation concerns the experience of the ordinary man. Let it be; it is the false everyday world; it exists only in virtue of an unfounded belief in the reality of a personal self,
69 which is a pure misbelief. It is the condition for the maturation of favourable qualities leading to liberation in those pursuing it, so long as there is no realization of the true nature of things (*tattvam*). But you destroy this false everyday world by your wrong-headed understanding of the distinction between it and the higher truth (*paramārthasatyam*); you introduce inappropriate arguments.

I, being able to determine the true nature of the false everyday world, base myself on the viewpoint of the ordinary man. I refute one argument designed to invalidate the everyday world by matching it with another argument; like an old authority I refute you specifically when you go astray, using

[1] Subject and attribute. This is the topic of Chapter VII.

what is accepted by ordinary people. But I do not reject the everyday world. And so, if we take the experience of ordinary people, there will have to be something possessing characteristics as their subject, as well as the characteristics themselves. This is precisely the flaw in your argument. However, as in the higher truth there is no subject to be characterized, your dual definition falls away. How then can there be a duality of the means of knowledge?[1]

Furthermore you do not accept the traditional explanation of sentences as containing a connection between an action and its circumstances. That is indeed unfortunate. You yourself use sentences which express a real connection between action and circumstances, but you do not think that the meaning of a sentence consists of action, means, and so on. It is too bad that all this is based on nothing but your idiosyncratic views.

So long as, in this way, the dual nature of what is known – the universal and the particular – is not objectively established, there will be other means of knowledge such as knowledge from authority.

The unintelligibility of perception

And now a different matter. Your theory[2] does not make sense because your definition is too narrow. It does not comprehend such expressions of ordinary speech as 'there is a perception of a jar', and the speech of the unenlightened must be accepted as a base.

You may reply that blue and such qualities are perceptions which are the basis of the jar, because they are what perception, the means of knowledge, singles out. So, just as it is commonly said 'the birth of a Buddha is a happy event' where the cause is spoken of as the effect, similarly, though the jar is caused by the perception blue and such qualities, it is commonly said there is a perception of a jar where the effect is spoken of as the cause.

To speak thus of objects like jars does not make sense. Everyone experiences birth to be different from happiness. It is precisely unhappiness, the nature of temporal things being

[1] The controversy is too involved for footnote commentary; but it is clear that Candrakīrti must contest *any* theory of the everyday which claims to be true, because that would preclude his own understanding of the world as a rationally impenetrable magical play.

[2] Of the self-characterizing particular, the ultimate simple, as the object of perception.

what it is, and the sources of trouble being many and various. To maintain 'birth is happy' is indeed illogical, but, in this case, it makes sense as a figure of speech. But when one says 'there is a perception of a jar' there is no unperceived jar, experienced in some private way, of which one could say, in a figure of speech, that it was perceived.

If you say that, because there is no jar apart from colour and the other qualities, its being perceived is a figure of speech, such a figure of speech makes even less sense. There is no basis for it: one cannot speak 'metaphorically' of the sharpness of a donkey's horns.

Further, if it is agreed that the jar which is imbedded in
everyday verbal transactions does not exist apart from colour
and so on, its perception must be taken to be 'metaphorical'
(*upacārika*). And if this is so, then colour and the other qualities do not exist apart from earth and the other elements and
their perception must be taken to be metaphorical as well.
71 To quote, 'Even as a jar does not exist apart from form and so
on, so form does not exist apart from wind and the other
elements.'[1]

And so your definition is inadequate because you fail to grasp the nature of these everyday verbal transactions. From the point of view of the true nature of things (*tattvavid*) one cannot concede the perception of blue and such qualities or of jars and such things. In terms of the false everyday world, however, we have to accept the perception of jars and such things.

To quote from the *Catuḥśataka*, 'Who, knowing the true nature of things, could say "the jar is perceived" or "an unperceived jar is created from all perceived qualities"? By the same reasoning all such qualities as the fragrant, the sweet and the soft must be repudiated by the sovereign mind.'[2]

Or, further, the term perception means what is not mediated
(*aparokṣa*); what is immediately present is a perception. Jars
and colours and so on are accepted as unmediated perceptions
because it is agreed that they are immediately present to the
72 senses in particular instances. The act of knowledge distinct
from the object is considered to be perception as well, being
the cause of what is perceived even as we say 'a straw fire' or
'a chaff fire'.[3]

There is one[4] who explains the term perception as meaning

[1] *Catuḥśataka*, XIV, 14. [2] XIII, 1, 2.

[3] I.e. the straw or chaff is the cause of the fire but is the term which designates the effect.

[4] Praśastapāda of the Vaiśeṣika School.

'what is real for its corresponding sense'. This derivation is not intelligible because the senses are not the objects of perception, but sense objects are. 'Sense perception' would have to become 'object perception' or 'thing perception'.

Again it might be said[1] that the functioning of the act of perception depends on both factors. Perceptions are *named*, however, solely with reference to the sense organ because the degree of their acuteness conforms to changes in the sense organ. For example, we say 'visual perception'. Thus, although perception functions with reference to a specific object, none the less it is based on a specific sense organ. Because it is named with reference to this base it becomes 'sense perception'. Names customarily designate the specific base of anything: we say 'the sound of a drum' or 'a sprout of barley'.

These examples do not hold for the argument given. Because, according to it, if the type of perception were designated according to its object, we would say 'colour perception', and so on. The differences between the six kinds of perception,[2] however, could not be made clear in this way because the sixth sense, inner perception, functions with precisely the same
73 objects as does vision and the other five kinds of perception. That is, if there are six kinds of perception – that of colour and the others – and perceptions arise in strict dependence on the sense faculties, how can a perception, arising from one of the external senses be a mental or inner perception? If, however, the designation is according to the sense faculty, then the objects of vision and the other sense faculties can be the objects of mental or inner perception as well and the mutual differences would be clear.

In your[3] argument, however, which is concerned with a definition of the valid means of knowledge, you presume that perception is merely that from which the elaboration of thought is removed (*kalpanāpodha*) because you conceive of it in distinction from thought construction. You see no purpose in designating it by its special causes. As the actual number of the means of knowledge depends on the number of the kinds of objects of knowledge, and as the essential nature of the two means of knowledge has been determined exclusively by their conformity to the nature and reality of the objects of knowledge, nothing is served by designating them according to the

[1] A Buddhist view. Cf. *Abhidharmakoṣa*, I, 45.

[2] Or, types of consciousness: the five external kinds and perception of the contents of consciousness which is the sixth sense.

[3] The Buddhist logician.

faculty involved; the designation solely in terms of the object is, in every respect, the cogent one.

You may say that the designation rests solely on the faculty
because in the everyday world the term sense-perception is
74 accepted and object-perception is not, even if we mean object-
perception. It is true that the term sense-perception is commonly accepted but we alone use it as the ordinary man understands it. By distorting everyday things as they actually are,
the explanation you offer accepts a distortion of what is
'commonly accepted'; that is, there is no commonly accepted
sense-perception in your sense. A single visual perception
based momentarily on a single sense faculty would not be perception: it would lack an adequately wide sense; and what is
not perception in a single instance cannot be in many instances.

Your supposition is that perception is only that act of knowledge which is free of the elaboration of thought but this does not appear in the experience of the ordinary man at all although your concern is to give an account of knowledge and its objects in the experience of the ordinary man. This theory of perception as a means of knowledge turns out to be wholly futile.

You may quote the traditional text: 'A man had a visual
perception, blue, though he does not know "it is blue".' But
this scriptural pronouncement is not relevant to a definition
75 of sense perception; it is explaining that the five kinds of sense-
perception are inert. Nor do the traditional texts say that sense-
perception is limited to perception which is free of the
elaboration of thought; that would not make sense.

The Mādhyamika conclusion

It follows that in the everyday world (*loka*), everything, whether the subject of characterization (*lakṣya*), the self-characterizing particular or a general characteristic is unmediated because directly perceived. Sense perception is therefore defined as an object together with the act of knowledge. For cognition which is free of defect there is no perception of two moons; but for defective cognition the two moons are precisely 'sense-perception'.

An act of knowledge whose object is not directly given is an inference. It derives from a distinguishing characteristic which is unfailingly concomitant with what is to be inferred. The pronouncements of those especially gifted in the direct perception of matters beyond the senses constitute authority. Knowledge of something never experienced, like a gayal, because it resembles what we have experienced, a buffalo, is called knowledge by analogy. 'And so the attainment of knowledge by the ordinary man is defined in terms of the four means of knowledge.'[1]

Both means and object of knowledge however are established in reciprocal dependence: in so far as there are means of knowledge there are objects of knowledge; in so far as there are objects of knowledge there are means of knowledge. But most emphatically neither the means of knowledge nor their objects can be established as existing in themselves. The everyday world should be accepted exactly as it appears to be.[2]

Enough of these logical arguments. We will now give an account of the main subject-matter. The teaching of the truth by the illustrious Buddhas was based on the way the ordinary man regards things.

[1] Candrakīrti thus accepts four means of knowing, as Indian realists of the Nyāya school do.

[2] Again Mādhyamika repudiates any *theory* which would offer another reality in place of the everyday.

III

Enquiry into Conditions

Refutation of origination

76 At this point fellow Buddhists interject: 'You said that things do not arise of themselves and that makes sense because spontaneous origination is meaningless. That they do not arise both from themselves and from another makes sense too, because one of the terms has been invalidated. And it is right to repudiate the wholly absurd view that things arise without cause. But when you say "nor do things arise from what is other than themselves" that does not make sense. The illustrious one taught that things are caused by what is other than themselves.'

> 2 Four only are the conditions of arising: cause, objective basis, the immediately preceding condition, and the decisive factor; there is no fifth condition.[1]

77 Here cause (*hetu*) is taken to mean the actualizing factor; that which is determined as what actualizes something else is the causal condition (*hetupratyaya*). When a particular mind content (*dharma*) arises, it arises with reference to an object (*ālambana*) and that is its objective basis. The extinction of the immediately preceding factor (*anantara*) – the cause – is the condition for the arising of the effect; for example, the immediately preceding extinction of the seed is the condition for the arising of the sprout. The decisive factor (*adhipateya*) is the factor because of whose existence something else will come to be.

These are the four conditions of arising. Such factors as prior, simultaneous or subsequent origination are included in them. Conditions such as 'god' in no way exist. Hence the restriction 'there is no fifth condition'. It follows that things do arise from other existing things: this is called 'arising from another'.

[1] This puts a Buddhist opponent's view.

In reply we say that nothing whatsoever arises from conditions which are other than itself.

78 3 If there are conditions, things are not self-existent; if there is no self-existence there is no other-existence.[1]

If, in any way, things which arise as effects and which are other than their conditions truly pre-existed in them, either in all collectively or in each singly, or both together, or indeed elsewhere, then the effect would arise from them. But something cannot, in this sense, exist prior to its arising. If it could, it would be observed, and its arising would be purposeless. Hence if there are conditions of arising, there is no self-existence of things. But if there is no self-existence there is no other-existence (*parabhāva*). Coming into existence is to exist, which is to arise. To arise from what is other is to exist in dependence on the other. But there is no such thing. So it does not make sense to say that things arise from what is other than themselves.

Or again it might be argued that things caused, like sprouts, do not exist as such in their causes – seeds or whatever it is; their nature is to transform themselves; otherwise it would follow that there was no cause at all.

What is this relation of 'otherness' (*paratva*) of conditions? If Maitra and his fellow worker co-exist, their reciprocal relationship is 'otherness'. But there is no such co-existence of seed and sprout. So, as effects are not in fact self-existent, the seeds and so on cannot exist as other, i.e., there is no 'otherness'. As the very term 'other' does not hold, there can be no arising from an 'other'. This is sheer ignorance of the meaning of the scriptures. The fully realized ones could never utter pronouncements contrary to sense. The intent of the scriptures was explained earlier.

Refutation of origination from generative force

79 The proponent of origination from conditions is thus disposed of. There is a proponent of origination from generative force (*kriyā*). Vision, colour, and the other conditions do not generate visual consciousness[2] directly, but are called conditions because they give rise to the force which generates perceptual consciousness. It is this force which generates the perception (*vijñāna*). Therefore this force generating the perception inheres

[1] *Parabhāva*, existence-as-other, or existence-in-dependence-on-other.
[2] i.e., the sensation or perception as mental content.

in the conditions; the conditions do not give rise to perceptual consciousness. It is like the force which cooks rice.

Nāgārjuna says

4a Force is not inherent in conditions

If there were any such force it would, being inherent in the conditions, generate perceptual consciousness by means of the eye and the other conditions. But it is not so. Why? Should this force be supposed after the perception exists, or before it exists or even as it is generated? To suppose it after the perception exists makes no sense because a force produces something real. If something has been produced what need would it have of a force? This has been made clear in the *Madhyamakāvatāra* in such passages: 'A second birth of what is already born makes no sense.'

Supposing a force before the perception exists makes no sense either. To quote the *Madhyamakāvatāra* again: 'Generation cannot, intelligibly, take concrete form in the absence of
80 an agent.' Nor is force possible which is born simultaneously with the generation of the perception because there can be no generation independently of what is generated or not generated.

As has been said: 'What is being generated is not generated, because it is only half generated; else it follows that absolutely everything is in the state of being generated.' As, thus, a generative force is not possible in past, present or future it follows that such does not exist. That is why Nāgārjuna says: 'Force is not inherent in conditions.' In the *Madhyamakāvatāra* it is explained 'There can be no characterization without something characterized.' The son of a barren woman cannot be said to possess a cow.

It makes no sense either, Nāgārjuna says, that generative force is not inherent in conditions.

4b Nor is generative force not inherent in conditions.

If generative force is not inherent in conditions, how could it exist as non-inherent, for it would be non-causal? How could it be supposed to be sensible that if cloth is not inherent in threads it is inherent in coarse grass? It follows that generative force does not generate things. If someone objects: 'If it is impossible that causation stems from generative force, then conditions themselves will generate things', Nāgārjuna continues:

4c There are no conditions without generative force.

If there is no force then conditions will lack generative force, will have no inherent force, will be non-causal. How will they give birth to anything? But as they give birth to something they do possess generative force.

Nāgārjuna concludes:

81 4d But conditions have no generative force.

The negation derives from the *kārikā* as a whole; the word 'but' adds emphasis. The meaning is that generative forces do not exist. How can there be generative forces in conditions? As it was claimed that there is a force generating perceptual consciousness, so should similar forces be understood. There is no origination of things from forces. The very term 'arising' is devoid of meaning.

Refutation of conditions

Someone may object: What is the point of this discussion concerning conditions having inherent force? After all some things, such as perceptual consciousness, arise in dependence on other things, such as the eye, as their conditions. Therefore the eye and so on are 'conditions' because perceptual consciousness arises from them.

Nāgārjuna says that this makes no sense either:

5 Let those things, dependent on which something arises, be conditions; how will such things not be non-conditions so long as nothing arises?

If perceptual consciousness arises dependent on the eye, colour and so on as conditions, then these are said to be its conditions. But surely as long as what is called the perception – the 'effect' – has not arisen, the eye, colour and so on cannot fail to be non-conditions? The meaning is that they are non-conditions. There can be no arising from non-conditions, even as sesame oil cannot arise from grains of sand.

82 Again there might be this thought: What are at one time non-conditions become causally effective through relationship to some other condition. But this makes no sense either. The very condition which is other than the non-condition but is supposed to be its causal efficacy will itself be a cause only if it really is causally efficacious. In this case precisely the same consideration arises as before, and it does not make sense.

If, in this example, the eye, colour and so on are conceived as the conditions of perceptual consciousness, they must be conceived as the conditions of either an existing or of a non-existing perception. But Nāgārjuna says there is no way in which either can make sense.

6 A condition[1] either of what exists or of what does not exist makes no sense:

And so he says:

6 How could there be a condition of the non-existent and how can 'condition' apply to what exists?

If something is non-existent, how can there be a condition of what factually is not? If some future existent is meant, something that will be, this won't do. 'One may refer to a future something, but it cannot be created without a present force.'[2] This logical flaw has been dealt with previously. If something is factually existent, already produced, the idea of its condition is simply pointless.

Refutation of the four special conditions

83 Having, in this way, shown that conditions in general are inefficacious because of their inability to give rise to effects, Nāgārjuna goes on to show the inefficacy of the types of conditions one by one.

Someone may object: Even though, in this sense, conditions are impossible, none the less, because its definition can be given, the idea of condition is commonly accepted. For example, the definition of condition as cause (*hetu*)[3] is that it brings forth something. But to give the definition of something non-existent, like the son of a barren woman, does not make sense.

We reply: There would be condition as cause if it had a definable nature (*lakṣaṇam*). So:

7 As no putative element of existence, whether existent, non-existent or both is brought forth, how can it make sense that a cause brings something forth?

Here 'to bring forth' means to produce. If the element of existence (*dharma*) which is to be brought forth were really

[1] *Pratyaya.* In this passage one would think 'cause' in English.
[2] *Madhyamakāvatāra*, VI, 58.
[3] This is the first of the four kinds of condition given in *Kārikā* 2, p. 65.

brought forth the producing cause would 'produce' it. But it does not come forth: nothing, whether existent, non-existent or both, is brought forth. Nothing existent is brought forth, because it is in existence; nothing non-existent is brought forth because it is not in existence; nor anything both existent and non-existent, because no one thing has mutually contradictory attributes and because of the faults of each view already given. So, as no effect is produced, there is in consequence no cause. Therefore the claim that cause must be factual because its definition can be given does not make sense.

Now, with a view to refuting condition as the objective basis (*ālambana*) Nāgārjuna says:

84 8 An existing mental content is, as such, held to be without an objective basis. If it exists without an objective basis, why would there be an objective basis subsequently?

Which mental contents (*dharma*) are held to be dependent on an objective basis?[1] According to scripture all the contents of consciousness (*cittacaitta*) are. Whatever objective cause – colour or other sense object – produces the contents of consciousness that is their objective basis. It must be thought of as the cause of either existing or of non-existing mental content. In the first case there need be no objective cause of mental contents which exist; indeed the objective cause is conceived in order to explain the arising of mental content; this exists in fact prior to there being an objective cause. The contents of consciousness being thus established as independent and without objective cause, why would a connection with an objective cause be supposed? Consciousness and its contents exist factually without objective causes. To say they have objective causes is the merest caprice, for there is no connection whatsoever between them and objective causes.[2]

Second, an objective cause of a non-existing content of consciousness is imagined, which makes equally little sense. 'Mental content is, as such, without an objective basis', as the *kārikā* says. There can be no conjunction of non-existing mental content with an objective cause.

85 'An existing mental content is, as such, held to be *without* an objective basis.' Our opponent would have to substitute the phrase '*with* objective basis'. 'If a mental content exists without an objective basis, why would there be an objective basis

[1] In the opponent's view.

[2] The Mādhyamika view is rather that objective cause and mental content are interdependent and singly unintelligible.

subsequently?' This is a question which gives the explanation. The meaning then becomes: If, thus, a mental content is without an objective basis, it is factually non-existent; how can it then have an objective cause? The thought is that because what justifies the objective cause does not exist, the objective cause itself cannot exist.

But in what sense do the contents of consciousness have objective causes? This is a characterization which holds for the delusive everyday world, but not for the higher truth; so it is not to be faulted.

And now Nāgārjuna refutes the idea of condition as the 'immediately preceding condition'.

86 9 The coming to an end of elements of existence which have never arisen is not logically possible. Hence the immediately preceding condition makes no sense: how could what has come to an end be a condition indeed?

In the last sentence of this *kārikā* the two halves should be transposed; and the word 'indeed' should precede 'come to an end'. The sentence would then be, 'If something has indeed come to an end, how can it be a condition? The immediately preceding condition makes no sense.' It was put the other way for the purposes of verse structure.

In this argument the definition of the immediately preceding condition (*anantara*) is this: the immediately preceding cessation of the cause is the condition of the effect arising.[1] This should be examined. If elements of existence in the form of effects, for example a sprout, do not in fact arise, it is not logically possible that their 'cause', for example a seed, could cease to exist. There being, in this way, no cessation of a cause, what could be the immediately preceding condition of the sprout? Perhaps it is held that the seed ceases to exist before the effect arises. If this is so, when the seed has ceased to exist, is non-existent, what will be the cause of the sprout? Or what will be the cause of the extinction of the seed? Both are without cause; as Nāgārjuna put it: 'If something has indeed come to an end how will it be a condition?' The word 'indeed' refers back to the phrase 'which have never arisen'. It follows that if the sprout does not come into existence because the seed and the other factors are considered to have

[1] Existence is conceived as a series of discrete moments, each perishing before the next arises, yet each being, as it were, the material cause of its successor.

ceased to exist, it must be that both[1] are without cause. The 'immediately preceding condition' does not make sense.

Or it might be that Nāgārjuna had in mind the general rejection of causation of the first *kārikā*[2] when he said, 'The coming to an end of elements of existence which have never arisen is not logically possible. Hence the immediately preceding condition makes no sense.' The remaining part: 'How could what has come to an end be a cause indeed?' can be explained exactly as before.

And now Nāgārjuna, with a view to refuting, independently, the idea of condition as 'decisive factor' says:

> 10 Things lacking in self-existence are never real; therefore the principle[3] 'this being, that becomes' is not intelligible in any way.

87 The definition of condition as 'decisive factor' (*adhipateyam*) assumed here is this: a factor which, on being present, something arises, is the decisive factor of the latter. But as nothing is self-existent, all things arising in mutual dependence, how can the 'this' be represented as a cause (*kāraṇatva*)? And how can the 'that' be represented as an effect (*kāryatva*)? So, though 'decisive factor' is defined, it has not been established.

Final repudiation of condition, origination and effect

Someone may object: Having seen that cloth and such things are made of threads and so on it is said that threads are the condition of the cloth. We reply: But cloth and such things do not emerge truly as self-existent effects; how will the causal efficacy (*pratyayatva*) of conditions be established?

In what sense there is no emergence of cloth and such things as effects Nāgārjuna expounds in this way:

> 11 The effect is not in its conditions, either singly or collectively; how could something which was not in conditions emerge from them?

In this case the cloth does not exist in any of the conditions taken singly, i.e. in the threads, the weaver's brush, the loom, the shuttle, the pins and so on, because it is not perceived in them and because from multiple causes, multiple effects would

[1] I.e. the extinction of the seed and the arisal of the sprout.

[2] P. 36.

[3] The earliest formulation of the Buddhist conception of 'causality'; it is attributed to the Buddha. Cf. p. 34, note 1.

follow. Nor does the cloth exist in the threads and the other conditions taken collectively. As the effect as such is not present in any part, it would have to arise part by part. It follows from the absence of a self-existent effect that there can be no self-existent conditions.

12ab If an effect which does not even exist can issue forth from its conditions

88 This would be the opinion of our opponent.

12cd Why should an effect not issue forth from non-conditions?

An effect cannot pre-exist in non-conditions either. Therefore cloth cannot issue forth from straw and other such non-conditions. No self-existent effect ever arises.

You may object: If the effect (*phala*) were one thing and its conditions quite another then the question whether the effect pre-exists in its conditions or not would be understandable. But the effect is not distinct from its conditions. On the contrary it is the conditions themselves.

Nārgārjuna replies:

13 If the effect consists of its conditions then the conditions are not, strictly speaking, conditions; if the effect arises from conditions which are not strictly conditions, how can it consist of conditions?

It does not make sense to say that an effect consists of its conditions or is a mode of them, because these very conditions are not, strictly, conditions. That they are not self-existent conditions is what is meant. The opponent thinks that cloth
89 consists only of threads. Cloth would consist only of threads if self-existent threads themselves were real. But they consist of small parts, are modifications of small parts; they are not real as self-existent. So, as the effect, which has the name 'cloth', arises from these small parts which have no self-nature and are not self-existent, how can it consist of threads?

It has been said: 'Cloth is supposed to be realized from a cause and this cause from another cause; but how can what is not realized in its own right be the cause of something else?'

14a Therefore not as its conditions themselves. . . .

does an effect exist. If we assume, on the contrary, that it is its non-conditions:

14b Nor does an effect exist as its non-conditions.

If cloth does not consist of threads, how could it consist of straw?

Our opponent objects: There may be no effect as such but there is in fact an inherent regularity (*niyama*) in both conditions and non-conditions. You say: 'If a non-existent effect can issue from its conditions why should it not equally well issue from its non-conditions?' But, if the effect – whether cloth or straw mat – did not exist, it would not make sense that the conditions – threads or straw – should be causally effective. Therefore the effect too is real.[1]

We reply. The effect would exist if conditions and non-conditions existed. If the effect existed we could say such are its conditions and such are its non-conditions. After thorough investigation, however, that is not the case.

14cd As the effect is non-existent, how could there be either conditions or non-conditions?

90 The point is the same for conditions and non-conditions.

The conclusion is that things do not arise as entities having their being in themselves (*svabhāvataḥ*).

As is said in the *Ratnākara Sūtra*: 'One who lives the absence of being does not exist as a fact, like the flight of a bird through the air; what in no wise possesses self-existence will never be a cause of something else.

'What does not possess self-existence, how can it, lacking self-existence, be caused by anything else? How can what is lacking in self-existence give birth to anything else? Such is the nature of cause as taught by Buddha.

'All the elements of existence are by nature immovable, not variable, beyond affect and blissful; they are imperceptible like a flight path in the sky and the unenlightened misconceive them.

'As the rocky mountains are immovable so are the elements of existence immovable. They do not pass away nor do they arise: in this way has the victorious Buddha taught the truth.'

91 And from another source, 'The truth of things as revealed by the victorious one, the lion among men, is neither born nor does it arise, it does not decay, it does not die. In it are merged all living beings.

'What is not self-existent in any sense, cannot attain other-existence either from within or from without, the lord is

[1] I.e. certain 'conditions' are in fact connected with certain 'effects'.

realized everywhere. Buddha has revealed the way of being at peace though no definable way has been attained; there you will walk what is called the way of liberation. Yourself free, you will free many other beings.'

IV

Motion and Rest

92 One may interject that, although, by denying origination as an attribute of the true way of things, it is established that neither perishing nor any of the other attributes hold for the true way of things, still, in order to prove that neither coming nor going hold of the true way of things,[1] what additional arguments can you offer for denying to and fro movement as this is commonly understood?

Denial of past, future and present movement

We reply that, if there were something called movement (*gamana*), it would have to be conceived of as relating either to a path of motion already traversed (*gata*), or not yet traversed (*agata*), or just being traversed (*gamyamāna*). Nāgārjuna says that in none of these ways does movement make sense.

> 1 There is no motion, first, in what has been traversed, nor in what has not yet been traversed, nor in what, as something distinct from what has and has not been traversed, is just being traversed.[2]

Where, on the path of movement (*adhvajāta*), the activity 'motion' (*gamikriyā*) has ceased is said to have been traversed. That sector which is just being entered by a present activity of motion is said to be where movement is (*gamyate*). What has been traversed – where the activity 'motion' has ceased – because it is associated with a present activity of motion is spoken of as being 'in motion'. As this statement is clearly illogical it is not tenable to say what has been traversed is in

[1] See p. 32.

[2] An alternate translation might be: What has moved does not move, or is not in motion; what has not moved does not move; and what, as something distinct from what has and has not moved, is just moving, does not move. Nāgārjuna's analysis gains some of its strength from the fact that his Sanskrit terms are both spatial and temporal, inextricably.

motion.[1] The word 'first' indicates the sequence of refutation.

93 And now the statement 'There is no motion in what has not yet been traversed.' The sector of the path of movement which has not yet been traversed is where the activity 'motion' has not yet arisen, it is the future (*anāgata*). But to be in motion is present, and because future and present are irreconcilable it is equally untenable to say what has not yet been traversed is in motion. If a sector has not been traversed how can there be motion there? Where there is motion how can one say it has not been traversed?

Nor is there movement in the sector just being traversed, for 'There is no motion in what, as something distinct from what has and has not been traversed, is just being traversed.' The thought here is that the space which the mover has passed through is for him traversed and the space he has not yet passed through is for him not yet traversed. But we never observe another, third sector of the path of movement unrelated to what has and has not been traversed called 'in traverse' (*gamyamāna*).[2] In this sense, therefore, there is no motion in what is just being traversed. Being in motion cannot be expressed intelligibly (*na prajñapyate*). The conclusion is that there is no 'being in traverse'. Hence there is no passage there of an activity 'motion'; that is, there is no motion. There is no movement in what is being traversed either.

Again, one might think that the place where one walking actually places his feet would be just being traversed. But this won't do, because feet are an aggregate of minute particles. A place which is earlier for a minute particle located in the tip of the toe falls for it within the sector of the traversed, while for a minute particle located in the tip of the heel that place is later and falls within the sector of what has not been traversed. But there is no foot apart from minute particles and so there is no space just being traversed apart from what has and has not been traversed. An analysis, similar to this one of the foot, should be carried out of the spatial relationships of ahead and behind for the minute particles as well. As for what is just being traversed being half traversed, this was analysed earlier in connection with 'being brought forth'.[3] It is thus established that there is no motion in the sector just being traversed.

[1] Or, that past motion moves.
[2] Or, just being traversed.
[3] P. 67.

Denial of present movement

Someone might object that there *is* motion in what is just being traversed, as:

2 Where there is bodily effort there is motion, and as there is bodily effort in space just being traversed, but no bodily effort in what has or has not been traversed, it follows that there is motion in space just being traversed.

94 Here bodily effort can be taken to be the lifting up and stretching out of the foot in walking. When one is walking there is motion in the very place where there is the bodily effort of lifting and stretching out the foot. This bodily effort is not possible either in space (*deśa*) which has been traversed nor in space which has not been traversed but only in space which is just being traversed. There is, therefore, motion in space just being traversed. Where motion is directly perceived there space is just being traversed, that is, is being entered into in virtue of the activity 'motion'; so there emphatically is motion just where space is being moved through. In these arguments the one verb root '*move*' means first 'to comprehend', and second 'to reach another point in space'.[1]

But even on these suppositions there is no motion in what is just being traversed, Nāgārjuna says.

3 How can movement be intelligibly attributed to what is in traverse, as a dual movement in what is in traverse is not intelligible?

You, good sir, are using the expression 'in traverse'[2] only because of its association with motive activity, and you say there is motion there. But there is only one motive activity in virtue of which you may, if you will, use the expression 'in traverse' with respect to a path of movement. But to say 'it moves' is an additional connection with motive activity and does not make sense. 'How can movement be intelligibly attributed to what is in traverse?' Nāgārjuna explains why not: 'As a dual movement in what is in traverse is not intelligible.' His meaning is that 'in traverse' and 'moving' are synonyms.

[1] Candrakīrti might have added a third meaning, namely, 'to attain' or 'to achieve'. The entire chapter could be taken in either of these two alternate senses. The primary reference, however, is to motion in space and the chapter has been so translated.

[2] 'In traverse' includes both (a) what is traversing and (b) the space being traversed.

'Dual movement' means a movement found in two things. As 'in traverse' is fully absorbed by the one motive activity (*gami-kriyā*) and as there is no second motive activity, and as to use
95 the expression 'there is motion' in the absence of motion is obviously contrary to reason, so, to say 'what is in traverse is in motion' is not a statement with a completed sense. Such is Nāgārjuna's meaning. It is possible to say only 'what is in traverse' but, as there is no second motive activity, not that 'it is in motion'.

On the other hand you may want to connect the motive activity with the motion itself. In such case there is no connection of the motive activity with what is in traverse. Nāgārjuna says such a statement lacks a completed meaning.

> 4 For one who holds that there is movement *of* what is in traverse, for him it must follow that what is in traverse is devoid of movement; that is, for such a one 'what is in traverse moves'.

The one arguing the view that what is in traverse *has* motion, must think that, as what is in traverse is a mere name devoid of motive activity, motive activity is adventitious to it. According to this view it must follow that what is in traverse is devoid of motion; that is, movement would be without motion! For such a one what is in traverse moves. The abbreviation 'that is' means 'hence'. As what is in traverse lacks motion entirely, for one of such view it follows that it moves, because the activity of motion is fully appropriated by the 'it moves'. The undesirable consequence follows, therefore, that what is at present in traverse lacks motion.

Again you may want to connect motion with both what is in traverse and with movement. Even so,

> 5 If movement is of what is in traverse it will follow that there must be two movements: one in virtue of which there is present traversing and the other *in* which there is motion.

96 The one movement (*gamana*) is the sector of the traverse (*adhvā*) which, by association with movement, is said to be present in traverse; the second movement, which is based on what at present is in traverse, is that in virtue of which traversing actually moves. These two movements necessarily follow if there is movement *of* what is in traverse.

Both movement and mover are unintelligible

If you say: 'Let there be two movements, what is the harm', there would be this unacceptable consequence:

> 6ab Given two movements it must follow that there are two movers.

Nāgārjuna says why it follows that there must be two movers:

> 6cd Movement in default of a mover is not intelligible.

As an activity necessarily requires certain factors for its realization, either an agent or an object, the activity of motion must reside in an agent and so requires a mover (*gantā*). But in the very Devadatta[1] who is walking there is no second agent. As there are not two agents there cannot be two movements, and so it is logically impossible to say that what is just in traverse is moving.

One might suggest that even while Devadatta is standing, may he not talk, may he not look; may not the one agent be seen to engage in several activities? In this sense there will be two movements in the one mover.

This will not do. The agent is not an object, but a specific energy (*śakti*). From the difference of activity the difference of specific energy which engenders activity is established as well. There is after all no agent of speaking by reason of the activity of standing. If you say but the object[2] is the same,
97 there is no objection. The object, however, is not the agent, but rather the specific energy is, and specific energies differ. Nor is someone in one locus ever observed to be the agent of two similar activities. So there cannot be two movements of one mover.

You may object that even if this is so none the less movement is directly perceived in Devadatta the mover because we say 'Devadatta is going'. Hence movement does exist, because the mover, on which movement is based, exists as a fact.

We reply that this would be so if there were a mover as the base of movement. But there is not. Nāgārjuna says how this is so.

> 7 If movement is not intelligible in default of a mover, then, if there is no movement how can there be a mover?

It was stated[3] that a movement not based in a mover was

[1] The 'Mr Smith' of Sanskrit.
[2] Devadatta.
[3] *Kārikā* 6cd, above.

unreal. So if the mover is denied, there is no movement related to him; and then, in the absence of movement, how can there be a mover who lacks a *raison d'être* (*nirhetuka*)? Hence there is no movement.

You may object that movement does exist because we commonly say that the mover is endowed with movement (*gamanavat*). Here the thought is that the mover is joined with movement and because he is so joined, he moves. If there were no movement we would not commonly say of Devadatta who moves, that 'he moves'. If there were no staff we would not speak of 'the bearer of a staff'.[1]

We reply that there would be movement if the expression 'he moves' were acceptable. For,

> 8 The mover does not move, nor does the non-mover move. What third thing, neither mover nor non-mover, moves?

98 The thought is, that, to say 'he moves' there must be a mover. In the first alternative the mover does not move. In what sense he does not move Nāgārjuna will expound in the three following verses. But neither does the non-mover (*agantā*) move; for what is called a non-mover is devoid of movement. But the word 'moves' takes its meaning from its connection with the activity of motion. If such is a non-mover how will he move? On the other hand, if he moves, he will not be a non-mover. If you think something quite apart from these two moves, it is not so. What third thing unconnected with a mover or a non-mover could be thought of as 'moving'. Hence there is no movement.

You may object that it is not a non-mover which moves, nor one other than mover and non-mover, but rather it is the mover itself. But this too is false (*asat*). Why? Because,

> 9 How will it be intelligible that 'the mover moves', as the mover himself is not intelligible without movement?

In the statement 'the mover moves' there is only one activity of motion in virtue of which we say 'he moves'. What we call the mover is not a second activity of motion. A mover without movement is not moving, so if the mover is not possible it will not make sense to say 'the mover moves'. One may say 'moves' if one wishes to, but 'the mover' is not possible and so the entire sentence does not make sense.

[1] A reference to the wandering mendicant whose insignia was a staff.

Perhaps the mover is by nature mobile, being joined with motion. Here as well Nāgārjuna says that, because there is no second activity of motion, the expression 'the mover moves' is not acceptable.

> 10 For one holding the view that the mover moves, for him, thinking that movement belongs to the mover, it must follow that the mover is without movement.

99 For one holding the view that it is the mover who is joined with the activity of motion, for him, thinking that movement belongs to the mover because of the expression 'the moving mover', the statement 'the mover moves without movement' would have to follow, as there is no second activity of motion. Hence it makes no sense to say 'the mover moves'. In the phrase 'a mover without movement', the word 'mover' has the meaning 'to move'.

Perhaps one thinks that in the sentence 'the mover moves' motion is joined with both parts. This too is futile.

> 11 If it is the mover who moves there will necessarily be two movements: the one in virtue of which we say 'mover' and, the mover being given, the other in virtue of which we say 'he moves'.

The movement in virtue of being joined with which one says 'mover' is referred to as the one movement; the mover existing, there is the movement in virtue of which he 'moves', that is, the activity of motion he carries out (*karoti*). These are the two movements which necessarily follow. The necessary consequence (*prasaṅga*) that there must be two movers should be pointed out, as this fallacy (*duṣaṇa*) was previously. Hence it will not do to say 'the mover moves'.

You may object that, even though this be so, none the less, because we do in fact say 'Devadatta goes' movement does exist. It is not so. The only thing based in Devadatta is the enquiry how a mover who exists can move, or again how a non-mover can move or something quite separate from both. As none of these alternatives is intelligible the point is quite irrelevant.

Denial of the commencement of movement

You may object that there *is* movement because its commencement (*ārambha*) is a fact (*sadbhāvāt*). The thought here is that
100 Devadatta, by ceasing to be at rest, commences to move. But

one does not commence something which does not exist like a woollen garment made from tortoise hair.[1]

We reply that there would be movement if its commencement existed. For,

> 12 Motion (*gantum*) does not commence in what has been traversed, motion does not commence in what has not yet been traversed, motion does not commence in what is in traverse. Where does it commence?

If there were commencement of movement it would have to be in the sector of the path of motion traversed, or not yet traversed, or just in traverse. Movement does not commence in the sector traversed as it is so called because it is devoid of the activity of motion. If movement commences there it would for that reason not be already traversed because past and present are contraries (*virodhāt*). Movement cannot commence in what has not yet been traversed because future and present are contraries. Nor in what is in traverse because that does not exist, because it would follow that there were two motions, and because it would follow that there were two movers. Thus Nāgārjuna says that nowhere can the commencement of movement be observed: 'Where does motion commence?' In what further way movement is not possible Nāgārjuna expounds thus:

> 13 Prior to the commencement of movement there can be no present nor past traversing where movement could begin. And how could it begin in what has not yet been traversed?

The thought is that so long as Devadatta is unmoving in one place he does not begin to move. Before he commences movement there is no sector of a path of movement (*adhvajāta*) which is being traversed nor a sector already traversed where movement could commence. As what is in traverse
101 and what has been traversed do not exist, movement cannot begin in them. You might suggest that, even though prior to the commencement of movement there is no present nor past movement, none the less there is the sector not yet traversed and it is there that movement would begin.

We reply: How could it begin in what has not yet been traversed? The not yet traversed is the sector where the activity of motion has not yet arisen, has not yet begun. That

[1] A common equivalent of the 'married bachelor'.

movement should commence there is incoherent (*asaṁbaddha*) Nāgārjuna says: 'How can there be movement in what is not yet traversed?'

If you suggest that, although movement does not begin in what has been, what has not been and what is being traversed, these distinctions themselves exist, because, if there were no movement, they would have no meaning.

We reply that there would be movement if these distinctions existed. You are supposing that if an activity of motion has commenced, where that activity of motion has ceased has been traversed, where it is present is in traverse and where it has not arisen is not yet traversed. As, however, there is no commencement of movement, so

> 14 What past, present and future movements are being presumed, as the beginning of movement is not observed in any of these ways?

If no beginning of movement is observed what delusive (*mithyā*) tripartite path of movement is being presumed (*vikalpyate*)? How can movement be the basis for such terminology? This is absurd (*ayuktam*).

Denial of rest

You may object that movement is a fact because its opposite (*pratipakṣa*) is a fact. That of which there is an opposite exists, as in the case of light and darkness, this side and other side, doubt and certainty. And there is an opposite of movement, namely rest (*sthānam*).

We reply that there would be movement if there were its opposite, rest. But how could rest, so conceived, be supposed to apply to a mover, a non-mover or what is other than these two? Nāgārjuna says that this does not make sense in any way.

> 15 A mover does not come to rest; a non-mover does not come to rest; what third body, other than mover and non-mover, then comes to rest?

102 In what way a mover does not come to rest (*tiṣṭhati*)[1] is explained in the next *kārikā*. The non-mover does not come to rest either because he is by nature at rest. What would be the purpose of his coming to rest a second time? In virtue of one 'coming to rest', he is a non-mover; in virtue of a second he is

[1] Or 'is at rest'; this is as much an act as movement is.

'at rest'. This involves the necessary consequence of two acts of resting and of two bodies resting. There is no third body quite separate from a mover and a non-mover, a fallacy pointed out earlier.

You may object that it is not the non-mover who rests, nor a body other than mover and non-mover, but rather it is the mover himself who rests.

It is not so, for,

> 16 How will it be reasonable to say 'the mover comes to rest' as a mover without movement is not intelligible?

If it is said that the mover comes to rest, then there can be no movement as the opposite of rest; in the absence of movement the term mover does not obtain; hence to say the mover is at rest or comes to rest is unintelligible.

You may object that movement is a fact because its cessation (*nivṛtti*) is a fact. The thought is that the ceasing of motion is the commencement of rest. But if there were no movement it could not cease.

We reply that there would be movement if its cessation were a fact, but it is not. For,

> 17ab One does not come to rest either from present, past or future movement.

The mover does not cease moving on the sector already traversed because there is no motion there; nor from the sector not yet traversed as there is no motion there either; nor does he cease on the sector in traverse, because such is never experienced and because there is no activity of motion there. Hence there is no cessation of motion.

103 You may object that if motion (*gati*) is non-existent because its opposite state rest (*sthiti*), does not exist, still, for the sake of establishing movement we will establish rest, and that being established, movement will be established. So let rest be real because its opposite state is a fact: movement is the opposite state to rest. It exists and so rest exists as well because its opposite state is a fact.

But this too is untenable, for,

> 17cd Movement, commencement and cessation are the same as for motion.

Here the term movement, used to establish rest, is the same as motion; that is, it suffers from the same fallacy as motion.[1] This is what the verse means. As in the verse 'The mover does not come to rest'[2] and the others the fallacy of adducing rest as the ground for establishing motion was pointed out, so in the same way here the fallacy of adducing movement for the sake of establishing rest can be shown by rewording the two verses thus: 'The one at rest does not move' and so on. Movement does not exist; and as it does not exist, neither does its opposite state, rest. In this sense movement is to be rejected as was motion.

One might argue that rest is a fact because the commencement of rest is a fact. The thought is that rest commences in virtue of motion coming to an end. How could this not be so?

We reply that the commencement of rest is to be thought of in the same way as was the commencement of motion. The commencement of movement was denied earlier in the verse, 'Motion does not commence in what has been traversed . . .'[3] and so on. Similarly in this case one could say, 'Rest does not commence in what has already come to rest; rest does not commence in what is not yet at rest; rest does not commence in what is resting; where will it commence?' By re-wording
104 the three verses[4] in this way the commencement of rest will be analogous to motion. And the cessation of rest as well is to be denied as was the cessation of motion. In the refutation of motion the fallacy was stated in this way. 'One does not come to rest from present, past or future motion.'[5] Similarly in the refutation of rest the fallacy will be the same as for motion. 'One does not start moving from being at rest, from having been at rest, from not yet being at rest.' Thus the fallacy as for motion. There is no state of rest. As it does not exist how can motion be established by those who argue for it on the ground of its opposite, rest?

Concluding denial of movement and mover

Further, if there were movement it would exist either quite apart from (*vyatirekeṇa*) a mover or not so apart. Nāgārjuna says that neither alternative, on being critically analysed, is possible:

[1] By an appeal to movement one cannot establish the commencement and cessation of rest.

[2] *Kārikā* 15, p. 84; cf. also *Kārikā* 12, p. 83.

[3] *Kārika* 12, p. 83.

[4] *Kārikās* 12 to 14, pp. 83–4.

[5] *Kārikā* 17ab, p. 85.

18 To say that movement itself is the very mover does not make sense; to say that the mover is wholly other than movement does not make sense.

Nāgārjuna explains in what way it does not make sense:

19 If movement itself were the very mover it would follow that doer and deed were one thing.

If the activity of motion itself were not quite apart from, that is wholly other (*anya*) than the mover, then agent and activity would be identical; and the distinction 'this is the activity, this the agent' would not be possible. But the activity of cutting and the cutter are not one and the same. Hence to say that movement itself is the very mover does not make sense.

105 How mover and movement are not wholly other (*nānyatva*) either, Nāgārjuna expounds in this way:

20 If, on the other hand, the mover is thought to be wholly other than movement, there would be movement without anything moving and something moving without movement.

If mover and movement were wholly other, then there could be a mover unrelated to movement, and movement would be understood as unrelated to a mover which existed separately, even as a cloth is separate from a pot. But movement is not understood as existing separately from a mover. So it has been established that it does not make sense to say the mover is wholly other than the motion.

This being so,

21 How can a pair of things exist at all if they cannot be proved to exist either as identical or as different?

According to the argument given mover and movement do not exist either as identical or as different. In what other way could their existence be established? That is why Nāgārjuna says, 'How can a pair of things exist at all.' He means to say that mover and movement cannot be proved to exist (*nāsti siddhiḥ*).

You may object that it is common convention to say, 'Devadatta, the mover, moves', as it is common convention to say, 'the speaker speaks sentences', or 'the agent carries out an activity'. In the same sense the mover carries out the motion by which he realizes himself as mover. The fallacy urged does not hold.

But this too is false. For,

22ab The mover does not carry out that motion in virtue of which he is called the mover.

Devadatta, an existing mover, does not carry out that very motion in virtue of which he realizes himself as mover. He does not attain it if you like; the idea is that he does not carry it out as agent.

22c Because he does not exist prior to the motion.

'Prior to the motion' means the agent prior to the motion. If the mover existed prior to the motion he would be able to effect it. Why? Because

22d It is a someone who moves toward a something.

It is commonly observed that someone – 'Devadatta' – moves toward a village or a city spatially removed from himself. But there is no realized (*siddharūpa*) 'mover' independent of motion prior to the motion in virtue of which he is 'the one moving' who could carry out that very motion.

You may think, as against this, that the mover does not carry out that very motion in virtue of which he realizes himself as mover, but rather another motion.

But this cannot be either:

23 The mover does not carry out a motion other than the one in virtue of which he is called a mover, because, as there is only one mover, two motions are unintelligible.

107 A mover who is already in existence does not carry out a motion other than the one in virtue of which he realizes himself as mover, because it would follow that there were two motions: one, that in virtue of which he is realized as a mover, the second, that other motion which he – already a mover – carries out. These would be the two entailed motions. But in the one mover there are not two motions; this would go against reason (*ayuktam*). On the same grounds the statements 'the speaker speaks sentences', 'the agent carries out an activity' are to be rejected.

This being so,

24 An existing mover does not carry out movement in any of the three ways; a non-existing mover[1] does not carry out movement in any of the three ways.

[1] That is, one not actually moving.

25ab A mover who both exists and does not exist does not carry out movement in any of the three ways.

In these verses movement means 'being in motion' (*gamyate*), and an existent (*sadbhūta*) mover is one connected with an activity of motion. A non-existent (*asadbhūta*) mover is one who is devoid of the activity of motion. A mover who is both existent and non-existent embraces both possibilities. It should be realized that movement too is three-fold according to its relation to the activity of motion. In this context a real mover does not carry out movement in any of its three modes – as real, unreal or both. This will be explained in the chapter 'The Agent Subject and his Doing'. Similarly an unreal mover does not carry out movement in any of the three ways. That a mover both real and unreal does not, Nāgārjuna will demonstrate in the same place. It follows, thus, that neither mover, movement nor space traversed (*gantavyam*), on being critically examined, exist.

25cd Therefore there is no motion, no one moving and no space traversed.

108 As is said in the *Akṣayamati Nirdeṣa Sūtra*, ' "Coming", venerable Śāradvatīputra, is a word meaning union; "going", venerable Śāradvatīputra, is a word meaning separation. Where there is no word for either union or separation, that is the language (*padam*) of the wise ones, because theirs is a language beyond ordinary words (*apadayogena*). The movement of the wise ones is neither coming nor going.'[1]

If the seed itself passes over into the sprout, the sprout would be seed and not sprout which entails the fallacy of eternalism. If the sprout arises from something other than the seed that would entail the fallacy of causelessness. But nothing can arise uncaused, for example the horns of a donkey.

That is why the illustrious one said, 'Given a seed there will be a sprout; but the seed is not one with the sprout. It is not other than nor identical with it. In the same way the nature of things is neither perishable nor imperishable.

'The seal becomes visible in the imprint but does not in fact pass over into it. It is neither in the imprint nor divorced from it. Even so compound things are neither perishable nor eternal.'

And 'A man catches sight of a pretty female face in a
109 mirror or a dish of oil. The foolish man, conceiving a desire

[1] The further meanings of the verb *gam* must come to mind here: (a) attainment; (b) comprehension. Cf. note 1, p. 32.

for her, starts in pursuit of his love. But as the face does not pass into and exist in the reflection, he will never attain it. As he generates his passion in error, even so, you should know, are all the elements of existence.'

V

Vision and the Other Sense Faculties

113 Some might interject here that although motion, the one in motion and the space traversed do not in fact exist, nevertheless the existence of the one who sees, the object of sight and seeing itself should be accepted because this is established in the authoritative commentaries (*Abhidharma*). There it is said,

> 1 Vision, hearing, smell, taste, touch, thought are the six senses. Their objects are the visible, the audible and so on.

It follows that vision and the other senses are self-existent.

The concept of vision is unintelligible

We reply that they do not so exist. According to this way of thinking the act of seeing (*paśyati*) is vision (*darśana*) and this is eyesight (*cakṣu*). What the eye sees is said to be object. That vision does not see anything as object (*rūpa*) Nāgārjuna expounds in this way:

> 2 Vision does not see itself. How can something which does not see itself see other things?

114 He means that the very act of vision does not see itself because it is contradictory that an act (*kriyā*) should be directed at itself. It follows from vision not seeing itself that it does not see colours and such things; and hearing and the other senses are the same. There is, therefore, no such thing as vision.

It may be argued that although vision cannot see itself, nevertheless it can see other things. Even as fire burns other things but not itself, so vision will see other things but not itself. But this does not make sense either, as

> 3ab The example of fire is not conclusive for proving the reality of vision.

Nāgārjuna means that the example of fire adduced to prove

the reality of vision is not conclusive, that is, it is not appropriate, not adequate and is not logically tenable. For

> 3cd Like vision it is refuted by the analysis of movement, past, present and future.

'Like vision' means 'along with vision'. This example of fire adduced to establish the reality of vision is refuted, along with vision, for which it stood as the example. You may ask how it is refuted. By the analysis of movement, past, present and future: what has been traversed is not in motion, nor is what has not been traversed, nor is what is being traversed. The same can be said of fire: what has been burned by fire is not being burned nor is what has not been burned, and so on.[1] As what has been traversed, what is at rest, and what is traversing are not in motion, similarly: 'Neither what has been seen nor, emphatically, what has not been seen is being seen. And what is just being seen, as something wholly other than the seen and the not seen, is not being seen.'[2]

115 As was said, 'The mover does not move', and so on, so it can be said 'the agent of burning is not burned', and so on. Similarly 'the one seeing does not see', is entailed, on the model of fire, by the analysis of motion. As there is the same fault, the proof of the reality (*siddhi*) of vision makes as little sense as the proof of fire. So it is established that, as vision cannot see itself, it cannot see other things either. This being so, then

> 4 As there can be no vision at all which is not actively seeing, how can it make sense to say vision sees?

As, that is, there cannot be any vision at all which does not see (*apaśyan*) – because there is no relation between the power of vision and an unseeing thing like a post – to say 'vision' is 'what sees' does not make sense.[3] Although the text has, for reasons of metre, 'vision sees', in exposition one should read it 'how can it make sense to say "vision" "sees" '.

Further, in this way of thinking to say ' "vision" is "what sees" ' is to suppose a connection of an act of seeing with the sense of sight, either as endowed or not endowed with self-existent vision (*darśanasvabhāva*).

[1] See Chapter XI, 'Fire and Fuel'.

[2] This quotation has the form of a *kārikā*, but it is not so treated by Candrakīrti.

[3] The thought is: vision, distinct from an agent and an object of vision, is unintelligible; or vision *is* seeing.

Nāgārjuna explains that neither possibility makes sense:

5ab Neither vision as such nor non-vision as such is what sees.

It is not logically possible (*nopapadyate*) to add the idea 'it sees' to a self-existent vision which is by nature the activity of seeing; because this would imply that both the act of seeing and vision are uselessly duplicated. Nor does non-vision see because it is devoid of the activity of seeing as are things like the tip of the finger. This is the meaning.

116 If 'Neither vision as such nor non-vision as such is what sees' then, '. . . how can it make sense to say "vision" "sees"?' In this way we see the connected thought.

Some, however, think that there are imperishable elements[1] (*dharmamātra*) which enter into existence, but are inactive at the moment when they do so. No one sees any object if there is no activity of seeing. They think that what we are trying to prove, namely, that 'vision does not see' is already established.

Our answer to this is that if an activity does not exist as a factor in the transactional world (*vyavahārāṅgabhūta*) then there is no corresponding imperishable element either. Being destitute of activity, like the sky-flower, how can such a dormant, imperishable element exist? So, if, for the transactional world one should accept that, given an imperishable element, there must be activity as well so, for the way things truly are (*tattvacintā*), one must acknowledge that even as there is no activity there is no imperishable element either.

As Āryadeva says in the *Catuḥśataka*: 'Nothing eternal has activity, nor is there activity in the all-pervading; yet the non-active is like the non-existent. Why do you not value what is neither (*nairātmya*)?'

And so this stricture is not an obstacle; nor do we incur the fault of proving the obvious.

The concept of an agent of vision is unintelligible

117 But our opponent objects. We do not suppose that vision derives its name from being the agent of seeing (*kartā*); rather it derives its name from being the means of seeing. So we do not incur the fault you charge us with. The one who, by vision as the means, sees something is the seer (*draṣṭā*) which is either

[1] 'Vision', for example. This is a view of the Vaibhāṣika school of Buddhism. The elements become 'active' on entering into existence.

consciousness or an enduring self. Because the agent of vision truly exists, vision is proved as well.

Nāgārjuna replies

> 5cd It must be accepted that the seer is accounted for as was vision itself.

As the inadequacy of the concept of vision was shown in the verse beginning, 'Vision does not see itself', so the inadequacy of the concept seer should be understood in the same way. The following quotation, among others, bears on the subject: 'The seer does not see himself by means of vision. How will something which does not see itself see other things?'[1]

Thus the agent, like vision itself, has been proved not to exist.

Our opponent objects. The seer does exist because the object of seeing (*karma*) and the means of seeing (*karaṇa*) exist intact. That is, there can be neither object nor means of something, for example the son of a barren woman, which does not exist. But the means exist, namely, the act of vision and the object as well, namely, the thing seen. Therefore an agent whose means and whose object factually exist does himself exist, like one who splits wood.

We reply. There is no object of vision (*draṣṭavya*) and no act of vision (*darśana*); so how could there be an agent of vision (*draṣṭā*)? Object and act require an agent. On being investigated, however,

> 6ab No agent of seeing exists either detached from or not detached from the act of seeing.

This means that if an agent of seeing existed, he would either be dependent (*apekṣa*) on the act of seeing, or not. If he is considered to be dependent then he is not detached from the act of seeing. The seer will be dependent on seeing either as having seen or as not having seen. If the seer has seen, he is not dependent on seeing; how can a seer who has already seen still be dependent on seeing? For what has been accomplished
118 need not be accomplished (*siddha*) again. Then there is the seer who has not seen (*asiddha*) but who is dependent on, i.e. related to, seeing. Because he has not seen he cannot be dependent on seeing any more than the son of a barren woman can be. Thus, in so far as he is not detached from seeing, the seer cannot exist in dependence on it; that he cannot exist

[1] i.e. the very notion of 'one who sees' yields no sense. Cf. *Kārikā* 2, p. 91.

detached either because then he does not require seeing was explained earlier. Thus, as the seer, whether separate or not separate from seeing, does not exist, so:

6cd How can there be seeing and an object of seeing if the seer does not exist?

If the seer does not exist, an object and an act of seeing, thus lacking any basis, will not be possible; how then will the seer be established by *their* existence?

Consciousness cannot be urged as proof of vision and its object

You may object that the act of seeing and its object do exist because their consequences exist as fact. That is,

7 The birth of a son is held to depend on the mother and father; similarly the genesis of consciousness is held to depend on the faculty of sight and its object.

Consciousness comes into existence dependent on the act of seeing and its object. From the conjunction of these three there is contact with things which results in afflicted existence (*sāsrava*),[1] and simultaneously there is feeling. Dependent on feeling there is craving for existence. These four factors of existence[2] are caused by the act of seeing and its object.
119 Therefore, as their effects are real, seeing and its object must be real.

We reply that these two could be real if the four factors – consciousness and the others – were real. That is,

8abc Because the act of seeing and its object do not exist, the four factors – consciousness and the others – do not exist.

The thought is that as the agent of seeing does not exist neither do seeing and its object, as has been explained. How then can the four factors – consciousness, contact, feeling and craving existence – be real? It follows that they are not real (*na santi*).

You may argue that they do exist because their effects are fact. One says 'Because of craving for existence there is appropriation of things.' From the existence of the four factors the

[1] The three *āsravas* (harmful influences or conditions of affliction) are desire, belief that being is particular, and ignorance.

[2] Consciousness, contact, feeling, craving for existence.

entire series[1] – grasping, existence, birth, old age and death – arises. Consciousness and the other factors exist therefore because their effects are fact.

We reply. If the four factors – consciousness and the others – existed, then the entire series – grasping and so on – would exist too. As, however, because vision and its object do not exist, the four factors – consciousness and the others – cannot exist either, so,

> 8d How will the entire series – grasping and so on – exist?

The meaning is that the entire series – grasping and so on – does not exist.

The analysis applies to the other sense faculties

Finally, in order to apply this exposition of the faculty of vision to the remaining sense faculties, Nāgārjuna says

120 9 It should be realized that by this analysis of vision, the agents and objects of hearing, smell, taste, touch and thought have been analysed as well.

As the illustrious one has said, 'The eye does not *see* material objects nor does the mind *know* ideas; but that is the surpassing truth where the ordinary person does not penetrate. When the teacher, who is aware of the surpassing truth, explains vision in terms of causes he is speaking in a modified way to serve a purpose.'

And again, 'It is commonly supposed that visual consciousness arises in dependence on the organ of sight and the object; but the object is not based in the organ nor does the organ enter into the object. The putative elements are ill and without substance, but are thought to have substance and to be good; visual consciousness has the same origin: it is a misconception,
121 a non-existent figment. The wise one discerns, in meditation, how the contents of consciousness arise and vanish, are born and destroyed; he understands that consciousness neither comes nor goes, that it is a magician's trick, and devoid of being.'

And from the *Upālipṛcchā*: 'The eye sees in conjunction with all the enabling conditions, it does not see in default of these. The eye does not see an object because conjunction and

[1] This is the twelvefold 'causal' account of afflicted existence or *saṁsāra* accepted by all Buddhists.

disjunction are just ways of thinking. The eye sees differentiated, coloured, pleasant objects in conjunction with light; because the eye depends upon this conjunction the eye never sees. Again, when a pleasing sound is heard it never enters into the mind; one cannot perceive its passage; it is by a theory that we explain the origin of sound.'

VI

Material Objects and the Other Factors of Personal Existence

123 Some may argue that, although vision and the other sense faculties are not real, the constitutive factors of personal existence (*skandhas*)[1] are, because they have not been explicitly denied. The sense faculties, however, belong to the factors of personal existence and therefore will exist as well.

Matter cannot be understood as the cause of material objects; nor can these be understood as the effects of matter

We reply that they would if the factors of personal existence were real. With reference to material objects (*rūpa*),[2] Nāgārjuna says:

> 1 Objects are not perceived apart from matter as their cause; matter as cause is not perceived apart from objects.

Here 'objects' means particular material objects (*bhautika rūpa*), and their material cause (*kāraṇa*) are the four elements.[3] One does not perceive objects – the physical particulars designated sights, sounds, smells, tastes, and touch – separated from the four elements and existing by themselves as a piece of cloth is separate from a jar.[4] And matter as cause (*rūpa-kāraṇa*) is not perceived existing by itself apart from objects. Wishing to establish this double claim Nāgārjuna says:

> 2 If objects exist apart from matter as their cause, objects must be uncaused; but nothing is ever without a cause.

124 As a piece of cloth, being another thing than a pot, cannot be caused by the pot, so objects – material particulars –

[1] There are five: body or material object, feeling, ideation, character dispositions and consciousness.
[2] Objects within the fields of perception.
[3] Earth, air, fire, water.
[4] That is, a perceived object is inseparable from a material base.

cannot be caused by the four elements if thought of as separated from them. But, 'Nothing is ever without a cause.' Therefore, because causelessness is logically absurd, it cannot be accepted that objects are separate from matter as their cause.

Now, to show that matter as cause cannot exist apart from objects, Nāgārjuna says:

3ab If matter as cause were separate from objects –

If, that is, matter as cause were separate from objects as its effects then, just as the frying pan taken as separate from the pot cannot be the cause of the pot, so if matter as cause is conceived as existing separated from its effects,

3c Matter as cause would be without any effect.

It would be effectless. The condition for the causality of a cause is that it produces an effect. There is no production of an effect if this is thought of as separated from a material cause unrelated to the effect. Nāgārjuna says that a cause without an effect, because it does not cause anything, does not exist, like the horns of a man or of a snake or of a horse.

3d There is no cause without an effect.

Further, what is taken to be the material cause of objects must be taken as the cause either of an object which exists or of one which does not exist. Nāgārjuna says that neither way is logically possible.

4 Matter as cause of an object which exists is not logically possible; matter as cause of an object which does not exist is not logically possible.

If an object is in being (*sant*), that is, factually exists (*saṁvidyamana*), what would be the point of its having a material
125 cause? If an object is not in being, that is, does not factually exist, what could be the meaning of its 'cause'? What would one suppose such a cause to be the cause of? So, if an object does not exist, its cause is not logically possible.

You may say: Although a material cause of objects is in this way not logically possible, none the less objects exist in fact as effects and because of their real existence matter as cause will exist as well. This would be so if the object as effect existed, but it does not. So,

5ab An object without a material cause is not, repeat not, logically possible.

How it is that there is no material cause has been shown. But if there is no material cause, how could there be an object as an effect which has no cause? By the double rejection of the emphatic 'not, repeat not' Nāgārjuna makes clear the harmfulness of the view that things can be without causes.

And thus, on being considered from every aspect, a perceptible material object (*rūpa*) is not possible. Therefore the wise one (*yogī*), who sees things as they really are,

5cd Should not form any theories at all concerning objects.

The meaning is that he does not take objects to be the external base (*ālambana*) to which are attributed such characteristics as penetrable or impenetrable, veridically perceivable or not veridically perceivable, past or future, light or dark.

Whether one thinks that matter as cause gives rise to an effect which is identical with or not identical with itself, neither alternative is logically possible. Nāgārjuna says:

6 It is not logically possible that an effect is identical with its cause. It is not logically possible that an effect is not identical with its cause.

126 It is commonly supposed that matter (*rūpakārana*) is by its inherent nature solid, liquid, warm and mobile. Particular material objects (*bautika*), however, whether they are personal like the eye and the other sense faculties which are by nature of a subtle matter and are the base of visual and the other types of sense consciousness, or whether they are the external sense fields like the visible whose nature it is to be perceived *in* the various types of sense consciousness, do not possess the inherent nature of the four elements. It follows that, because they have different characteristics, cause, i.e. matter, and effect, i.e. material objects, are not identical, as in the case of *nirvāṇa.*[1] 'It is not logically possible that an effect is identical with its cause.'

Further, one never sees the real dependence in the relationship of cause to effect, even when they are identical like the rice seed and the ripe grain. 'It is not logically possible that an effect is identical with its cause.'

And again, 'It is not logically possible that an effect is *not* identical with its cause.' The meaning here is that it is so because they have different characteristics, as in the case of *nirvāṇa.*

[1] Candrakīrti seems to be saying that cause and effect, like *saṁsāra* and *nirvāṇa* are so different that no statement about their relationship is possible.

So perceivable material objects, on being investigated, are not logically possible in any way at all. Nāgārjuna extends this conclusion to feeling and the other constitutive factors of personal existence as well.

The same procedure holds for the other factors of personal existence

7 The inquiry into material objects holds in every essential for feeling, consciousness, ideation and personal dispositions – for all the factors of personal existence.

127 Feeling and all the constitutive factors of personal existence may suitably be considered in the same way as material objects have been.[1] Precisely as the absence of being (*śūnyatā*), as conceived by Mādhyamika, is expounded for one thing (*dharma*), precisely so is it to be expounded for all things. And so:

Any refutation of mādhyamika must beg the question

8 If a counter-argument has been given in terms of the absence of being and someone would offer a refutation of it, he refutes nothing because everything he says presupposes what has to be proved.

Here 'counter-argument' means discrediting the view of another; 'in terms of the absence of being' (*śūnyatayā*) means by showing that objects are without a self-existent nature so the view that they have a self-existent nature is ruled out. If an opponent would offer a refutation of this, saying, 'but as feeling, ideas and so on are real, so objects must be real too', everything he says lacks the force of a refutation because the actual existence of feeling, ideas and so on must be known in the same way as the actual existence of objects: which is what has to be proved.

Even as material objects, on being thoroughly investigated, do not actually exist whether they are one with their material cause or different, so feeling, which is dependent on contact with objects, ideation which is simultaneous with consciousness, personal dispositions which are dependent on ignorance, and consciousness which is dependent on dispositions, on being thoroughly investigated, do not exist either as being

[1] That is, each factor appears to be dependent on appropriate causes; on being examined, however, it is found to be unintelligible either as caused or uncaused: it is devoid of being.

one with their cause or different. They are like contact and the other factors of the death–birth cycle: all of these are just what has to be proved. And as feeling and so on are the same as what has to be proved, so attributes and the subject of attributes, effect and cause, whole and part and such concepts are things which, like material objects, are just what has to be proved. How could an opponent offer a refutation? His every assertion will be just what has to be proved. Throughout this treatise Nāgārjuna teaches that for Mādhyamika it is to be taken as a rule that refutations offered by opponents are instances of *petitio principii.*[1]

Even as this is the invariable rule concerning the invalidation of the view of an opponent, so, concerning an expository statement, Nāgārjuna says:

> 9 If, after an exposition has been made in terms of the absence of being, someone were to offer a criticism, nothing he says will be a criticism because it will be just what has to be proved.

If during an exposition some pseudo-disciple raises a critical objection, that very objection, it should be known, will be just what has to be proved, as in the case of a counter-argument.

To quote: 'Who sees one thing truly, it should be remembered, sees all things truly. The absence of being in one thing is the absence of being in all things.'

And from the *Gaganagañjasamādhi Sūtra*: 'The one who by examining one putative element realizes that all putative elements are like a magical show, like a mirage: unintelligible, false, deceptive and perishable, he is the one who progresses directly to the haven of enlightenment.'

And from the *Samādhirāja Sūtra* as well: 'Just as you have understood the concept of the self, so should you turn your mind to all things; all putative elements have the same nature as the self: they are as transparent as the heavens. The one who from one thing knows all things and from one thing sees all things, in him, whatever the paths of his thought, there will be no egomania.'

[1] A succinct restatement of Chapter I.

VII

The Primal Elements or Character and Characteristic

129 Someone may object that the primal elements (*dhātu*) exist because they have not been disproved. And the illustrious one said, 'The individual person, O great king, consists of the six primal elements.' Therefore, because of this scriptural pronouncement, even as the primal elements exist, so do the constitutive factors of personal existence and the bases of cognition (*āyatana*).

We reply that the factors of personal existence and the bases of cognition would exist if the primal elements did. Nāgārjuna explains how that is.

Character and characteristic unintelligible

1 There is no space which exists prior to its distinguishing characteristic; if it existed prior to its distinguishing characteristic it would follow that it was without character.

The six primal elements referred to in the scriptural quotation are: earth, water, fire, air, space (*ākāśa*) and consciousness. The stanza, using space as a paradigm, shows the vitiating difficulty of understanding them as self-existent natures. Openness (*anāvaraṇa*) is commonly taken to be the distinguishing characteristic (*lakṣaṇa*)[1] of space. Prior to its characteristic, openness, space could not be something characterized (*lakṣya*)[1] because it could not be such before its characteristic was actual: before openness characterized it.

If it is so that, 'There is no space which exists prior to its distinguishing characteristic; if it existed prior to its distinguishing characteristic it would follow that it was without character'

[1] The problem is both logical and ontological. Some Buddhists, specifically the Vaibhāṣika school, held that the elements of existence were a small number of irreducible reals, *dharmas*, which persisted through all time in their proper natures, even when they were not actual.

then let space be actual without its distinguishing characteristic. But such a thing, like a flower in the sky, cannot be. 'There is no space . . .' Nāgārjuna says:

> 2ab No thing whatsoever can be actual anywhere lacking its distinguishing characteristic.

130 You may interject that a distinguishing characteristic could be actual (*pravṛtti*) only in something characterized and as this actual characteristic is a fact (*sadbhāvāt*) what is characterized must exist as well. But this is not so either. Because

> 2cd As a thing lacking a distinguishing characteristic does not exist to what would a distinguishing characteristic be applied?

It was said that no thing (*bhāva*)[1] lacking a distinguishing characteristic can exist prior to its distinguishing characteristic. It follows that the distinguishing characteristic cannot be actualized. How can a distinguishing characteristic become actual in something which is not, which in no way at all exists, which is without distinguishing characteristic, which is quite lacking in distinguishing characteristic? Further, this actualized distinguishing characteristic would be actual either in something with or in something without a distinguishing characteristic. Nāgārjuna says that neither alternative is intelligible:

> 3 A distinguishing characteristic can be actualized neither in something without that distinguishing characteristic nor in something with it. Nor does the characteristic become actual otherwise than in something which either has or does not have it.

In the one case no distinguishing characteristic can be actualized in something lacking that distinguishing characteristic, as it would be like a donkey's horns. In the other case the actualizing of a distinguishing characteristic is something which is already so characterized is unintelligible because pointless. What would be the purpose of a characteristic becoming actual once more in something known to possess that characteristic? That would lead to an infinite regress. But such a thing would never be without a distinguishing characteristic, from which it would follow that the actualized characteristic

[1] This discussion can be read as an attack on the possibility of eternal *dharmas* unrealized in time and space; or as an attack on the realist (common sense) conception of the nature of 'things' in time and space.

was permanent, but this is not desirable. Hence it is unintelligible that a distinguishing characteristic should become actual in something which possesses that characteristic: it would be pointless.

Again there could be the view that the characteristic becomes actual otherwise than in something which either has or does not have the characteristic already. Nāgārjuna says, 'Nor does the characteristic become actual otherwise than in something which either has or does not have it.'

131 Why is this? Because such a thing does not exist. If something possesses a characteristic it is not without it and if it is without a characteristic it does not possess it. So, to 'possess a characteristic' and 'not to possess it' are contradictory (*vipratiṣiddha*). But what is contradictory cannot be (*na saṁbhavati*). For this reason, precisely because it is simply impossible, Nāgārjuna says it is unintelligible that a characteristic could become actual either in something that possesses it or in something that does not.

Again one might think that, even though characteristics cannot be actual, none the less the subject of characterization (*lakṣya*) exists. But this cannot be either because

4ab A subject of characterization is unintelligible without actual characteristics.

So long as there are no actualized characteristics how could there be something characterized? Nāgārjuna means that that is completely impossible. If you interject that we have rejected as false the actualization of distinguishing characteristics but not distinguishing characteristics themselves and that therefore the subject of characterization does exist because the characteristic is a fact, Nāgārjuna replies:

4cd If the subject of characterization is not established characteristics become impossible as well.

It was shown that: 'A subject of characterization is unintelligible without actual characteristics.' So it follows: 'If the subject of characterization is not established characteristics become impossible as well', because they would have no substrate (*aśraya*). In so far as, thus, characteristics do not exist, the argument given, namely that the subject of characterization does exist because the characteristic is a fact, does not hold. This being the case, therefore

5ab It follows that neither the subject of characterization nor distinguishing characteristics exist.

Space neither entity nor non-entity

This is the conclusion. Someone may interject that even though the subject of characterization and characteristics do not exist, none the less space does. As it exists as something real it must be either the subject of characterization or a characteristic. Hence, the subject of characterization and characteristics do exist. But Nāgārjuna says that this makes no sense either.

132 5cd Nor can anything exist except as characteristic or what is characterized.

That characteristics and what is characterized do not exist, was established previously. If these two do not exist there can be no space lacking both characteristics and something characterized as it would be like a flower in the sky.

If space does not exist as an entity (*bhāva*) let it exist as a non-entity (*abhāva*). But this does not hold either. Because

6ab If something *is* not at all, of what will there be non-existence?

In so far as space does not exist as an entity, that is, there is no such thing, of what is there supposed to be non-existence? Nāgārjuna will say later[1] 'If existence is not accepted, non-existence cannot be established. Because people say that non-existence is being other than existence.' Hence, because it is not a something, space cannot possibly be a non-entity either.

Space is the total absence of external form (*rūpa*) – thus it is defined. Now if form existed then space could be the total absence of form. But as, according to the line of thought already developed,[2] form does not exist itself, of what would space be the absence?

Nor does the enquirer exist

Someone may interject that there *is* existence and non-existence as the one enquiring into them exists in fact. 'You yourself', he might say, 'are the one enquiring into existence and non-existence. You are the one who says, "If something is not at all, of what will there be non-existence?" Hence, as the one enquiring into existence and non-existence is a living fact, existence and non-existence too as the subject of the enquiry, must be real.' Our reply is that this makes no sense either. Because

[1] P. 157. [2] Chapter VI.

> 6cd Who would it be who enquires into existence and non-existence contrary to the logic of existence and non-existence?

133 If it is accepted that there is both existence and non-existence, then the one who inquires would be either existent or non-existent. If he is thought of as existing, the crippling difficulty already given holds: 'Nor can anything exist except as characteristic or as what is characterized.' If, on the other hand, he is thought of as non-existent, in this case the crippling difficulty already given is, 'If something *is* not at all of what will there be non-existence?' There is no third kind of entity which, contrary to the logic of existence and non-existence, would be the one grasping these two. There is no enquirer into existence and non-existence.

That is why the illustrious one said, 'Whoever comprehends things as non-things in no way clings to anything at all; whoever clings in no way to anything at all attains that state where there are no causes.'

And again: 'Whoever thinks the elements of existence are merely empty is foolish and walks a dangerous path. Imperishable are the empty elements and yet not imperishable are the imperishable elements said to be.'

134 'To think the elements of existence are at peace, utterly at peace, such a thought can never be true. The entire manifest world arises from discriminative thinking; the elements should be realized to be subtle and beyond the reach of thought.' And so on.

Being, non-being and nirvāṇa

Now Nāgārjuna, with a view to summing up what has been established, states

> 7ab Space is neither existent nor non-existent, nor is it something characterized nor yet a characteristic.

And

> 7cd The other five primal elements are exactly like space.

Earth, air, fire, water and consciousness are the remaining five primal elements. This means that they are to be clearly known as lacking, as space does, existence, non-existence, character and characteristics – a nature which is merely imputed (*parikalpa*) to them. Even though the true nature (*svabhāva*) of things has thus been established, there are some who, because their mind's vision has succumbed to the optical defect of ignorance from entanglement in the beginningless cycle of birth and death, view things falsely as existing or not existing and so on. These have fallen away from the true path of seeing things unerringly as not self-existent, the path which leads to *nirvāṇa.*

135 8 Those who see being and non-being in things are of small mind; they do not comprehend the beatific coming to rest of the manifest world.

The coming to rest of the visible world (*draṣṭavyopaśama*), which is of the nature of beatitude is free of the entire network of conceptual thinking (*sarvakalpanājāla*); its very nature is the cessation of knowing and the known; its very nature is the beatitude of the higher truth. Those who, because of weak mind are rooted in the prejudices of being (*astitva*) and non-being (*nāstitva*), cannot understand a *nirvāṇa* of the higher truth which does not age nor die, which is not of the realm of named-things, and whose quintessence is the absence of both being and non-being (*śūnyatā*).

As it is said in the *Ratnāvalī*, 'The one who thinks "it is not" walks a difficult path; the one who does not think "it is not" walks a favourable path. The one who is freed from both attains liberation from a clear grasp of the way things really are.'

In the *Samādhirāja Sūtra* the illustrious one says, ' "It is", "It is not" are two dogmas; "purity", "impurity" are two dogmas; and so the wise man abandons both dogmas without taking up a position in the middle. "It is", "It is not" is mere disputation; "purity", "impurity" is mere disputation; afflicted existence is not terminated by engaging in disputation; afflicted existence is brought to an end by not engaging in disputation.'

It follows that it is utterly impossible to attain *nirvāṇa* by any path based on the everyday world.

VIII

Desire and the Other Afflictions

137 Some hold that the factors of personal existence, the bases of cognition and the primal elements exist in fact. On what grounds? Because of the direct perception of the state of affliction (*saṁkleśa*) which is based on these. The reasoning here is that there can be no direct perception of a state of affliction based on something which does not exist, as, for example there is no perception of the daughter of a barren woman by the son of a barren woman. So desire (*rāga*) and the other afflictions (*kleśa*)[1] exist because they are the necessary basis of the state of affliction.

As the illustrious one said, 'The ordinary, unsophisticated man, o monks, succumbing to the everyday world of names and having beheld things with the eye, cleaves to those things which promise happiness. From so cleaving desire is born; seized by desire he carries out – in deed, thought and word – karmic acts born of the three afflictions, desire, aversion and illusion. . . .'

Desire presupposes one desiring

138 In reply we say that the factors of personal existence, the bases of cognition and the primal elements would exist if desire and the other afflictions themselves existed. The reasoning here would be that desire, conceived of as real by unsophisticated, ordinary people, would presuppose a person who desires and that he would either exist or not exist. Nāgārjuna says that neither alternative makes sense.

1 If the one desiring were to exist prior to his desire, that is, quite apart from desire, desire would depend on the one desiring; given one desiring there would be desire.

[1] These are the structures of everyday existence; sometimes ten are given, sometimes six; Mādhyamika can accept any number but invariably takes three as basic: desire (*rāga*), aversion (*dveṣa*), and illusion (*moha*). Cf. Chapter XVII.

Here 'desire' embraces being attached, the effort of desiring, cupidity and devotion. Desire has its base in the one desiring (*rakta*). If the one desiring exists prior to his desire, that is, quite apart from it, he would be devoid (*rahita*) of desire; in such case desire would be based on a desiring person who was quite separate from desire. In this way it makes sense to say that desire could arise in an existing person who desires. But this cannot possibly be – a desiring person devoid of desire – and it would necessarily follow that even the wise ones could have desires.

If, in this way, there can be no desire in a desiring person who exists, then let there be desire even if the desiring person does not exist.[1] But this makes no sense either, Nāgārjuna says:

> 2ab If the desiring one does not exist, how, precisely, will desire arise?

As there can be no desire if the desiring person exists, how can there be if the desiring person does not exist? Will a desire, which is without a basis, be conceded existence? For a fruit which does not exist cannot possibly ripen.

One desiring presupposes desire

Someone may interject: 'Even though you repudiate desire none the less the one who desires exists as he has not been repudiated; but one who desires does not make sense in the absence of desire; therefore desire exists as well.' Our rejoinder is that desire would exist if the one desiring existed. That is, if one postulates a person who desires then one must suppose either that desire exists or that it does not. But Nāgārjuna says that neither alternative is intelligible.

139 2cd If the desiring one himself exists the consequence is the same whether desire exists or not.

If one postulates a desiring one on the supposition of an existing desire, it will follow that in this case too desire is unintelligible, paralleling the argument just given where the one desiring was supposed to exist. 'If desire were to exist prior to the one desiring, that is, quite apart from anyone desiring . . .'[2] and so on. Or one can consider the one desiring

[1] i.e., if there is no person prior to the act of desiring.

[2] *Kārikā* 1, p. 109. The argument is now applied to desire instead of to the one desiring.

on the supposition that the desire does not exist. But this makes no sense either. Because 'If the desire does not exist, how can there be one who desires?'[1] It follows that the one desiring does not exist. As then neither desire nor the one desiring exist, the factors of personal existence, the bases of cognition and the primal elements do not exist.

Simultaneity or conjunction of desire and the one desiring

Someone may interject that desire and the one desiring do not arise one after the other as our attack supposes. Rather, the desire and the one desiring arise simultaneously (*sahaiva*).[2] It is by a desire arising simultaneously with a state of mind that the latter is desirous, and that is the 'one desiring'. So both desire and the one desiring exist in fact.

Nāgārjuna replies that here too

> 3ab The simultaneous arising of desire and the one desiring does not make sense;

that is the simultaneous origination of desire and the one desiring does not make sense; because,

> 3cd Desire and the one desiring would arise independently of one another.

Because of their being simultaneous, like the right and left horns of a cow, is the meaning.

Now the simultaneity (*sahabhāva*) of these two, desire and the one desiring, would have to be conceived either as resting on their identity (*ekatva*) or on their difference (*pṛthaktva*).[3] The first case, that they are identical, does not make sense. Because

> 4a There can be no simultaneity in identity;

140 Nāgārjuna explains why that is:

> 4b There can be no simultaneity of something with itself.

The essential nature of a desire, which cannot be distinguished from the desire, cannot be held to be simultaneous with the desire.

Concerning the second case, Nāgārjuna says there is no simultaneity of what is separate.

[1] This adapts *Kārikā* 2ab, p. 110.
[2] Or, 'in conjunction'; the temporal factor predominates.
[3] Or, 'separateness'.

4cd Again, how can there be simultaneity of what is entirely separate?

Indeed one never observes the simultaneity of things each of which exists separately like light and darkness or *saṁsāra*, the death-birth cycle, and *nirvāṇa*.

5 If there could be simultaneity in identity, then there would be simultaneity even without the second component; if there could be simultaneity based on separate existence there would be simultaneity even without the second component.

If there were simultaneity in identity, then one could say 'wherever there is identity there is simultaneity' and then there would be simultaneity of even one of the two components. Again, if simultaneity is thought to rest in separateness on the principle 'wherever there is separateness there is simultaneity', then there would be simultaneity in one component which had been defined as different from the other as a cow is different than a horse and other animals.[1] Further,

Reciprocality of simultaneity or conjunction and separateness or difference

6 If there is simultaneity in separateness, how will the separateness of a desire and of the one desiring be established, on the basis of which they would be simultaneous?

141 The simultaneity[1] of a desire and the one desiring is imagined to rest on their separateness. How will their separate existence be established (*siddhi*)? How can the one desiring be established apart from dependence on the desire so that there could be simultaneity of both? After all, the simultaneity of cow and horse, which have been established as separate, is a matter of direct observation. But desire and the one desiring have not been established in this way; so there is no simultaneity of the pair.

Again, on the other hand it is clear that there is no simultaneity of two things established as separate.

7ab Again, if the total separateness of desire and the one desiring is established,

[1] In this passage the sense of conjunction becomes more prominent.

If the opponent supposes this, what then, Nāgārjuna asks, of this supposed, ineffective simultaneity?

7cd What purpose will you suppose the simultaneity of these two to have?

Simultaneity is conceived to serve the purpose of establishing desire and the one desiring. But there can be no simultaneity of two things if each is not established as separate, and the opponent is assuming that each has been established as separate. But if this is so what is to be achieved by establishing their simultaneity? That is,

8ab You suppose simultaneity even though separate existence is not established.

It is obvious that desire and the one desiring cannot be established separately if you consider only their simultaneity. And there can be no simultaneity unless these have been established separately.

8cd And yet you seize on separateness for the sake of establishing simultaneity.

It being thus clear that the opponent's proof is established on a reciprocal relationship, which of the two is the basis of proof and which is the proven? That is to say

142 9 If separateness does not exist, simultaneity cannot establish it; but if separateness does exist then what simultaneity can you have in mind?

There can be no separateness existing as such and unrelated to simultaneity, in which simultaneity could be established. Nāgārjuna says it is simply impossible: 'if separateness does exist then what simultaneity can you have in mind?' Thus, concluding the analysis carried out, Nāgārjuna says, insisting that desire and the one desiring have not been established,

10ab Thus desire cannot be established either in conjunction with or independently of the one desiring.

Even as desire and the one desiring cannot be established either one after the other or simultaneously, so, extending this conclusion to all things, Nāgārjuna says

10cd As in the case of desire, none of the elements of existence can be established either as simultaneous or as not simultaneous.

That is, one proceeds, as with desire and the one desiring, to show the non-existence of aversion and the one averse, delusion and the one deluded and so on for the other afflictions.

143 Precisely for these reasons the illustrious one said, 'Something which would be desire, either as the seat or the object of desire; something which would be aversion, either as the seat or the object of aversion, something which would be deludedness either as the seat or the object of delusion; such an element of existence one never discerns directly nor perceives in any way. The one who does not discern such an element directly nor perceive it in any way is said to be without desire, without aversion, without delusion, to have a mind free from false belief: to be a realized man. He is said to have crossed to the other shore; to have attained peace . . . to have done away with all harmful influences. He is said to be free of the afflictions, master of himself, one whose everyday thinking is perfectly liberated and whose insight is perfectly liberated; one of noble origins, a mighty serpent, one who has done what is to be done, who has done what he had to do, who has done away with his burden, has fulfilled his own duty, has achieved the complete annihilation of the thirst for existence, whose mind is perfectly liberated by right practice, who has attained complete mastery over all thought. Such is called a *śramaṇa*.'[1] And so on.

Then there is this verse: 'Those who have understood that the nature of desire, aversion, infatuation and delusion springs from a will engendered by falsity give up vain imaginings; for such there is not even renunciation in this world; they have fully realized the nature of all things.'

[1] *Samādhirāja Sūtra.*

IX

The Agent Subject and his Doing

Refutation of realism

180 You may object that the compound elements of existence (*saṁskṛtā dharmā*)[1] – consciousness and the rest – do exist in fact, it being their nature to exist as compounded; this is because their cause, the agent subject and his doing (*karma-kāraka*), exists in fact. As the illustrious one said, 'A human person, o monks, who is in the grip of ignorance develops meritorious qualities or unmeritorious qualities of a special kind', and so on. This passage speaks of the agent subject and his doing and teaches that the consequences of his doing – consciousness and the other factors[2] – are compounded. That of which there is a productive agent must itself exist, as, for example, a pot. What does not exist can have no producer, as, for example, a garment made of tortoise hair.

We reply that there would be compounded factors like consciousness if the agent subject and his doing existed as their cause; but they do not. Because

> 1 An agent subject, actual as such, does not give rise to a product, actual as such. Nor does an agent subject not actual as such realize a product not actual as such.

The verse says the agent subject 'gives rise to' or 'produces' (*karoti*), that is, he is the doer (*kartā*). The term agent subject, or producer, is used only of someone who produces something, not of one who does not produce something. One must conceive of such an act of production as the act of an agent who is actual as such (*sadbhūta*) or who is not (*asadbhūta*) or who both is and is not. 'What is produced' – the product, what is

[1] Topic of a chapter not included in this translation.

[2] The allusion is to the Buddhist paradigm of causality, the cyclical linkage of causal factors in existence: ignorance, character disposition, consciousness, individuality, sense organs, etc., leading to re-birth.

done (*karma*) – is the primary object of the agent; it too may have three modes: actual, non-actual or both.

181 The two themes of this verse are, first, that an agent subject, actual as such – one conjoined with the activity (*kriyāyukta*) of agency – does not give rise to a product which is actual as such, that is which is conjoined with the activity of being produced; and, second, that an agent not actual as such – one devoid of the activity (*kriyārahita*) of agency – does not give rise to a product which is not actual as such, that is which is devoid of the activity of being produced.

With a view to establishing the first thesis Nāgārjuna says

> 2ab If there is no activity of an agent subject who is actual as such, a product would be without a producer.

Because what is called an agent subject is essentially conjoined with the activity of agency, only an agent who exists as such conjoined with the activity of agency gives rise to something and receives the name agent or producer. It follows that for one such, who is called agent or producer because of his activity of production, there cannot be another activity by which he gives rise to a product. If, because of the absence of this second activity the agent does not give rise to anything, then a product would be unrelated to an agent, that is, would be without a producer (*akartṛka*). But a product is not possible without a producer, it would be like the making of a pot by the son of a barren woman. This being so, 'If there is no activity of an agent subject who is actual as such, a product would be without a producer.' Because of this unacceptable consequence an agent subject actual as such does not give rise to any product.[1]

And now, explaining that an agent does not give rise to a product actual as such, Nāgārjuna says

> 2cd If there is no activity of an agent subject actual as such the agent would be without a product.

What is called a product actual as such (*sadbhūta karma*) is essentially conjoined with the activity of being produced. Of such a product, which gets its name from the activity of being produced, there is no second activity by which it would be produced. In this sense there is no activity of being produced

[1] A producer is such only when he is *producing*; i.e. he must be a producer *before* he enters into the activity of producing a product. Yet a producer can produce nothing but a product. Therefore he cannot be a producer before he produces a product.

of a product already actual as such. If there is no second activity of being produced then the producer most certainly does not produce a product actual as such. And if he does not produce because there is no second activity of being produced on the part of the product, then the producer of such a product would be without a product (*akarmaka*) – a producer of a non-existing product. But this makes no sense: it is contrary to experience that there could be a perpetrator of an unforgivable deed which has not been perpetrated.

Refutation of idealism[1]

Having thus established that an agent actual as such does not
182 give rise to a product actual as such, Nāgārjuna, expounding how it is that an agent not actual as such (*asadbhūta kāraka*) does not give rise to a product not actual as such (*asadhbūta karma*) now says

> 3 If an agent not actual as such gives rise to a product not actual as such then such a product would be uncaused and the agent would be non-causal.

An agent not actual as such is one devoid of the activity of agency. As the activity of agency is the basis (*hetu*) for the expression agent, an agent not actually producing would be non-causal (*nirhetuka*); and as well a product not actual as such would be uncaused (*nirhetuka*). If we accept the doctrine that things can exist without a causal basis (*hetu*)[2] then, Nāgārjuna says, effect and cause and all related concepts would be denied validity.

> 4ab In the absence of the causal principle there will be no cause and no effect.

If we accept the causal principle in general (*hetu*), what is produced in virtue of causality is the effect. What gives rise to the effect may appropriately be called direct cause (*kāraṇa*). For example clay is the material cause (*hetu*) of a pot and the pot is the effect. The potter's wheel and so on are the co-operating direct causes. If, however, we assume that there is

[1] This section refutes the Buddhist (Sarvāstivada) view that elements of existence persist even when not actual in space and time; it can also be taken as a critique of views like Plato's theory of forms.

[2] Either material cause or causal principle in general. This is an attack on the view, held by some Buddhists, that *dharmas*, the elements of existence, subsist, when not actualized in time, without a material basis and causally inactive.

no causal principle there could be no pot because it would be unrelated to a material basis, like a pot made from the crest-jewel taken from the head of a frog. If there is no pot how could there be a cause of it? So, as Nāgārjuna put it, 'In the absence of the causal principle there will be no cause and no effect.' Therefore

> 4cd In their absence there will be no activity, no agent and no means.

183 'In their absence' means in the absence of cause and effect. What effect would make the activity of an agent conceivable? In which activity would there be an independent agency of the potter? Nor does it make sense that the effective means should be merely the pot having the same nature as the clay. So much for 'In their absence there will be no activity, no agent and no means.' Therefore

> 5ab If activity, agent and means are impossible there would be no right and no wrong.

The thought here is that if Devadatta is an actual agent because, of his own free will, he engages in the activity of refraining from taking life, he gives rise to the activity of refraining from taking life because of a freely chosen purpose and through the appropriate means. In this way a meritorious deed has arisen for him. This can be applied to the remainder of the ten favourable paths of action which are produced by favourable activities and also to the favourable observances laid down such as honouring the triple jewel,[1] one's mother and father, other worthy people and so on. And in the case of wrongdoing as well, that is the taking of life and so on, the opposite of the favourable paths, it should be emphasized that the consequence will necessarily follow that, if there are no activities, no agents and no means, there are no deeds. If, in this sense, there is no good deed and no ill deed then they can obviously have no moral consequences.

Nāgārjuna expounds this saying

> 5cd If there is neither good nor ill deed no fruit can arise from them.

If neither good nor ill deed (*dharmādharma*) exists there could be no fruit, no moral consequences (*phala*), whether desirable or undesirable, born of good and ill deeds. Hence

[1] The Buddha, the (Buddhist) Truth and the community of Buddhist monks.

6ab In the absence of moral consequences such as fruition a path leading to heaven or to liberation is unintelligible.

184 If there were desirable or undesirable consequences on the lower path (*laukika mārga*) which aims at composed insight beyond phenomena through meditation, that is to say, heaven, then the spiritual pursuit of the lower path would be the best means of achieving this and it would include the fruits of renouncing the kinds of action which conduce to a wasted life. And if *nirvāṇa*, understood as liberation, were a fruit of action then with it in view the spiritual pursuit of the higher path (*lokottara mārga*), the eightfold path of the wise, would bear fruit. But as there are no fruits of action, 'In the absence of moral consequences as fruition, a path leading to heaven or to liberation is unintelligible.'

If in this way there is no fruit, what then?

6cd It follows that all activities whatsoever are without purpose.

Further, such activities as farming, commerce and governing are taken up with a view to their fruits; all such activities as well, if there are no fruits, will be unintelligible. In this sense it would follow that all activities as such are without purpose. But they are not without purpose. That is why this theory is the source of the poisonous growth of all the fallacies. It denies both heaven and liberation, it is the source from which
185 hell arises and the great troubles which descend on us, it contradicts both the seen and the unseen reasons for things. This being so the thesis that an agent subject who is not actual gives rise to deeds which are not actual is a debased theory and is to be rejected by the wise.[1]

Exhaustion of the formal possibilities

Having in this way established the two theses Nāgārjuna now says that an agent subject by nature *both* actual and non-actual does not give rise to a product which is by nature *both* actual and non-actual.

[1] This sweeping rejection of the non-actual agent because of causal inefficacy, reminds of Aristotle's rejection of the separate, i.e. 'non-actual' existence of Plato's forms. Mādhyamika cannot tolerate the claim to existence of anything other than the actual; and, of course, even that claim is merely commonsensical.

7ab An agent subject both actual and non-actual does not give rise to a product both actual and non-actual.

Here a product both actual and non-actual means a product which is both conjoined with and not conjoined with the activity of being produced. An agent subject who is both actual and non-actual does not give rise to such a product. Because

7cd As to exist and not to exist are reciprocally contradictory[1] how can they hold of one and the same thing?

That one and the same thing at one and the same time can be both conjoined with the activity of being produced and not so conjoined is clearly nonsensical. Therefore an agent subject actually both existing and not existing does not give rise to a product actually both existing and not existing either. The thought is that they are not real (*avidyamāna*).

Having exposed in this way the faultiness of the homogeneous form[2] of the three theses, Nāgārjuna, wishing to repudiate the heterogeneous form of the three theses as well says

8ab A non-actual product is not produced by an actual agent subject, nor is an actual product produced by a non-actual agent subject.

A non-actual product, not actual *as* product, that is not conjoined with the activity of being produced, is not produced by an actual agent, one existing *as* agent, that is one engaged in the activity of producing. Because

8cd All the previous fallacies will necessarily follow.

186 'If there is no activity of producing in an actual agent the product would be without agent.' In this sense an actual agent does not produce a product. But neither is a non-actual product produced by one such. A non-actual product would be an uncaused (*ahetuka*) product. That is why 'In the absence of the causal principle there can be no cause and no effect.' From this all fallacies ensue.

And so, as the grounds are exactly the same as given before, the reason for the faultiness of the heterogeneous form of the thesis will not be adduced again. Even as it has been shown how an actual agent subject cannot give rise to an actual

[1] *Parasparaviruddha*. One of the many passages explicitly stating the law of non-contradiction.

[2] That is, where agent and deed are *both* either actual or non-actual or both. In the heterogeneous form the agent will be existent while his deed will be non-existent, and so on.

product, it should be shown, by following the method given, how a non-actual agent subject, that is one not connected with the activity of production, does not give rise to an actual product. Having thus far pointed out the fault in the heterogeneous form of the thesis by relating the terms singly, Nāgārjuna now points out the fault in each term by relating them in pairs.

> 9 An actual agent subject, for the reasons already given,
> gives rise neither to a non-actual product nor to one
> both actual and non-actual.

The very agent subject who is actual does not produce a non-actual product nor one both actual and non-actual. Why? Nāgārjuna says 'for the reasons already given'. As 'If there is no activity of production in an actual agent subject', an actual agent subject does not produce. Because of the difficulties adduced: 'a non-actual product is not produced'; 'such a product would be uncaused'; 'if there is no causal principle there can be no cause and no effect' – and so on. In short, a product both actual and non-actual cannot be produced. To quote again: 'As to exist and not to exist are reciprocally contradictory how can they hold of one and the same thing?' And so an actual agent subject can give rise neither to an actual product nor to one both actual and non-actual.

187 Now Nāgārjuna says that a non-actual agent subject as well can produce neither an actual product nor one both actual and non-actual:

> 10 A non-actual agent subject does not give rise to an
> actual product nor one both actual and non-actual for
> the reasons already given.

An agent subject who was not actual would be without causal efficacy (*nirhetuka*); so, because of the fallacy already given, 'If there is no causal principle there can be no cause and no effect', a non-actual agent subject cannot produce. It follows from the statement 'If there is no productive activity of an agent subject actual as such the agent subject would be without a product' that an actual product is not produced. No more is a product produced which is both actual and non-actual: 'As to exist and not to exist are reciprocally contradictory how can they hold of one and the same thing?'

And now Nāgārjuna expounds how it is that even an agent subject who is, singly and jointly, both actual and not actual does not give rise to a product of such different attributes as to be both actual and non-actual.

> 11 An agent subject both actual and non-actual does not give rise to a product both actual and non-actual; this should be realized for the reasons already given.

188 The reference is 'As to exist and not to exist are reciprocally contradictory how can they hold of one and the same thing?' So an agent subject both actual and not actual does not produce anything. It follows from the statement 'If there is no activity of production in an actual agent subject as actual agent subject does not produce' that an actual product is not produced. Nor is a non-actual, uncaused product produced because of the fallacy given in the statement 'If there is no causal principle there can be no cause and no effect.'

Conclusion: the self-existence of things is without sense

In this way, in both the homogeneous form of the thesis and in the heterogeneous form, the existence of both the agent subject and his product – his doing, his deeds – is, however taken, without sense. It follows that what was said earlier, namely, 'The compound elements of existence – consciousness and the rest – do exist in fact it being their nature to exist as compounded: this is because their cause, the agent subject and his doing, exists in fact'[1] does not make sense.

You may ask: Do you assert positively that things do not exist? Indeed we do not. But for you, who hold the view that things have their being in themselves, the rejection of all things as real becomes possible just because they are denied self-existence. We, however, because things arise in dependence, discern no self-existence in anything at all. Of what then would we deny self-existence.[2]

As is said in the *Ratnāvalī*: 'One who takes a mirage to be water and who, arriving at the spot, persuades himself that the water is non-existent, is befuddled. The basic illusion is to hold that the personal world, this mirage, either exists or does not exist. So long as this illusion persists there is no freedom. At first the imaginings of ignorance, later the disclosure of the truth of things. If one does not insist on the reality of things what could their unreality be?'

[1] P. 115. The opponent's view.

[2] This puts the Mādhyamika position succinctly: he is not a disillusioned realist, therefore he is not a nihilist.

189 This being so, how could the existence of things, whose nature is to be without self-existence, be established in any of the three ways? So, Nāgārjuna says, it is by succumbing to conventional misbelief and accepting the real dependence of one thing on another, and not in any other way, that the existence of everyday illusory things, which are thought constructs like the water of a mirage, becomes acceptable.

> 12 An agent subject can be held to exist only on the presupposition of a product, and a product can be held to exist only on the presupposition of an agent subject. We discern no other basis for establishing their existence.

That is because an agent subject who is unrelated to a product cannot be productive; but an agent subject related to a product is productive. There is no product – something done – not resulting from the activity of an agent because the term product is reserved for what is produced or done. The product exists as such in dependence on the producing agent. In this way, except for a proof of the existence of agent and product which depends on their reciprocality (*parasparāpekṣa*), 'We discern no other basis for establishing their existence.'

Extension of conclusion to all things

The idea that the proof of the existence of agent and product depends on their reciprocality Nāgārjuna extends to other things.

> 13abc One should grasp the factors of personal existence in the same way by giving up the idea of the agent subject and his doing.

'In the same way' refers to the immediately preceding terms 'agent subject' and his 'product'. 'Factors of personal existence' (*upādāna*) means appropriation (*upātti*). Nāgārjuna uses the expression 'factors of personal existence' as a synonym for the activity of appropriation. This, in its concrete realization, embraces the agent subject as appropriator and his doing as the appropriating. Precisely as for agent subject and his doing the appropriator and what is appropriated can be established as reciprocally dependent, but not as self-existent. They cannot be established as self-existence because of 'giving up the idea of the agent subject and his doing'. The quotation marks indicate the reason; 'giving up the idea' means renouncing. The

190 sense of the verse can be given thus: It should be understood that the reasons for rejecting the appropriator and what is appropriated are precisely those given for renouncing the agent subject and his doing. But it should be understood that the refutation of the agent subject and his doing is not the proof that only these two are reciprocally dependent, but further, that

> 13d One should think of all other things on the model of agent subject and his doing.

'One' means the wise man. The wise man, seeking freedom for the sake of release from the bonds of birth, ageing and death, having discredited the self-existence of agent subject and his doing would realize that they can be established only in utter dependence on reciprocality. 'All other things' are all those things without exception other than agent subject and his doing and appropriator and what is appropriated, such as, what is born and what gives birth, what moves and movement, what is seen and seeing, the subject of attribution and attributes, what is produced and the producer; and as well whole and part, quality and substance, means of knowledge and object of knowledge.

A detailed investigation of these topics can be had in the *Madhyamakāvatāra* and other works. You may think it is not necessary to mention appropriation a second time as the phrase 'One should think of all other things' comprehends both appropriation and appropriator. This is true, yet for the purpose of making clear their importance for the investigation into the way things truly are they are mentioned separately. Indeed, in the chapters still to come there will be repeated investigation of these two terms.

X

Self as Subject of Perception

The personalist thesis

192 Some may object that the *kārikā* in the previous chapter, 'One should grasp the factors of personal existence in the same way by giving up the idea of the agent subject and his doing', does not make sense, because

> 1 Some hold that prior to seeing, hearing and the other kinds of perceiving as well as to feeling and the other factors of personal existence, the one whose they are must exist.

It is the view of the Sāṁitīyas that seeing, hearing, smelling, tasting and the other kinds of perceiving as well as feeling, touch, ideation and the other factors of personal existence are of an appropriating perceptor (*upādātā*) and that he exists prior to appropriative percepting (*upādāna*). What is their argument? This:

> 2 How can seeing and the other kinds of perceiving belong to a non-existent entity? Therefore a determinate entity exists prior to these.

The thought is that it is an existing Devadatta who effects possession of wealth not the non-existent son of a barren woman. Similarly, in this sense, if there were no person (*pudgala*) existing as such (*vyavasthita*) prior to seeing and the other kinds of perceiving he would not have been able to
193 appropriate seeing and the other kinds of perceiving as his own.[1] Therefore, even as Devadatta clearly existed as such prior to his wealth, the person exists prior to perceiving as the one who effects possession of it.

[1] This pleonasm seems appropriate.

Mādhyamika critique of the personalist thesis

We reply:

> 3 How can this determinate entity which exists prior to seeing, hearing and the other kinds of perceiving and to feeling and the other factors of personal existence be spoken and thought of sensibly at all?

In what way can one speak and think sensibly (*prajñapyate*) about this determinate person who exists prior to perceiving, as perceiving is the basis for the idea (*prajñapti*) of person? If he is imagined to exist as such prior to perceiving then he would exist independently of it, as cloth is independent of a clay pot. But what is not related to its own material cause, for example wealthy persons who have no relation to wealth, is without a basis in reason. What is more,

> 4 If this person exists as such even without seeing and the other kinds of perceiving these will quite certainly exist without him.

If you think a so-called person exists prior to perceiving, he will appropriate for himself the appropriative activities of seeing and the other kinds of perceiving. Now if this is so, perceiving will, incontestably, exist without the person.

As a wealthy Devadatta, existing prior to any connection with and apart from wealth in the usual sense, would have to appropriate wealth of a different kind attained in a special way, so the appropriator would have to appropriate a different sort of perceiving because it would be other than usual. But Nāgārjuna says this is impossible.

194

> 5 Every effect implies a cause, every cause implies an effect; how can there be an effect without a cause, how can there be a cause without an effect?

The thought here is that by virtue of a cause, for example a seed, some effect or other, for example a sprout, becomes evident, and by the effect some cause or other is clearly implied: the seed being the cause of the sprout and this being the effect of the seed. Similarly, if by virtue of appropriative perceiving a self-existent person is clearly implied, he would be the appropriator of such perceiving. And if, by virtue of a person, appropriative perceiving is clearly implied, this being what the person appropriates, then in such case the reciprocal dependence of appropriator and what is appropriated would be established. So long as perceiving is accepted as existing in a special way, without the appropriator, then, being without dependence, it would be simply non-existent. It follows that neither of the two has been established. In sum, it makes no sense to say that a determinate (*avasthita*) appropriator exists separate from seeing and the other kinds of perceiving.

A separate subject for each kind of perceiving

You may counter the statement 'How can this determinate entity which exists prior to seeing, hearing and the other kinds of perceiving and to feeling and the other elements of personal existence be spoken and thought of sensibly at all?'[1] by urging that it would be an error to suppose that a determinate subject exists prior to all perceiving *in general*. If however,

> 6ab No one subject exists prior to seeing and other perceiving in general;

but rather prior to each kind of perceiving singly; if this is so then

> 6cd Each kind of perceiving implies a different prior subject at different times.

If a subject of seeing (*draṣṭā*) is implied by seeing he is not in that case to be thought of as presupposing hearing and the
195 other kinds of perceiving apart from seeing. Your earlier reproach is therefore inappropriate.

Mādhyamika critique

We reply. This is not tenable either because it is impossible for something to exist which is bereft of seeing and the other kinds of perceiving, which does not appropriate, lacks causal efficacy (*nirhetuka*)[2] and cannot manifest itself.

> 7ab If there is no subject prior to seeing and other kinds of perceiving in general,

if this is supposed,

> 7cd How can there be a different subject prior to each kind of perceiving?

What cannot be a subject (*yaḥ*) prior to (*pūrvaḥ*) all perceiv-

[1] *Kārikā* 3, p. 126. [2] Or, 'lacks any basis in reason'.

ing in general cannot be a subject prior to each kind of perceiving singly either. There is for example no forest before all the trees nor before each of the trees singly; and oil is not extracted from sand in general nor is there oil in any one grain of sand.

What is more, a subject prior to each singly must be accepted as no less prior to all as well; because there is no totality apart from single particulars. That is why it does not make sense to say that the subject is prior to each kind of perceiving singly.

There is a further absurdity.

8ab If the subject of seeing is the same as the subject of hearing and it the same as the subject of feeling

then

8c it would be prior to each singly.

It makes no sense to say that the seeing subject is the same as the hearing subject. If this were so then the subject of hearing would be a subject of seeing even without the activity of seeing and the subject of seeing would be a subject of hearing even without the activity of hearing. But we never observe a seer devoid of the activity of seeing nor a hearer devoid of the activity of hearing. That is why Nāgārjuna says:

8d But this makes no sense either.

196 How could this be as there is a different agent (*kārakā*) for each and every activity (*pratikriya*), is what Nāgārjuna was explaining. And so this thought as well is tenable.

Buddhapālita[1] explained it this way. If there is only one self (*ātman*), it follows that the subject must move from one sense to the other like someone moving from one window to another. Bhāvaviveka faulted that explanation in this way: if the self is all-pervasive it need not move from one sense to another, so Buddhapālita's criticism does not hold. But this itself does not hold because the context of Buddhapālita's refutation was the doctrine of the separate person (*pudgala*) as conceived by our fellow Buddhists who do not accept the all-pervasiveness of the self. Thus the fault we pointed out does stand.

Again, if, attempting to escape the difficulty pointed out, one supposes that

[1] See p. 36, note 3.

9ab The subject of seeing, the subject of hearing and the subject of feeling are each different,

that would not make sense because if one wished to think in that way,

197 9cd The subject of hearing would exist at the same time as the subject of seeing and there would be a plurality of selves.

For example, a horse is other than a cow. But it is not the case that because a cow exists a horse cannot exist at the same time. So if the subject of hearing were other than the subject of seeing he would have to be able to exist at the same time as an existing subject of seeing; but this is not what one wished to establish. Thus subjects are not totally different. What is more, on this thesis the plurality of selves is implied because each of the subjects of seeing, hearing and feeling is established entirely separately. Thus there is nothing whatsoever called a person existing prior to seeing and the other kinds of perceiving each taken singly, either.

The concrete individual as subject

At this point you may object: There is indeed a self prior to all the activities of seeing and the other kinds of perceiving generally. Earlier it was asked 'If there is such how will it be spoken and thought of?' This should be explained. It is accepted that, prior to seeing and the other kinds of perceiving, the four elements (*mahābhūta*)[1] exist in the form of a potential individual as a body-mind entity (*nāmarūpāvasthā*). In their turn the six sense faculties, seeing, hearing and the rest, based in the potential individual, arise out of these elements. Therefore the four elements do exist prior to seeing and the other kinds of perceiving as their base.

Mādhyamika critique

But this is not tenable either.

10 Nor does a self exist in the elements from which seeing, hearing and the other kinds of perceiving and feeling and the other personal factors arise.

That is, seeing and the other kinds of perceiving arise from

[1] Earth, air, fire, water.

the four elements; but a subject of perceiving which would both exist in the elements and yet be the agent of perceiving them makes no sense for the reason given earlier. This is Nāgārjuna's thought. We may quote the earlier line 'How can there be an effect without a cause, how can there be a cause without
198 an effect?' It fits here exactly. A subject which could exist prior to the perceiving of the four elements would be the base of the four elements. But this cannot be so because such a subject would be without any causal efficacy. How can what does not exist appropriate the four elements? As the difficulty of appropriating the four elements is the same as pointed out in the appropriating of seeing, it need not be gone into again.

Perceiving itself proves the existence of the subject

You may object that although in this way the self has been disproved, perceiving exists because it has not been disproved. There is no necessity of seeing and the other kinds of perceiving connected with things whose nature it is to have no self, like pots and such things. It follows that that with which there is this essential connection, namely the subject as self (*ātman*), does exist.

We reply that there would be a subject as self if there were perceiving. But there is no perceiving. If the one for whom perceiving functions does not exist as we have shown, then as this appropriating subject itself does not exist, how, Nāgārjuna asks, can perceiving, which is appropriative by nature, exist.

> 11 If the subject of seeing, hearing and the other kinds of perceiving, and of feeling and the other factors of personal existence does not exist, these do not exist either.

If the one *of* whom seeing and the other kinds of perception are imagined to be does not exist as has been argued, then it has been made evident that seeing and the other kinds of perception do not exist. It follows therefore that because perceiving does not exist the subject as self does not exist.

Conclusion. The subject neither exists nor does not exist

You may ask whether indeed we are certain that there is no subject as self. We explained this in what was just said, namely that because perceiving does not exist there is no perceiving subject as self either. This we said but you have not adequately grasped the purport of the statement. It was that the perceiving

subject conceived of as an ontic entity (*bhāvarūpa*) cannot have self-existence. What was said was solely to dissipate obstinate clinging to its *self-existence.* It was a counter-argument
199 using the false concept (*viparyāsa*) 'non-existence' (*asad*). But it is not to be thought of as non-existent (*abhāva*). Both the obsession with things as realities and the obsession with things as unrealities are to be repudiated.

As Āryadeva said,[1] 'What for you is self for me is non-self; the self does not exist because it is beyond grasping. Is speculation not born among perishable things?' Expounding precisely the same point Nāgārjuna says

> 12 Speculations concerning existence and non-existence
> are silenced in the face of something which exists
> neither before, at the same time as, nor after seeing and
> the other kinds of perceiving.

In the first place there is no subject as self prior to seeing and the other kinds of perceiving because it would lack a *raison d'être* (*astitvābhāvāt*). Nor is there a subject simultaneously with seeing and the other kinds of perceiving because one never experiences simultaneous existence of two things each of which by itself does not exist, like the two horns of a rabbit: subject and perceiving do not exist by themselves, independent of each other. So simultaneity is not possible either. No more is there a subject subsequently. If there were first perceiving and in a later moment a subject, then it would be possible. But it is not so because no act can be without an
200 agent. After a searching investigation it is clear that there is no perceiving subject as self either before, after or simultaneously with seeing and the other kinds of perceiving. What man of insight would in such case ontologize about the existence or non-existence of something whose very nature it is never to be perceived (*anupalabdha*)? The conclusion is that, exactly like the agent subject and his doing, the subject of appropriation and the activity of appropriating can exist only in
200.3 reciprocal dependence, not each in its own right (*svābhāvikī*).

[1] *Catuḥśataka*, X, 3.

XI

Fire and Fuel

The initial alternative: identical or different

202 Some may object that what we have just stated, 'Exactly like agent subject and his doing, neither the subject of appropriation nor the activity of appropriating exists in its own right', does not make sense. This is because even dependent things are observed to be self-existent; fire (*agni*) is dependent on fuel (*indhanam*) yet it is not lacking self-existence, as heat and the capacity to burn something are directly experienced as its peculiar effects. In the same way fuel is dependent on fire, yet it is not lacking in self-existence because the four material elements are self-existent. Similarly the subject of appropriation, though dependent on what is appropriated, exists in his own right; and what is appropriated is dependent on the appropriator like fuel and fire. These two, appropriator and appropriated, exist as a pair.

We reply that this would be so if fire and fuel existed as such; but they do not. How is that? The thinking is that if fire and fuel exist they must be either identical with (*ekatva*) or different from (*anyatva*) one another. But Nāgārjuna says that neither makes sense:

> 1 If fire is fuel that would be identity of agent and act. If fire is wholly other than fuel then it could exist even without fuel.

203 In this argument fuel is what is ignited and consists of wood and such things which are to be burned. That which burns the fuel is the agent, fire. If one thinks that the fuel itself is the fire then agent and act would be identical. But things are not taken this way because the untenable consequence would be the identity of the pot and the potter and of the woodcutter and the wood, and because this is not commonly found to be so.

On the other hand it is no better if they are wholly other (*anyatva*). If fire were wholly other than fuel then we would directly perceive fire as being independent of fuel. There is no cloth, wholly other than a pot, which is not seen to be independent of it. But fire is not independent of fuel in this way and so this does not make sense. Furthermore, if fire were wholly other than fuel then

> 2 It would flame forever uncaused by bursting into flame; to re-kindle it would be pointless, an act without action.

If fire is conceived of as existing independently (*pṛthagbhūta*) of fuel then it would burn forever; and it would not be caused by rekindling; it would be pointless to start it afresh. In such case it would be an act that did not act on anything.

Desiring to explain this very meaning Nāgārjuna says

> 3 Because it is unrelated to anything else it is not caused by bursting into flame; as it burns forever it follows that it is pointless to kindle it again.

The thinking is that what actually flames is the fuel bursting into flame; bursting into flame is the 'cause' (*hetu*) of fire; that is what 'caused by bursting into flame' means. 'Not caused by bursting into flame' means that bursting into flame is not the cause of fire. If fire were something entirely different than bursting into flame then it would be independent of fuel. What is wholly other than something else is in fact seen to be independent of it, as cloth is other than a clay pot.
204 Therefore fire, being independent (*nirapekṣatva*) of anything else, would not have bursting into flame as its cause. But if fire were dependent on bursting into flame it would go out if this failed. Yet if it were independent of ignition, not subject to the possibility of extinction, it would be alight forever. If fire burns forever then it would be pointless to try to prevent its extinction by fanning or blowing on the embers. In such case fire would be an agent without acting on anything (*akarmaka*). But no agent can be active if there is nothing for it to act on: the son of a barren woman does not exist. For this reason it is not tenable that fire is wholly other than fuel.

You may object that what was said earlier[1] 'If fire is wholly other than fuel then it could exist even without fuel' does not make sense. The thought here is that if fire and fuel were wholly different fire could exist without fuel. But the object which is enveloped in flames is the fuel and its definition is 'what is being burned' and fire is directly perceived to be

[1] *Kārikā* 1, p. 132.

dependent on it. Now if this is correct then fuel must be defined in terms of a necessary connection with fire. Fire is, in our experience, seen to be dependent on fuel and not separate from it. It follows that your statement 'If fire is wholly other than fuel then it could exist even without fuel' draws an absurd conclusion which is not appropriate.

Exposing the untenability of this line of thought Nāgārjuna says

> 4 If fuel is what bursts into flame, what will ignite the fuel as that is its essential nature.[1]

If you think that fuel is what is enveloped in flames and is defined as 'what is burning' and that fire is based on that; if you speculate thus it is not logically possible to say that fire burns fuel because 'what will ignite the fuel as that is its essential nature'.[2]

205 If one imagines, as is usual, that 'fire burns fuel' then fuel is what is being burned, enveloped in flames. But we never experience a fire entirely separate and distinct by which the fuel is burned; as fuel is of such a nature as to be perceived directly as enveloped in flames and nothing but what is being burned. If then fire is not separate, what is it that will burn the fuel? The expression 'as that is its essential nature' means to be nothing but what is in flames. Fire does not therefore burn fuel because a fire which is separate (*vyatirikta*) from fuel does not exist. If this is so then how would the idea of something being enveloped in flames not trouble you for the same reason?

The problem of interaction

Further, if we assume the complete otherness (*anyatva*) of fire and fuel, what is usually called 'burning' does not exist. How can fuel be burning and how will fire burn fuel? Nāgārjuna expounds this saying

> 5 Fire, being wholly other than fuel, cannot interact with it; not interacting it cannot burn; what does not burn cannot go out; and, not going out, it will persist in its own nature.

If fire were wholly other than fuel it could never, because

[1] *Iattāvanmātram*. That is, fuel is what is already alight.

[2] I.e. if fire burns only fuel that is already ignited, what ignites the fuel initially?

of this otherness, interact[1] with fuel as it can never interact with darkness, nor will it burn fuel because it has not acted upon fuel. It is as if it were situated in a remote region. That is why it is simply not logically possible to say 'fuel bursts into flames'. It follows that fire cannot be extinguished and being unextinguished it would enjoy its own specific nature, that is, it will remain alight. The word 'and' in the *kārikā* offers alternative possibilities. It may mean either–or, that is, either that fire will persist in its own nature or that there is no difference in this respect between fire and fuel. It may mean conjunction, that is, that fire, wholly other, neither interacts, nor burns, nor goes out and persists in its own essential nature. It is therefore untenable that fire is wholly other than fuel.

Though other, fire and fuel are not independent of each other

You may object that it does not make sense to say that the otherness of fire and fuel is untenable because 'fire cannot interact with fuel; not interacting it cannot burn; what does not burn . . .'. It is, after all, common experience that a man and a woman, though different, do interact with one another. In the same way there can be interaction of fire and fuel.
We reply

206 6 Fire, though wholly other than fuel, would interact with fuel if it were as it is with the woman interacting with the man and the man with the woman.

This would be so if fire and fuel existed independently of each other as man and woman do. But Nāgārjuna says they do not:

7 Fire, though wholly other than fuel, would interact with fuel naturally if fire and fuel existed in isolation from each other.

It is, however, not possible that fire exist independently (*nirapekṣa*) of fuel and fuel independently of fire. The example given is therefore invalid. The example adduced must be valid for such beings as, even though wholly other, are inherently dependent on one another, and between whom alone interaction could take place.[2] Such are not, however, possible;

[1] *Prāpsyate*, 'be affected by', or literally, 'reached by'. The problem of *prāpti*, how one entity can have an essential relationship to another, is endemic to the Buddhist doctrine of separate reals (*dharmas*).
[2] I.e. fire and fuel.

your statement 'though different they do interact with one another' is not tenable.

You may object that, even though fire and fuel do not exist in reciprocal independence as man and woman do, none the less there is at least reciprocal dependence. Therefore both fire and fuel, because of their reciprocal dependence, do have a nature of their own. After all, reciprocal dependence is never empirically observed between a non-existent son and daughter of a barren woman.

Fire and fuel as reciprocally dependent

We reply that this too is untenable.

207 9 If fire is dependent on fuel and fuel is dependent on fire, which of the two arises prior, that on which fire is dependent or that on which fuel is dependent?

Fire is what burns fuel, it is the 'agent' (*kartā*). If fire is defined as dependent on fuel, that is, if this very fuel is the 'object' (*karma*) of fire – what fire acts upon – and so if fuel is in this way dependent on fire, which of these two arises prior? Would it be fuel on which fire depends? Or would it be fire on which fuel depends? It would be absurd to think that fuel exists prior because there can be no fuel for a fire which is independent of it and which is burning nothing; and because it would follow that grass and absolutely everything would be fuel. On the other hand if one thinks that fire exists prior and fuel subsequently that too would be absurd because it is impossible for fire to exist prior to fuel because this would entail fire being without a material basis, and because dependence on what is subsequent is meaningless. There is therefore no prior existence of either in dependence on which the other could base its existence.

If you still think that fuel is prior and fire subsequent there is this further thought:

9ab If fire depends on fuel, the existence of fire is presupposed.

If it is supposed that fire is dependent on fuel this would be to establish the existence of an already existing fire. The dependence of an existing thing of established nature makes sense; but a non-existent Devadatta cannot be dependent on anything in his home. So if there were no existing fire, fuel could not be dependent on it. The existence of fire is thus presupposed. What then is achieved by a second dependence on fuel? As an existing fire is not re-lighted by fuel its dependence on fuel would be totally meaningless. In sum, it does not make sense to say that fire is dependent on fuel.

If one supposes that fire is dependent on fuel there is a further point:

> 9cd This being so fuel will exist as fuel without relation to fire.

208 If fuel did not exist fire could not be related to it because of the impossibility of relation to the non-existent. Then the existence of fuel unrelated to fire must be posited; but this cannot be the case and is untenable.

You may offer this possibility: Fire comes into existence simultaneously (*yaugapadya*) with the coming into existence of fuel and fuel comes into existence simultaneously with the coming into existence of fire. Because the priorness of neither is presupposed, what was asked does not make sense, namely 'which of the two arises first, that on which fire is dependent or that on which fuel is dependent?' We reply. Even if one attempts to think in this way neither can be established. Because:

> 10 One thing is established as dependent on the very thing which is dependent on it. If what is to be dependent is posited as already existing, which depends on which?

That is, if an entity called fire exists in dependence on an entity called fuel and this entity called fuel is that with respect to which the independent existence of fire is to be established; and if this fuel is to exist in dependence on this very entity fire, in such case, pray tell, which exists in dependence on which? There is no fuel strictly speaking so long as fire is non-existent, as there can be no fuel which is not the cause of fire. How will fire, whose material base is fuel, be established as existent?

In the same way let there be an entity called fuel which exists in dependence on an entity called fire and this entity called fire is that dependent on which the independent existence of fuel is to be established. Now if this fire is to exist in dependence on the entity called fuel, in such case, pray tell, which exists in dependence on which? As there is no fire so long as fuel does not exist – as there can be no fire which does not burn fuel – how will fuel, whose *raison d'être* is fire, be established as existent?

Further, fire and fuel do not exist in dependence on one another because there is no dependence either of what is real or of what is not real. Nāgārjuna, expounding, says

209 11 How can a supposedly dependent entity be dependent if it does not exist? On the other hand it does not make sense that an existing entity should be dependent on a dependent entity.

Something called fire depends on something called fuel: it will be dependent on the fuel either in so far as it – the fire – exists or does not exist. If it is non-existent then because of its non-existence it will not, like the horns of a rabbit, be dependent on the fuel. Again let it be the case that it exists. Then because it already exists how could it depend on fuel? So not even as existing does it exist in dependence because that would be meaningless. The case of fuel is to be demonstrated in the same way. In sum, fire and fuel cannot exist in dependence on one another simultaneously either.

From this it follows:

12a Fire does not depend on fuel.

You might think that therefore fire will exist independently. But Nāgārjuna says this is not tenable either:

12b Fire is not independent of fuel.

Because its separate existence has been refuted and because it would follow that fire was uncaused. As fire is impossible either dependent on, or independent of, fuel, so fuel shares the same incapacity. Nāgārjuna says

12cd Fuel is not dependent on fire and fuel is not independent of fire.

This argument is the same as that just given and to expound it again would be superfluous.

Fire is not latent in fuel. Rejection of Sāṁkhya

You may ask: What is the purpose of this overly subtle analysis for us? We claim that fuel is directly perceived by the senses
210 to be burned by fire; and that therefore both fire and fuel
exist.

We reply: This would be so if fire did burn fuel. If fire were possible in fuel it would burn fuel. But Nāgārjuna says it is not possible:

13ab Fire does not exist in the fuel; fire does not spring from any other source.

Fire does not derive from any source at all distinct from fuel because such source is never observed; and because no fire can arise which is without a cause, without relation to fuel; and because there would be no purpose in a fire starting up which was already connected with fuel. Nor again does fire exist in the fuel because the same objections would apply equally and would lead to an infinite regress. Fire does not arise from elsewhere than the fuel. Nor is it possible to be in the fuel because it is never observed there.

It may be argued[1] that an existing fire is not at first observed[2] because the conditions which would make it manifest (*abhivyañjakapratyaya*) are lacking as in the case of underground water and such things. Subsequently, however, from the rubbing of sticks together, because the conditions which make fire manifest are realized, it is observed.

This theory should first be clarified. What is additionally effected by the conditions of manifestation in the case of underground water and such things? Their intrinsic nature (*svarūpa*) is not at first brought into being by the conditions of their manifestation, because it exists already. If you say that it is the manifestation (*abhivyakti*) itself which is brought into being, what is this which is called manifestation? If it is 'becoming visible' then this becoming visible itself is what is created because it did not exist previously. To think this way is to abandon the theory according to which something exists in its intrinsic nature prior to its being caused, because the manifestation is created, at one time not existing and at a later time existing. If the intrinsic nature of a thing is independent of the conditions of its coming into being these would be, like a flower in the sky, without reality.

Further, this manifestation itself would have to be conceived as either of something already manifested or of something not yet manifested. In the first case something already manifest cannot be manifested because of the meaninglessness of its manifestation and because it would entail undesirable logical consequences. Again, what is not manifest can equally well not be manifested because of its not being manifested. It would be like a flower in the sky. Thus manifestation is not possible.

211 You may argue again that it is the coarse form (*staulya*) of a pre-existing thing which is brought into being by the

[1] The Sāṁkhya view. [2] In fuel.

conditions of manifestation. Here again, the coarse form itself does at a prior time not exist but is brought into being later. But how can there be manifestation as the actual production of the coarse form? Because the subtle form (*saukṣmya*),[1] lying outside causal efficacy, cannot exist, of what would there be a manifestation consisting of the production of the coarse form? It is thus clear that in no way is there a potentiality of fire in fuel: fire does not exist in fuel. Nor can the burning of fuel arise from a fire that does not exist. So what you claim to perceive is quite unreal.

Further, there are the objections developed earlier[2] in connection with motion and rest.

> 13cd The remaining arguments as given for motion and rest apply in this case to fuel.

'In this case' refers to the statement 'Fuel is perceived to be burned by fire.' With reference to fuel, that is, it should be understood that all the remaining objections are the same as those given for motion and rest. To adapt the passage referred to: What has burned is not burning, nor is what has not burned burning, and what is being burned – something other than what has burned and what has not burned – is not burning. In this way it is to be understood that fire does not burn fuel.

Review of the five possibilities

Nāgārjuna, in order to sum up what has been expounded, now says:

> 14 Fire is not identical with fuel; nor does fire arise elsewhere than from fuel; fire is not of the nature of fuel; fuels are not in fire nor fire in them.[3]

212 It was stated earlier, 'If fuel is fire that would be identity of agent and act.'[4] In this way the identity of fire and fuel was refuted; fuel is not fire. It was further stated 'If fire is wholly other than fuel it could exist even without fuel.'[5] In this and other arguments the complete otherness of fire and fuel was refuted. Fire cannot arise elsewhere than from fuel. From the refutation of both theses, that of identity and that of complete

[1] The 'intrinsic nature of'. The coarse form is the manifestation of this.
[2] Chapter IV.
[3] This fivefold formula is introduced again in the Chapter 'The Perfectly Realized One'. Cf. p. 193.
[4] P. 132, *Kārikā* 1. [5] Ibid.

otherness, the various other theses: that fire is of the nature of fuel, that fire contains fuel, that fuel contains fire are, by implication, refuted. Summarizing them Nāgārjuna says, 'fire is not of the nature of fuel; fuels are not in fire nor is fire in them'.

Fire is said not to be of the nature of fuel (*indhanavān*); 'of the nature of' means either that fuel is *of* fire or that fire is *in* fuel. Here fire is either separate, or it is not separate except in an etymological sense. An example of the first would be 'Devadatta has a cow'. An example of the second would be 'Devadatta has a body, a mind and so on'. The refutation of the two theses – identity or complete otherness – concerning fire and fuel entails the refutation of fire being of the nature of fuel.

It is commonly said that the dish, the completely other, is the container of the curd. But fire is not completely other than fuel so it does not make sense that fuel is contained in fire. Nor can fire be in fuel because their complete otherness has been refuted. So, in this way, the theses of container and contained have been implicitly refuted.

Extension of the argument to the self and all objects

As fire, on being thoroughly investigated in the five ways, is not possible, so it is, Nāgārjuna says, extending his argument, with the self as well.

> 15abc Everything expounded in terms of fire and fuel is, without exception, applicable to self and the factors of personal existence.

What the self (*ātman*) possesses is what is appropriated (*upādāna*), namely, the five appropriative factors of personal existence. What is commonly thought of as being based on these factors is the appropriator, the conceiver, the active agent and this is said to be the self. Because the 'I-me' sense (*ahaṁkāra*) is made into an object, the illusion of the 'I' is
213 conceived as in and of personal existence. The argumentation concerning the self and what it possesses is to be understood as exactly parallel to that expounded for fire and fuel.

What is the distinction between 'everything' and 'without exception'? The term 'everything' means the five theories taken consecutively. All these five theories are to be tied together in an orderly way for self and the factors of personal

[1] Cf. Chapter XIV.

existence as they were for fire and fuel. The expository argumentation given earlier applied to the refutation of self and the factors of personal existence with nothing omitted is what is meant by 'without exception'. This is the meaning. It should be understood that Nāgārjuna said 'everything without exception' with a view to emphasizing that the refutation of the self and the factors of personal existence is identical in every essential with that of fire and fuel. It is not tenable to say that the factors of personal existence are the same as the self because it would follow, absurdly, that agent and act were identical. Nor are the factors of personal existence one thing and the self another, because from that it would follow that the self could be perceived apart from the factors of personal existence and because it would follow, absurdly, that the self was without relation to anything other than itself. Because of the refutation of both identity and difference the self cannot be of the nature of the factors of personal existence. Because they are not wholly other the factors of personal existence are not 'in' the self nor is the self in them. It is clear, thus, that in none of the five ways is the self a reality. The reciprocally dependent existence of self and factors of personal existence, exactly like agent and act, is thus beyond doubt.

However, this extension of the argument is not limited to self and the factors of personal existence.

15d And to pot, cloth, and so on.

The exposition is to be understood as applying to all things without exception in every respect.[1] Pots and other things may be thought of in terms of cause and effect, or of part and whole, or of characteristic and the bearer of characteristics, or of quality and the possessor of quality. In the first case clay, stick, turntable, thread, water, the strength of the potter and so on would be the causes of the pot; the pot would be the
214 effect. In the second case the bare pot, its blue colour and so on would be the parts; the pot would be what the parts are in, the whole. Again, a broad base, turned-down edge, long neck and so on would be the characteristics of the pot; the pot would be the bearer of the characteristics. Last, colour and so on would be the qualities; the pot would be the possessor of qualities. In these ways the conclusions concerning fire and fuel are to be applied in extension. Concerning both self and

[1] It is characteristically Buddhist to apply the same kind of argument to the self and to things. This seems restrictive, but it serves to expose the inadequacy of relational thinking sweepingly.

the factors of personal existence, and such things as pots, the exposition may be found in the *Madhyamakāvatāra.* In this way the existence of self and the factors of personal existence as well as of pots and such things has been established as reciprocally dependent existence like agent and act.

Some, in their arrogance, believing they are aware of the true teaching of the realized one, in their confusion of mind conclude that the categories of things established by non-Buddhists accord with the true teaching.

Dependent origination

> 16 Those who teach either that the self and entities co-exist or that they exist separately I do not hold to understand the doctrine.

To exist by virtue of something else is the meaning of 'co-exist' (*satat*). A co-existing entity enjoys co-existence. The thought is that it is not separate, not wholly other, but makes a unity. Those who give this account of co-existence Nāgārjuna does not consider to be well-versed in the Buddhist doctrine. For example the self is conceived of in terms of the factors of personal existence and only together with these is it possible. This means that self does not exist separately, apart from the factors of personal existence. In the same way a pot is conceived in terms of its causes – clay, potter and so on; it exists unseparated from them, not isolated by itself. Those who give this account of the co-existence of self and of entities do not
215 discern the truth of the surpassingly deep idea of dependent origination – the way things really are – which is free of both ontology and nihilism and which is known as an idea based on the everyday but which conduces to enlightenment.

Those who espouse the separate existence of things see the self and the factors of personal existence each as separate and cause and effect as separate and so on: they see only complete otherness. Nāgārjuna does not believe that such understand the meaning of the Buddhist doctrine. As it has been said, 'You should be aware of the world as neither eternal nor perishable and the things of the world as neither identical nor different but like echoes, and so be beyond reproach.' When the *yogī* has comprehended the supreme truth of the teaching by means of this analysis of fire and fuel then his body cannot be burned by the world holocaust nor by the flames of passion, hatred and delusion.

XII

The Absence of Being in Things

237 As was shown in the preceding chapter,[1] the arising of things, on being examined, is neither spontaneous nor caused by another, nor both, nor random; nor is there any other way for things to arise. Yet to the unenlightened whose wisdom eye is afflicted with the disease of ignorance they appear to arise. This is why things, though wholly without self-existence, deceive, as an illusory elephant or horse, the unenlightened who do not comprehend them as they are, but do not deceive those of insight. And so the compassionate Buddha, the awakener of all creation, who has the vision to see all things without mediation (*aparokṣa*) as they are in themselves, uprooted totally all the illusions of ignorance and teaches unerringly the absence of being in things to protect helpless beings who, due to the four misbeliefs,[2] conceive things falsely.

The Mādhyamika view

> 1 Whatever is not what it pretends to be is unreal, declared the illustrious one. All compound things are not what they pretend to be and are therefore unreal.

The *sūtra* says,[3] 'What is not what it pretends to be (*moṣa-dharma*) is unreal (*mṛṣā*) and the realm of the compounded is that. The higher truth, o monks, does not pretend to be what it is not: it is *nirvāṇa*. All compound things pretend to be what they are not and are unreal.' Further, 'In this world there is
238 no truth of things nor absence of untruth: these too are not what they pretend to be; they too are empty talk.' Thinking in this way the illustrious, realized one declared that what pretends to be what it is not is unreal, that all compound things pretend to be what they are not, that, therefore, because

[1] Not included in this translation; the same point was dealt with in Chapter III.

[2] See Chapter XVII.

[3] Cf. p. 44.

of this false pretence, they are unreal. They are like the mechanical puppets made by craftsmen or like the mechanical elephant of great verisimilitude with which Udayana, King of Vatsa, was tricked. In these cases the falseness lies in their ultimate incongruence (*visaṁvādaka*); it is like the error of perceiving the circling torch as a circle of fire.

Thus all things pretend to be what they are not because they lack self-existence and because they are unreal. They are like mirages and other illusory appearances of water. The true (*satya*), however, is what does not pretend to be what it is not; *nirvāṇa* is the sole instance of this. Both the arguments we have advanced and the authority of the texts establish that all things are devoid of self-existence, and for this reason that there is an absence of being in all elements as such. We can read this in the *Ardhaśatikā prajñāpāramitā Sūtra.*

You may object that, if, in this way the illustrious one taught that all things are unreal because they are not what they pretend to be, then, if this is so, all things must be non-existent (*na santi*). But the denial (*apavāda*) of the reality of things would be a Buddhist heresy.

We reply. The fact is that the deceptive pretence of things is confusing you even now. For indeed,

> 2ab If whatever is not what it pretends to be is unreal, what is it in that case that pretends?

239 When we say, 'What pretends is unreal', and 'What in that case pretends?' we mean, How, then, can the non-existent (*abhāva*) exist (*bhavati*)? If any object whatsoever existed then the denial of it and the theory of non-existence would constitute a Buddhist heresy. So long, however, as we discern no actual object whatsoever, then what can do the pretending? No non-existent object can exist. So your accusation is not appropriate. You may ask, if the theory of non-existence is not taught by this text, what, then is?

We reply:

> 2cd The illustrious one said this in elucidating *śūnyatā*, the absence of being in things.

What the illustrious one uttered was not the elucidation of the non-existence of things, but rather the absence of being in things: that self-existent things do not arise. This is the meaning of the *Sūtra*. The *Anavataptahradāpasaṁkramaṇa Sūtra* says, 'What is born of conditions is not truly born; and it does not arise as self-existent; what depends on conditions is said to lack being. Whoever comprehends the absence of being in things is free of delusion.'

Absence of being as changeableness

240 You may object that this text[1] does not state that self-existent things do not arise, but rather that things are without self-existence in the sense that their essential nature is inconstant and perishable.[2] If you ask how this is meant:

3ab Things are without an essential nature because they are seen to alter.

Alteration (*anyathātva*) in things means that their transformation is directly observed. That is to say, if there were no essential nature in things, that is, if things were not self-existent, their alteration could not be perceived. But transformation is directly observed and so it should be recognized that the *sūtra* is speaking of the changeableness of the essential nature of things.

This is so, because

3cd No thing is without an essential nature as all things are without being.

A thing lacking an essential nature does not exist, as the absence of being is conceived of as an attribute of all things. But it is not logically possible that an attribute could be based in a non-existent subject, as the skin colour of a non-existent son of a barren woman is not logically possible. There is therefore an essential nature in things.[3]

241 Furthermore,

4ab If there were no essential nature, what would this becoming other be of?

If there were no essential nature in things what would this becoming other – which has the character of transformation – be of?

[1] The one quoted in *Kārikā* 1, p. 144.

[2] This view predominates in the early *sūtras*; the radically new depth given the notion of *śūnyatā* by Nāgārjuna can mark the philosophical maturation of Buddhism.

[3] To hypostatize *śūnyatā* is virtually irresistible; within metaphysics it is inescapable.

Unintelligibility of change

At this point we reply. Allowing this way of conceiving things to stand, still,

> 4cd If there is an essential nature what would this becoming other be of?

A characteristic which is invariable in a thing is commonly said to be its essential nature; that is, it is not conjoined with any other thing. For example, heat is said to be the essential nature of fire because in all experience it invariably accompanies fire. Heat is not the essential nature of water because it arises from extraneous conditions and because it is something artifically produced. But if this invariable essential nature is something real, then because of its invariableness it could not become other. After all coldness cannot become a property of fire. Thus, if we accept an essential nature in things, alteration is not possible. But alteration *is* directly perceived in things so there can be no essential nature.

Further, this becoming other of things, from the observation of which it is thought that there is an essential nature in things, is simply not possible.

> 5 Becoming other is not comprehensible either of the same thing or of another thing. So the young man does not grow old nor does the old man grow old.

242 The alteration of something which continues to exist just as it did in a previous state is not logically possible. For example a young man cannot alter so long as he exists in his state of youthfulness. You may suppose that the alteration is realized in the immediately succeeding state, but that is not logically possible either. Alteration is just a synonym for old age. And if you try to think that the alteration is not in the young man, but rather in the other – the old man – that too is impossible. A second conjunction of ageing with the old man would be pointless. What would be achieved by attributing old age a second time to an old man? As an old man does not exist before the advent of old age it makes no sense to say 'an old man becomes old'. On the other hand, it makes no sense to say that the alteration is in the youth because the term youth is used of the stage in which old age has not been attained, and because the two stages – youth and old age – are mutually exclusive.

What is more,

6ab If one and the same thing becomes other, then milk itself would be curd.

It may be thought that it is only by passing beyond the state 'milk' that the state 'curd' comes into existence, so that it is not the milk itself which becomes curd.

We reply. If you do not wish to think that milk becomes curd because they are mutually exclusive, then,

6cd Curd will arise from anything whatsoever other than milk.

Is curd to arise from water? Thus it is illogical to say that curd arises from what is other than itself. As, in this way, alteration is impossible, how can it be established that things have an essential nature from the observation of change? That would be absurd.

243 As is said in the *Ratnākaramahāyāna Sūtra*, 'The truth of things as revealed by the victorious one, the lion among men, is neither born nor does it arise, it does not decay, it does not die. In it are merged all living beings.

'What is not self-existent in any sense, cannot attain other-existence either from within or from without; the lord is realized everywhere.

'Buddha has revealed the way of being at peace, though no definable way has been attained; there you will walk what is called the way of liberation. Yourself free, you will free many other beings.

244 'Buddha, you declare all elements of existence devoid of self; you liberate men from belief in the individual being. Free from any path you have attained liberation; you have reached the other shore without leaving this one.

'Having crossed the ocean of existence you have reached the other shore. But there is no individual as such who has gone beyond. There is neither a shore here nor there; it is merely a manner of speaking to say you have crossed over.

'Neither do the words you utter exist, nor does what you speak about exist, nor does he with whom you speak exist nor he who comprehends.

'The whole world is deluded because it clings to false obses-
245 sions. The self-existent Tathāgata has been seen by those who clearly comprehend that all elements of existence are at peace.

'One who fully knows that the subtlest elements of existence are at peace attains happiness and makes other beings joyful. Overcoming the afflictions of existence, he becomes a conqueror.

'And he knows the pure mind of the victorious ones and enlightens all creation.'

Absence of being as the exhaustion of all views

You stated earlier that no thing was lacking an essential nature as absence of being is to be attributed to all things. That is, there is an essential nature in things which is the base for the absence of being in them. Nāgārjuna says that this does not make sense either.

> 7 If there were something not devoid of being there would be something devoid of being; but there is nothing not devoid of being, so how will anything be devoid of being?[1]

246 If there were something called devoidness of being[2] there would be an essential nature in each thing as its basis (*āśraya*). But it is not so. The reasoning here is that, if we suppose devoidness of being to be the universal characteristic of all elements of existence there can be no non-devoidness (*aśūnyatā*) because there is no element which is not devoid. If there are no non-devoid entities, that is if there is no non-devoidness, then because it will not be related to its antithesis (*pratipakṣa*), there will certainly not be any devoidness either, as there is no garland of flowers in the sky. If there is no devoidness of being no entities will exist as basis for it. This is dead certain.

You may object that the illustrious one, for the purpose of liberating those who follow him, taught three ways to liberation, namely, devoidness, causelessness and desirelessness. These are not learned in the systems of non-Buddhists but only in the teaching of Buddha. The illustrious Buddhas, the sole light of all creation, are born solely for the purpose of these three truths. They are born into this world which is given over to the dark confusion of false teachings and are the unquenchable flame of the truth of the absence of being in things. But you,[3] sir, by a deceitful interpretation of the teaching of the realized one, are about to destroy this very absence of being.

Good gracious! Like one whose head is held high in pride, you have overlooked, through a total misconception, the

[1] This implies that meaningful statements derive from pairs of opposite concepts. And 'absence of being' cannot be asserted of things: one of the variants of the Mādhyamika paradox.

[2] I.e. if devoidness were ontic. [3] Candrakīrti; opponent still speaks.

superior, blissful, direct path to the city of *nirvāṇa*. You thirst for liberation and depend on a path which, though it seems to lead to the city of liberation, winds through the forests of the cycle of death and re-birth. You are confused by a stubborn predilection for reality and roam about in the forests of the cycle of death and re-birth. The wise should reproach you, but you, subject to the obstinacy of pride, reproach them. Indeed, according to the great monarchs of medicine who completely cure the disease of the afflictions:

247 8 The spiritual conquerors have proclaimed the absence of being in things to be the exhaustion of all theories and views; those for whom the absence of being is itself a theory they declared to be incurable.

The exhaustion (*niḥsaraṇam*), the ceasing to function of all ways of holding to fixed concepts stemming from theories or views (*dṛṣṭi*) of any kind whatsoever, is the absence of being in things. But the mere ceasing to function of what stems from holding views is not itself a real thing. With those who obstinately hold to the reality of things, even in the case of the absence of being, we can have no dialogue. How could we, who teach that liberation ensues on desisting from all conceptual thinking whatsoever? It is as if one man said to another, 'I have no wares at all to sell you.' If this other man were then to say, 'Give me what you call those "no wares at all" ', how
248 would he be able to take hold of any real wares? Similarly, how can there be an end to the pertinaceous holding to reality (*bhāvābhiniveśa*) on the part of those who pertinaceously hold to reality even in the case of the absence of being? That is why the great healers, the realized ones, greatly wise, having diagnosed this disease in the light of the great art of healing, do not attend to them.

As the illustrious one said in the *Ratnakūta Sūtra*, 'It is not devoidness of being which renders the elements of existence devoid of being; rather the elements are devoid by nature. It is not causelessness which renders the elements of existence causeless; rather the elements are by nature without cause. It is not purposelessness which renders the elements of existence purposeless; rather the elements are purposeless by nature. Just this way of regarding things, Kāśyapa, I call the middle way; it is the true way of regarding the elements of existence. But those, Kāśyapa, who seize on the absence of being as an object they assail the absence of being and such, I say, are hopelessly lost. Indeed, Kāśyapa, it were better if one resorted to a belief in the reality of the individual as unshakable as Mount Sumeru, than to hold to a theory of the absence of being through the stubborn belief in the unreality of things. Why is that? Because Kāśyapa, the absence of being is the exhaustion of all theories and views.

'One for whom, in turn, the absence of being itself becomes a dogmatic view I call incurable. It is, Kāśyapa, as if a sick man were given a medicine by a doctor, but that medicine, having removed his ills, was not itself expelled but remained in the stomach. What do you think, Kāśyapa, will this man be freed of his sickness? No indeed, illustrious one, the sickness of this man in whose stomach the medicine, having removed all his ills remains and is not expelled, would be more violent.
249 The illustrious one said: In this sense, Kāśyapa, the absence of being is the exhaustion of all dogmatic views. But the one for whom the absence of being itself becomes a fixed belief, I call incurable.'

XIII

Self-Existence

Refutation of the realist thesis

259 Some argue that things in fact have essential natures which exist as such (*bhāvānāṁ svabhāva*) and take such essential natures to be produced, as effects, from certain causes and conditions (*hetupratyaya*).[1] They do not take things which have no ontic existence (*nāsti*), like the sky-flower, to be the effects of causes and conditions. But they take a seed, for example, to be the cause which has the sprout as effect, or primal ignorance (*avidyā*) to be the cause which has personal dispositions (*saṁskāra*) as its effect. Thus, things do have essential, self-existent natures, they say.

In reply we say that if things like personal dispositions and sprouts have self-existent natures what would be the purpose of their being caused, as they exist already? As personal dispositions truly exist one does not have to posit primal ignorance as their cause for the sake of producing them a second time, nor for sprouts must one posit seeds. Thus nothing other than itself is required for the genesis of anything, because its essential nature is in existence. Nāgārjuna puts it this way:

> 1ab The genesis of a self-existent nature from causes and conditions is not intelligible.

You may agree that before its genesis there can be no self-existent nature (*svabhāva*) of anything, as, being in existence, its genesis would be pointless. But, you may say, what if a self-existent nature which does not exist before its genesis arises subsequently from causes and conditions? If one so thinks, Nāgārjuna continues:

> 1cd A self-existent nature which arises from causes and conditions would be something created.

260 You may say: But that self-existent natures are created

[1] Or 'causal conditions', i.e. conditions of the nature of material cause.

(*kṛtaka*) because they issue from causes and conditions, is just what we mean, and, as we presuppose that self-existent natures are created, the logical objection of their being created does us no harm. Nāgārjuna says that this too is not intelligible:

2ab How can a self-existent nature be something created.

As the terms 'created' and 'self-existent nature' are contradictory (*parasparaviruddhatva*) there is no intelligible meaning in such a statement. Self-existent nature means, etymologically, what is itself through itself. A created thing, for example, the heat of water, which is produced by fuel or the activity of spirits, or such things as quartz appearing to be a ruby is not commonly spoken of by anyone as self-existent. On the other hand, what is not created, for example, the heat of fire or the genuine rubiness of rubies, is a self-existent nature, it is commonly said. Whatever it is in such things that is not born from conjunction with something else, is said to be a self-existent nature.

Although it is the convention in everyday transactions (*lokavyavahāra*) to say that the self-existent is uncreated, we claim further that even the very heat of fire must be understood as not being self-existent because it is created. In this case the dependence of fire on causes and conditions is directly perceived when lens, kindling and sun conjoin or when sticks are rubbed together. But heat does not occur in the absence of fire; and so heat itself is born of causes and is therefore created. It is clear and certain that, being created, it, like the heat of water, is not self-existent.

You may say: It is evident even to the womenfolk of the
cowherds that heat is the self-existent nature of fire. But did
we say that it was not evident? What we claim is that it is not
capable of being a self-existent nature because it lacks the
261 characteristics of a self-existent nature. The unenlightened
person, however, victim of misbelief due to primal ignorance,
treats all things as if they had self-existent natures, though
they have not.

As those of defective eyesight, because of their defect, persist in treating non-existing hairs and such things as if they were self-existent, so unenlightened people, their spiritual vision being afflicted with the defect of primal ignorance, persist in treating things which have no essential, self-existing nature as if they did. They frame their definition according to this fixed prejudice. Heat is the unique, inherent characteristic (*svalakṣana*) of fire; because it is not perceived anywhere else, because of its uniqueness, it is the characteristic of itself only, they explain. The illustrious one, having regard for the unenlightened, in the *Abhidharma* pronounced upon the essential nature (*svarūpa*) of such things only in the everyday, veiled sense (*saṁvṛta*). And such general characteristics as impermanence[1] were defined as universal. When, however, the teaching was for the understanding of those with the clear eye of wisdom who are rid of the defect of primal ignorance, then, as explained long ago by the great ones, benevolent to others, there is no self-existent nature as imagined by the unenlightened, even as one cured of defective vision no longer sees hairs and such things which he perceived when diseased. For such there is no self-existent nature of things in this sense.[2]

262 As is said in the *Laṅkāvatāra Sūtra*, 'As those of diseased vision deludedly grasp after false hairs, so the unenlightened deludedly imagine the notion of reality in things. There is no self-existence, no knowledge, no reality and no ground of consciousness: these are the imaginings of unenlightened, effete sophists.' And again, 'Knowing that self-existence does not arise in time, I have declared, o Mahāmati, that all the elements of existence do not arise in time.'

The Mādhyamika position

You may ask: If you say that the heat of fire and such things are without a self-existent nature because they issue from causes and are created, what then is the definition of a self-existent nature and what is such a nature? You should make this clear.

The reply is,

> 2cd Self-existent nature is not created nor is it dependent on anything other than itself.

Here the intended meaning is that a self-existent nature is one which exists of and for itself (*sva bhāva*); it is the unique,
263 ownmost nature (*ātmīya rūpa*) of anything. What is unique and ownmost in anything? Whatever is not created in that thing; whereas what is created in something, like heat in water, is not unique and ownmost in that thing. Again, what is completely at the disposal of one, that too is ownmost, as one's servants or one's wealth. But what is available through someone

[1] There are three universal characteristics of things: impermanence (*anitya*), imperfection (*duḥkha*) and insubstantiality (*anātman*).

[2] I.e., the *particularity* of identical things is not self-existent.

else is not ownmost; something borrowed for limited time is not unconditionally one's own. Thus self-existence is not considered to be in what is created nor in what depends on something else. For this reason it makes sense to say that the heat of fire is not self-existent because it is dependent on causes and because it is created, being non-existent at one time and subsequently coming into existence. And this being the case it follows that the innate nature (*nija rūpa*) of fire, which is unvarying throughout all time, must be uncreated, i.e. it cannot
264 come into existence if at one time it did not exist.[1] What is
relative to certain conditions does not truly exist, like the heat of water, like 'this side' and 'other side' or like the long and the short. That is what is meant by self-existence. Is there, in this sense, an inherent nature in things like fire? The heat of fire neither exists nor does not exist as an inherent nature.[2] Although this is so, nevertheless, in order to dispel the fears of people, we say 'Things do truly exist' by employing ordinary language and so constituting the everyday world (*saṁvṛtyā samāropya*).[3]

As the illustrious one said, 'How can the unutterable truth be taught or learned? The unutterable is taught and learned only by a special use of ordinary language (*samāropa*).'

Nāgārjuna says elsewhere in this treatise[4] 'The terms "devoid of being", "not-devoid of being", "both-devoid-and-not-devoid of being", "neither-devoid-nor-not-devoid of being" should not be asserted as predicates (*na vaktavya*); they are however employed for the purposes of practical teaching (*prajñaptyartha*).'

You may ask: Well, if one afraid says, 'Things do truly exist' only after projecting (*adhyāropa*) the notion of self-existence, what does self-existence itself mean?[5]

Whatever is the quintessential nature (*dharmatā*) of the elements of existence, that and only that has a self nature (*svarūpa*). And what is quintessential nature of the elements? Their self-existent nature (*svabhāva*). And what is self-existent nature? Original, invariable nature (*prakṛti*). What is original, invariable nature? Devoidness of being (*śūnyatā*). And what is
265 devoidness of being? Not being of the nature of substantial

[1] A Parmenidean formulation.

[2] The initial Mādhyamika formulation; the remainder of the chapter is a development of this puzzling statement.

[3] A view familiar to Westerners in the twentieth century!

[4] P. 201, 11.

[5] The following three paragraphs constitute the strongest statement of Mādhyamika up to this point.

thing (*naisvabhāvya*). What is not being of the nature of substantial thing? The way things really are (*tathatā*). What is the way things really are? Being as they are (*tathābhāva*): invariableness, steadfastness throughout all time.

Whatever it is in fire and other things that does not come into existence at any point in time because it is not dependent on anything other than itself and because it is not created, that is said to be its self-existent nature.

In short: what, arising from the optical defect of primal ignorance is, in whatever way, taken to be the everyday world of things (*bhāvajāta*), becomes, in virtue of going beyond ways of taking things, the world of the wise (*āryānām viṣayatvam*) who are free of the optical defect of primal ignorance; that and nothing else has a nature of its own; the wise name it 'self-existence'. Remember that Nāgārjuna defined it: 'What is self-existent is uncreated and is not dependent on anything other than itself.' Self-existence in this sense – by nature not arising in time – is non-self-existence in the ordinary sense because it is simply non-existent ontically through not having a specific nature. This being so, it should be clear that there is no self-existence of particular things.[1]

As the illustrious one said, 'The one who wisely understands that things are non-things is never obsessed with things. The one who is never obsessed with things attains peace of mind beyond all definition.'

Existence of otherness

You may interject that, although there is no self-existence in things, still there is at least the relative existence of otherness (*parabhāva*) as this has not been refuted. And if there is existence of otherness there will be self-existence also, because existence of otherness cannot be established apart from self-existence.

Nāgārjuna replies:

266 3 If there is no self-existence, how can there be existence of otherness? For it is the self-existence of the existence of otherness which is called 'existence of otherness'.

In this way of thinking any self-existent whatsoever, in so far as it is related to another self-existent, is designated 'other' (*para*). If heat is the self-existent nature of fire, it is designated,

[1] I.e. only enlightenment (*nirvāṇa*) is self-existent.

with reference to fluidity, the self-existent nature of water, as 'other'. As nothing whatsoever is self-existent when examined by those on the way to liberation, how can there be otherness? As there is no existence of otherness, it is evident that there is no self-existence either.

You may argue that, even though there is neither self-existence nor other-existence, none the less there are existing things because this has not been ruled out. And such things will be either self-existent or will exist in otherness. It follows that there is both self-existence and existence in otherness.

Nāgārjuna replies:

4 How can there be an entity apart from self-existence and other-existence? If there is either self-existence or other-existence entities are already established.

If one thinks of an existent thing it must be either self-existent or existent-as-other. But, as explained previously, there is neither and because there is neither of these two it must be accepted that there can be no existent thing either.

Non-existence

You may say: Although you have ruled out the existence of things, none the less there is non-existence (*abhāva*) because you have not refuted that. Therefore there must be existence of things because its opposite, non-existence, is fact. We reply that there would be existence if there were non-existence. But Nāgārjuna says there is not:

267 5 If existence is not accepted, non-existence cannot be established. Because people say that non-existence is being other than existence.

According to this reasoning, if there were anything existent there would be non-existence as its otherness (*anyathā*). Pots and such things are commonly said to be non-existent if they cease from their present state and enter another. But if pots and such things have not been established as existing, how can non-existing entities be other than them? It follows that there is no non-existence either. So, self-existence, other-existence and non-existence are all unintelligible, total misapprehensions of those whose spiritual vision is crippled by the defect of primal ignorance.

Evidence from the Buddhist tradition

> 6 Those who think in terms of self-existence, other-existence, existence and non-existence do not grasp the truth of Buddha's teaching.

Such are those who delude themselves that they are faithfully expounding the teaching of the perfectly realized one when they explain the self-existent and essential nature of things, saying that solidity is the self-existent and essential nature of earth, that experience of the object is the self-existent and essential nature of feeling and that being reflected as an object is the self-existent and essential nature of consciousness. And they explain existence-as-otherness (*parabhāva*) saying that consciousness is other than object and that feeling is other than both. They explain that consciousness and the other factors of personal existence, when in the present, exist, and when they are in the past do not exist. They do not explain the supremely profound truth of dependent origination. So self-existence and existence-as-other are, as we have shown, contrary to reason (*upapattiviruddha*). The self-existence of things as expounded by the perfectly realized ones, however, is not contrary to reason because of their autonomous, incorrigible, perfect enlightenment about the true nature of all things.
268 Therefore the teaching of the revered Buddhas is valid know-
ledge (*pramāna*), the wise say, because it is in accord with
reason (*sopapattika*) and free from contradictions. And also
because it derives from realized ones who are completely free
of any faults. It has authority because it yields the authentic
269 truth of all things; and because it is an authentic guide for
those on the way; and because the ordinary man attains *nirvāṇa* if he bases himself on it. Authority (*āgamatva*) is defined as being the teachings only of the perfectly enlightened one. Doctrines differing from this, because they are not in accord with reason (*upapattiviyukta*), are declared not to be valid knowledge but spurious doctrine. Therefore these theories of self-existence, other-existence, existence and non-existence are destitute of intelligibility and are not the true ways of things.

So, for the guidance of those desiring liberation:

> 7 In the *Kātyāyanāvavāda Sūtra*, the illustrious one, who comprehends existence and non-existence, repudiated both thoughts: that something is and that something is not.

The illustrious one says in the *Kātyāyanāvavāda Sūtra*, 'So much the more, Kātyāyana, the unenlightened man, clinging tenaciously to the belief that things are either in being (*astitā*) or not in being (*nāstitā*), is not liberated in that way. He is not liberated from the distress of birth, old age, disease, death, grief, lamentation and sorrow. He is not liberated from the prison of unregenerate existence with its basis in personal existence. He is not liberated from the painful sorrow of a mother's death nor of a father's death.'[1] And so on. This *sūtra* is taught in all the Buddhist schools. So on this authority and from the arguments given, an intelligent man should not, in reason, be capable of holding to the theories of self-existence,
270 other existence, existence and non-existence, which are completely opposed to the words of the perfectly realized one and which he rejected.

Of what nature is the illustrious one exactly? He comprehends existence and non-existence. One whose nature it is to comprehend existence and non-existence is a comprehender of existence and non-existence. From his ultimate grasp of self-existence in the true sense as related to existence and non-existence, as we have explained it, only the illustrious one is said to be a comprehender of existence and non-existence. Therefore he rejects both views: that things are in being or that things are not in being. It follows that it does not make sense to insist that the true way of things can be seen in terms of existence or non-existence.

To quote: 'To say, Kāśyapa, "Something is", is one extreme; to say "Something is not" is one extreme. What avoids these two extremes is said to be without a specific nature, beyond proof, not related, invisible, without an abode, not to be known conceptually. It is, Kāśyapa, the middle way (*madhyamā pratipad*); it is the right way of regarding the true nature of things.'[2]

To quote: ' "It is", "It is not" are two dogmas; "purity", "impurity" are two dogmas; and so the wise man abandons both dogmas without taking up a position in the middle. "It is", "It is not" is mere disputation; "purity", "impurity" is mere disputation; afflicted existence is not terminated by engaging in disputation; afflicted existence is brought to an end by not engaging in disputation.'[3]

[1] Cf. *Kindred Sayings*, vol. 2, p. 12, Pali Text Society, Translation Series, Luzac, London, 1952.

[2] From the *Ratnakūṭa Sūtra*, one of the earliest Mahāyāna *sūtras*.

[3] *Samādhirāja Sūtra*.

The unintelligibility of change

You may interject: But if there is self-existence of fire and
271 such things what objection would there be?

There would be the objection already given: 'A self-existent nature which arises from causes and conditions would be something created', and so on. Moreover, if there were this kind of self-existent nature in fire and such things, it, existing already in fact, could never change. Nāgārjuna expounds:

> 8ab If it is the nature of something to exist, it cannot cease to exist.

If it is the nature of fire and such things to be self-existent, then such a self-existent, whose nature it is to exist, could not change.

> 8cd Real change of the nature of something is not logically possible.

If the nature of fire and such things were as one supposes, it would be self-existent; and then, because of the unchangeableness of a true nature (*prakṛti*), change (*anyathābhāva*) would never be logically possible. For example, the infinity of space could never possibly change; similarly there could be no change in such things as fire because it is their nature to exist as such. But one perceives the disappearance of things, either in so far as they change or as there is a disruption of continuity. So, because their nature is to change, this cannot be the inherent self-existent nature of things; it is like the heat of water. This should be clear.

You may object: If change is impossible in something which exists by its very nature and yet one perceives change you say there can be no true nature of such things. But then, indeed:

> 9ab If things have no inherent nature what is it that will change?[1]

272 That is, how can there be change in something which, like the sky-lotus, does not exist by virtue of its inherent nature (*prakṛtya svarūpeṇa*); one does not perceive change in something which by its nature does not exist; because one experiences change there must be inherent self-existent nature.

We reply. If, according to your thought, there is an inherent

[1] The opponent's argument.

nature in things because there can be no change in something which has no essential nature and yet there is direct experience of change, even so

9cd If things have an inherent nature what is it that will change?

Taking your case, how will there be change in something which by its inherent nature exists in present fact (*vartamāna eva*)? There can be no change in something which by its very nature exists. Thus change is impossible in every sense. It should be realized therefore that there is no inherent nature (*prakṛti*) in things.

When we said earlier that there could be no inherent nature because we experience change, that was said with reference to the experience of change as understood by others. We have at no time agreed that there is change in anything at all. Rather it is that an inherent nature of things is totally (*atyantataḥ*) non-existent, that all the putative elements of existence are non-existent and without an inherent nature and that change in such things is non-existent. One who, however, believes in the existence and non-existence of things, for him, so believing, it follows inevitably.

The twin dogmas of eternalism and naturalism

10ab To say 'Things are in being' is the eternalist view; to say 'Things are not in being' is the naturalist view.

273 It is implied here that these theories of eternalism (*śāśvata*) and naturalism (*uccheda*)[1] are obstacles on the way to the final beatitude of heaven, and that they cause great ill.

10cd Therefore a thinking man should not resort to the twin beliefs in existence and non-existence.

Why, given the theories of real existence and real non-existence do the dogmas of eternalism and naturalism follow? Because:

11 What exists by its inherent nature can never not exist: this implies eternalism. What does now not exist but once did: this implies naturalism.

What is said to exist by its inherent nature (*svabhāvena*) can

[1] Usually translated 'nihilism'. In the discussion which follows 'naturalism' seems more appropriate.

at no time not exist because inherent nature is indefeasible (*anapāyitva*). If, thus, one agrees that things are in being one espouses the eternalist view. Again, if one agrees that in a previous time something really existed of which, later, because it has been destroyed, one says 'it does not exist', one is caught up in the naturalist view. One for whom a self-existent nature of things is not intelligible, because a self-existent nature of things is never directly experienced (*anupalambha*), is not involved in the eternalist and naturalist views.

You may object that one who supposes there is no inherent nature in things, though he does not hold the eternalist view as he rejects the reality of things, is inevitably caught up in the naturalist view. We reply that the naturalist view does not arise in this way. One who supposes that at one time there is a self-existent nature of something and who perceives this at a later time to have disappeared, holds that things are not in being because he repudiates what he previously perceived to be self-existent. However, when one is rid of optical defect, not
274 perceiving things as the one with an optical defect sees hairs, says, 'Things do not really exist' he is not saying 'Everything is illusory' because in that case there would be nothing to be negated. For the purpose of removing the persistent illusion of the deluded, we declare, like one freed from an optical defect, 'Things as such do not really exist'. In saying this we are not caught up in the naturalist theory: we are concerned to be of help to others.

As the *sūtra* says, 'One who supposes the real existence of desire, aversion and illusion and later says they have ceased to exist, he indeed is the naturalist', and so on.

But, you may say, one who supposes that mind and its objects are real (*vastumātra*) only in reciprocal dependence (*paratrantra*) avoids the theory of eternalism because there is
275 no inherent self-existence in dependence as he conceives it; and he avoids the theory of naturalism because dependent mental states, which are the cause of the removal of afflictions, really exist.[1]

How can such a one avoid the twin dogmas? What is projected by the mind is non-existent; what is dependent on mind is existent; so both the eternalist and the naturalist dogmas are operative. Further, his exposition does not make sense because it has been shown that the self-existence of what is dependent does not make sense. Thus the Mādhyamika view alone is free

[1] The position of the Vijñānavāda school of Buddhism.

of the twin dogmas of eternalism and naturalism, but not the views of the Vijñānavādin and others.

So it is said in the *Ratnāvalī*: 'Ask the Sāṁkhyas, the Vaiśeṣikas, the Jains, the personalists, and the naturalists if their doctrine teaches the transcendence of existence and non-existence.' 'You should know the hidden depths of the immortal teaching uttered by the Buddhas, for its very essence is the transcending of existence and non-existence.'

276 Out of concern for the enlightenment of such people who need guidance, as a useful means to comprehending the ultimate truth, the illustrious one, in his limitless compassion, taught the doctrines of the Vijñānavādins and of the Sāṁmitīyas, who believe in the person. But only for the sake of the uninitiated (*neyārtha*), not for the initiated (*nītārtha*).

As is said in the *Samādhirāja Sūtra*: 'The one who can distinguish the higher truth in the *sūtras* knows that the Buddha held to the absence of being in things. All mention of persons, beings, and souls, he knows, are only for the sake of the uninitiated.'

This point is found repeatedly in the teachings of the *Akṣamati* and other texts. The cycle of death and re-birth endures as long as the entanglement in the twin dogmas – that things are in being or that they are not – endures. When those genuinely striving for liberation have realized this, being freed from the twin dogmas, they rightly embrace the middle way.

As the illustrious one said in the *Samādhirāja Sūtra*: 'Let
there be an end to the knowledge of existence and non-
existence; all is inaccessible to thought and all is unreal. Those
who follow their inclination to intellection will suffer in count-
277 less rebirths. The one who wisely understands that things are
non-things is never obsessed with things. The one who is never
277.4 obsessed with things attains peace of mind beyond all defini-
278.5 tion.' 'When Buddha, the sage, the king of truth, the revealer
of all truths appears, the refrain is sounded from grass and
bush and tree and plants, from the rocks and the mountains:
all elements of existence are without being.'

'Howsoever far mere words reach in the world realm, all are without being, none is real; and so far resounds the call of the realized one, the guide and teacher of all men.'

To say 'something is' is to say that it is in being. But eternal being as the self-existent nature of particular things is never a fact. All putative elements of existence are not real and devoid of being because as particulars they do not have self-existent natures. This is found in the *prajñāpāramitā* texts. The self-existence of particular things is contrary to thought. 'The refrain is sounded that all elements of existence are without being.'

The meaning of similar *sūtras* is to be understood in this sense.

279 'Howsoever far mere words reach in the world realm, all are without being, none is real.'

In sum, the intention is to repudiate the reality[1] of things; to say things are not real is precisely the same as to say they have no self-existence.

[1] Reading *bhāva*; the text has *abhāva* but this *must* be a mistake. It is true that Mādhyamika repudiates both *bhāva* and *abhāva*, but the tactical thrust of this chapter, as of most others, is against uncritical realism (*bhāva*).

XIV

Self and the Way Things Really Are

The problem

340 At this point someone may ask: If the basic afflictions, actions, personal existence, responsible agents and the fruits of action are all not the real way of things (*tattvam*) but rather, being like a fabled city and such things, precisely what is not real, merely appearing to the unenlightened in the guise of reality, what then for you is the way things are really (*tattvam*)? And how does one attain (*avatāra*) to the way things are really?

We reply. It is the utter cessation of I-ing (*ahamkāra*) and mine-ing (*mamakāra*) in both personal and non-personal regard through ceasing to take anything whatsoever, whether personal or non-personal, as real in its particularity, that is for us the way things are really. Concerning how one attains to the way things really are the *Madhyamakāvatāra* should be consulted for details. To quote: 'The *yogī*, discerning in his wisdom that all basic afflictions and defects whatsoever arise from holding the view that the person is real (*satkāyadṛṣṭi*) and having inseen that the self (*ātman*) is the central concept of this view, does away with the self.'

Discerning that the cycle of birth and death springs from holding the view that the person is real, and discerning that the self is the basis of this view that the person is real, the *yogī*, through not taking the self as real, abandons the view that the person is real, and having abandoned this view, discerning that all the basic afflictions come to an end, he enquires into the self: what is this so-called self which is the intended object of the notion 'I' (*ahamkāraviṣaya*).

The self identical with personal existence

The intended object of the notion 'I' must be thought of either as being of the very nature (*svabhāva*) of the factors of personal
341 existence (*skandhas*) or as being wholly other (*vyatirikta*) than

them. Because the other theses:[1] that the self is either the base of the factors of personal existence, or is based in them, or possesses them, are implicit in the alternatives that the self is either identical with or different from them, and because he wishes to express himself succinctly, Nāgārjuna, with a view to commencing the invalidation of the self, refutes both views: that of identity and that of difference.

> 1 If the self were identical with the factors of personal existence it would itself arise and perish; if it were other than them, it would not be characterizable in their terms.

If you ask: How is it that in the Chapters on the Realized One, and Fire and Fuel five theses are given whereas here only two alternatives are? We reply: just because in those two chapters five views are expounded they are not expounded again here. Only the two views are taken up for the sake of brevity.

In this *kārikā*, if the self (*ātman*) is conceived of as identical with the factors of personal existence, then, as it participates in arising and perishing, the self becomes something which arises and perishes because of its participation in the arising and perishing of the factors of personal existence. But the self is not so regarded because of the various faults which that would entail.

Nāgārjuna will say later, 'Something which once did not exist cannot come into existence, because of the logical fault involved. The self would be either something created or it would come to be without any cause.'[2] 'The self is not identi-
342 cal with what it possesses (*upādāna*)[3] because that both arises
and perishes. How then can the self be the possessor of the possessed?'[4] Further: 'If the self is identical with the factors of personal existence, this would render the self multiple as these are multiple. If the self were like a real object, it could not, as such, have contradictory states.'[5] 'The self would necessarily perish in *nirvāṇa*; so it would perish and arise in the moments preceding *nirvāṇa*. If the responsible agent perishes there can be no consequences of his acts for himself; the accumulated consequences would fall to the lot of another.' This much from the *Madhyamakāvatāra*. My point of view can be

[1] Cf. p. 141 and p. 193.
[2] XXVII, 12. Not included in this translation.
[3] The factors of personal existence, the *skandhas*.
[4] XXVII, 6. Not included in this translation.
[5] *Madhyamakāvatāra*, VI, 127, 128.

comprehended from the investigation carried out there and I shall not enter into a lengthy exposition again here.

The self other than personal existence

343 So much for the self not being identical with the factors of personal existence; that it is wholly other than them does not make sense either. If the self were other than the factors of personal existence it could not be characterized in their terms (*askandhalakṣaṇa*). As a horse, being other than a cow, cannot have the character of a cow, so the self, if it is thought of as entirely other than the factors of personal existence, cannot be characterized in their terms. Now the factors of personal existence, being compounded, come into existence as a result of causes and conditions and it is their character to arise, exist and perish. If the self is not of the character of the factors of personal existence, then according to this thesis it could have no connection with the characteristics of arising, existing and perishing. Such a thing is not taken to be the meaning of self, either because it would not actually exist, like the flower in the sky, or would be uncompounded as *nirvāṇa* is uncompounded. But it does not make sense that it could be the object of the sense of 'I'. So it does not make sense that the self can be wholly other than the factors of personal existence.

But then another argument is possible. If the self were wholly other than the factors of personal existence it would not be definable in their terms. The five factors of personal existence are (1) bodily form, (2) experiencing, (3) seizing on the specific character of things, (4) shaping one's dispositions, (5) becoming aware of objects.[1] The self conceived of as wholly other than the factors of personal existence, as con-
344 sciousness is other than a physical object, would be of a character peculiar to itself. And this character would be understood as peculiar even as mind is peculiar in relation to body. But the self is not so understood. Therefore it is not wholly other than the factors of personal existence.

You may object that non-Buddhists believe that the self is entirely distinct from the factors of personal existence and propound a special definition so that for them your reasoning is no logical impediment. How the non-Buddhists propound a special definition of the self is dealt with in the Madhyamakāvatāra.[2]

[1] An interesting statement of the five *skandhas*. [2] VI, 142.

'Non-Buddhists think of the self as eternal, as non-agent, as the enjoyer, as beyond all attributes and as inactive.[1] Depending on the different conceptions of the self, non-Buddhists arrive at differing doctrines.'

We reply. It is true that non-Buddhists claim that the nature of the self is quite distinct from the factors of personal existence. But they do not propound their definition from a grasp of the true nature (*svarsīpataḥ*) of the self. Rather, because not rightly understanding existential hypostatizations (*upādāya-prajñapti*), they do not understand, because of fear, that the self is merely a name (*nāmamātrakam eva*). Having gone astray
345 even from everyday common sense, by erroneous reification (*mithyākalpanā*) misled by simply a pseudo-inference, in their delusion they construct a theory of the self and define its nature. By giving the proof of the reciprocal dependence of self and the factors of personal existence in the Chapter 'The Agent Subject and his Doing', and elsewhere, the refutation of the non-Buddhists is offered even on the level of common sense. To quote: 'As the reflection of one's own face is seen depending upon a mirror, but does not exist in its own right; so the "I" is experienced depending on the factors of personal existence but is not anything existing in its own right, like the image of one's own face. As, in the absence of a mirror, one's own face is not seen, so neither is the "I" in the absence of the factors of personal existence. From hearing this kind of statement the noble Ānanda attained the eye of truth and spoke continuously of it to the other monks.'[2]

We do not therefore undertake the exposition of the same point again. It is nothing but existential hypostatizing which is, in the mature view of those aspiring to freedom, the root of the obsession with self among those who, as a result of primal ignorance are in the grip of false belief. The five factors of personal existence appear to be what the self is founded on. Is it of the same nature as the factors of personal existence or is it not? Having examined this question from every aspect, those aspiring to freedom do not take the self to be a self-existent entity (*bhāvasvabhavataḥ*).

If no self, no I or mine

For such,

> 2ab If the self is non-existent how will anything be one's own?

[1] This description fits the Sāṁkhya.

[2] *Ratnāvalī*, I, 31–4.

346 Because they do not directly experience the self, even less do they directly experience the five factors of personal existence, on which the hypostatization of the self is based, as their own (*ātmīya*). Just as, when a chariot has been burned, one does not perceive its parts because they have been burned too, so those on the way (*yogīs*), when they have realized that the self is not an entity, necessarily realize that their own factors of personal existence are not entities either.

To quote from the *Ratnāvalī*: 'The factors of personal existence arise from the sense of "I", but this "I" is, in truth, false. If the seed of something is false how can the resulting thing itself be true? Having seen that the factors of personal existence are unreal the sense of "I" is expelled. When the sense of "I" has been abandoned the factors of personal existence are no longer possible.'

The sun, at the end of a summer's day when it is throwing out fiery rays of light and just as it enters that part of the heavens where there is no cloud, emits slanting rays like elongated sparks from a blazing fire and warms the dry earth beneath. If one is in the vicinity of this dry area a visual illusion gives rise to a mirage which seems to be water. For those at a distance it seems to be clear blue water; but for those close by it does not give rise to a mirage.

347 Similarly, for those who are far removed from viewing the nature of self and own as they really are, who are caught in the cycle of birth and death, in the grip of the misbelief of primal ignorance, for such, a false thing – the self as hypostatized on the basis of the factors of personal existence – manifests itself as real. But for those close by who see the truth of these matters, no such false thing manifests itself.

As Nāgārjuna says: 'An object seen from afar is seen clearly by those close by. If a mirage is water why is it not taken to be so by those close by? The everyday world is not seen in the same way by those close to it as it is taken to be by those remote from it, but is without factual character (*animitta*), like a mirage. As a mirage, which looks like water, is not water, nor any real thing, so the factors of personal existence which are like a self, are not of the self nor of anything real.'[1]

And so, because he in fact has no sense of self and what is of self, the one on the way, having seen the higher truth from close by, naturally becomes

[1] *Ratnāvalī*, I, 29–30.

> 2cd Free of I-ing and mine-ing because the self and what is of the self have come to an end.

'Of the self' means what is in the interest of the self, that is,
348 the fivefold factors of personal existence taken as mine. The *yogī* – the one on the way – becomes free of the I-ing and mine-ing by the coming to an end of the self – the object of the I-sense – and by the coming to an end of what is of interest to the self, that is the factors of personal existence taken as real – the object of the sense of 'mine'. These are not allowed to arise because he no longer has any sense of them (*anupalambha*).

You may object that the one who becomes in this way free of I-ing and mine-ing must by that fact exist, and if his existence is established so too are self and the factors of personal existence. But this is not so. Because

> 3 One who is free of I-ing and mine-ing does not exist factually. Anyone who thinks he sees one free of I-ing and mine-ing does not truly see.

If self and the factors of personal existence are not perceived at all as self-existent entities, how will there be a different entity distinct from them – this one who is free of I-ing and mine-ing? And anyone who thinks he sees one free of I-ing and mine-ing – who does not exist at all as an entity – he does not see things as they really are (*tattvam*).

As the illustrious one said, 'Regard everything personal as devoid of being, regard everything external as devoid of being. No one at all factually exists, not even the one regarding things as devoid of being.' And again, 'Whoever thinks the elements of existence are merely empty is foolish and walks a dangerous path. Imperishable are the empty elements and yet not imperishable are the imperishable elements said to be.'

'To think the elements of existence are at peace, utterly at peace, such a thought can never be true. The entire manifest
349 world arises from discriminative thinking; the elements should be realized to be subtle and beyond the reach of thought.' Again: 'The factors of personal existence are devoid of self-existence and without being. Enlightenment is devoid of self-existence and without being. The one involved with both is devoid of self-existence. So think the wise but not the foolish.'

And so

> 4 When I-ing and mine-ing have wasted away both inwardly

and outwardly, possessive attachment comes to an end and from its cessation personal re-birth ceases.

As the *sūtra* says, 'The basic afflictions are rooted in the belief in the permanent self, arise from the belief in the permanent self and are caused by the belief in the permanent self.' This belief in the permanent self is brought to an end by no longer having a sense of self and of what belongs to self. From that sense coming to an end the fourfold possessive attachment – to sense pleasure, to dogmas, to moral pride and vows, and to belief in the permanent self – ceases. From the cessation of possessive attachment (*upādāna*) personal existence understood as re-birth is ended. The sequence of stages in the cessation of personal existence is definitively given in this way:

Absence of self leads to freedom

5a From the wasting away of the afflictions and karmic[1] action there is freedom.

350 Possessive attachment having wasted away, birth into personal existence, which depends on it, is no more. When personal existence has come to an end, how can there be the cycle of birth, old age and death? Nāgārjuna puts it precisely: 'From the wasting away of karmic action and the afflictions there is freedom.' But, you may ask, from the wasting away of what do karmic action and the afflictions cease? The answer is:

5bcd The afflictions and karmic action arise from hypostatizing thought and this from the manifold of named things. Named things come to an end in the absence of being.

The afflictions arise in the unenlightened from groundlessly (*ayoniśa*) hypostatizing (*vikalpayata*) external objects and the other factors of personal existence. Nāgārjuna will say, 'Desire, aversion and delusion are said to spring from hypostatizing thought. They arise dependent on misbelief and on taking things to be good or bad.'[2] As is said in the *sūtra*: 'Oh desire, I know where you spring from: you are born of the mind. I will dwell on you no more and then for me you will be no more.'

[1] Action proceeding from a belief in a permanent self; only such action has moral consequences.

[2] P. 207, 1.

Thus karmic action and the afflictions arise from hypostatizing thought. Hypostatizing thought springs from the manifold of named things (*prapañca*), i.e., from the beginninglessly recurring cycle of birth and death, which consists of knowledge and objects of knowledge, words and their meanings, agents and action, means and act, pot and cloth, diadem and chariots, objects and feelings, female and male, gain and loss, happiness and misery, beauty and ugliness, blame and praise.[1]

This world of named things (*laukikaḥ prapaña*) in its entirety finds its end in the absence of being, when there is immediate realization that all things are devoid of self-existence.

How is that to be understood? Once objects are taken to be real things, you have the entire world of named things as just described. However, if those thirsty with desire do not take the daughter of a sterile woman to be a beautiful young lady, that is to say if they do not take objects to be real, they will not bring the manifold of named things into existence with such things[2] as its objects. By not calling the manifold of named things into play they do not groundlessly bring hypostatizing thought into play with named things as its object. By
351 not bringing hypostatizing thought into play they do not allow the afflictions to arise which are rooted in the belief in a permanent self, a belief which springs from obsession with the I and the mine. Because the afflictions, which are of the very essence of the belief in the permanent person, have not been allowed to arise they do not perform acts which can be distinguished as either good or bad. Because they do not perform good or bad acts they do not experience the jungle of birth and death which is one great network of being born and ageing and dying, of suffering, lamentation, misery and sadness. The wise, thus steadfastly seeing all things as devoid of a self-existent nature, do not take the personal factors, the sense fields or types of consciousness to have being in their particularity. Because they do not take these supposed elements to have being in their particularity, they do not bring the manifold of named things into play which would have such real particulars as its object. Because they do not bring the manifold of named things, having real particulars as its object, into play, they do not invoke hypostatizing thought, they do not allow the afflictions, which are rooted in the belief in the permanent person, to arise because of obsession with I and

[1] This is the longest list of the fateful dualities Candrakīrti ever gives us.

[2] Knowledge and objects of knowledge, and so on.

mine. Because they do not allow the afflictions which are rooted in the belief in a permanent person to arise, they perform no karmic acts. Because they perform no karmic acts they do not experience the cycle of life and death called birth, ageing and dying. Thus, having attained to the true way of things (*śūnyatā*) which is the serenity of the coming to rest of the manifold of all named things (*prapañcopaśamaśiva*) there is an end to all named things as the base of hypostatizing thought. From named things being no more there is an end to hypostatizing thought, because hypostatizing is at an end all karmic action and afflictions are ended. Because karmic action and the afflictions are ended there is an end to personal existence.

It follows that it is nothing other than the absence of being in particular things, understood as the repose (*nivṛtti*) of the entire manifold of named things which is said to be *nirvāṇa*.

To quote from the *Catuḥśataka*: 'The perfectly realized ones hold, in brief, that the Buddhist truth is harmless and that the absence of being in things is itself *nirvāṇa*. These are the only two truths for us.'

Bhāvaviveka, however, not understanding the attainment of the absence of being in things by the disciples and the fully realized sages, as just explained, gives this account: The disciple, regarding the entire mass of experiences which perish
352 momentarily and which are generated externally, as not self nor what belongs to self, and regarding the self and what belongs to it as not being real entities, develops the view that there are pure elements of existence (*dharma mātra*) which are born and perish.

As against that we say that the self is the object of the I and as this does not exist neither does the self; because the self does not exist there is no reality which could be internal or external to self. And if the sense of mine is not functioning, one is free of I and mine and the I does not arise as a definitive entity, but is rather a conventional term for everyday purposes.[1] How much more this is true for the great *Bodhisattvas* who course in transcendent awareness without hypostatizing thought, and who regard all things as unborn. That is why Nāgārjuna says, 'One free of I-ing and mine-ing does not exist in fact.'

Therefore, Bhāvaviveka does not follow Nāgārjuna in this

[1] Candrakīrti gives, we might say, a phenomenological description of the way the self appears in experience. Bhāvaviveka, according to Candrakīrti, gives a metaphysics of the self.

353 matter, as I have shown in the Madhyamakāvatāra. 'In the seventh stage of the *Bodhisattva*'s career transcendent awareness governs.' So I do not again make the effort to show the fault in Bhāvaviveka's account.

The illustrious one says in the *Eight Thousand Sūtra*: 'One who is hungry to learn, o Subhūti, the enlightenment of the disciple can learn from this *sūtra* of transcendent awareness (*prajñāpāramitā*).[1] One who is hungry to learn, o Subhūti, the enlightenment of the realized sage can learn from this *sūtra* of transcendent awareness. One who is hungry to learn, o Subhūti, the unsurpassable perfect enlightenment of the great beings, he may learn from this *sūtra* of transcendent awareness.'

And it is said further: 'Whoever desires to become a follower
354 of the realized one or a realized one himself, or a monarch of the truth, without attaining this imperturbableness, will achieve nothing: a man who does not discern the banks of a river will not arrive either at this bank or the other.'

The Buddha's teaching concerning self

Someone may object: If, as you argue, the way things are really is the non-arising of the hypostatizations I and mine in either personal or non-personal regard by not taking anything, personal or non-personal to be real in its particularity, then what about the following sayings of the illustrious one?

'The self is master of the self. What other master could there be? The wise attain heaven by restraining the self. The self is master of the self. What other master could there be?
354.10 The self is the witness of the self in both good and ill.' And so on. Surely this contradicts you.

355.3 We reply: Did the illustrious one not also say: 'In this world neither person nor self exists, because they are causally dependent things.' And again: 'The body is not the self, nor does the self possess the body, nor is the self in the body nor the body in the self. In the same vein consciousness is not the self, nor does the self possess consciousness nor is the self in consciousness nor consciousness in the self.' And again: 'All elements of existence are without self.'

How is it that these scriptures do not contradict the ones quoted earlier? Because the purpose of the illustrious one's teaching in the former scriptures has to be understood. It is

[1] Commonly translated 'perfection of wisdom'.

the universal rule that a distinction between truth for the initiated (*nītārtha*) and what is merely truth for beginners (*neyārtha*) exists in the teaching of the illustrious Buddhas who are devoted to the awakening of the lotus-like mind of the entire creation which is to be guided, who are like a sun that never sets and who are great in the power of their insight, of their ducational wisdom and of their universal compassion.

> 6 Both 'The self exists' has been expounded and 'The self does not exist' has been taught too. And 'Neither self nor non-self exist' has been taught as well by the Buddhas.

356 The meaning is this. There are some[1] who, even though rooted in the world of everyday practice, do not correctly see everyday things though these are nothing but the objects which the person of normal vision sees; this is because the eye of their mind is completely covered as by a cataract simply by the erroneous view, arising from false belief, that the self does not exist. They are determined to accept as reality only the elements called earth, water, fire and air. They claim that mind arises solely from the gestation of the four elements, like a foetus; even as the gestation of various substances like roots, boiled rice and water results in intoxicating drink, anal wind and so on. So, actively denying a beginning and an end to life, they deny the self and future existence. This life (*loka*) is not real; the next life is not real; the matured fruits of good and ill deeds are not real; no individual creature is born, and so on. Because of denying all this, they turn their backs on the various endeavours like the rare and desirable goals of heaven and ultimate beatitude; they incessantly and forever perform ill deeds because of their innate disposition, and are headed for a mighty plunging into the hells.

In order to put an end to the belief of such people that the self does not exist, the illustrious Buddhas sometimes have
357 maintained, for teaching purposes, that the self exists. They, adjusting to the realm of living beings in which there are 8,400 categories of creature, devoted to fulfilling their vow to rescue the entire realm of living beings and flowing with a great store of universal compassion, practical wisdom and ultimate insight, who are peerless, bonded to this one creation, physicians to the great malaise of the afflictions, masters of the art of healing, willed to show kindness to those needing

[1] Materialists or naturalists.

guidance whether of the lowest, middle or highest level, they, in order to put an end to the ill acts of those of the lowest level, formulate their teaching in everyday terms.

The refutation of the theory that things can be without cause is given in the Chapter 'The Agent Subject and his Doing' of this treatise and in the verse 'or without cause'[1] and details may be found in the *Madhyamakāvatāra*. It is not necessary to refute that view again here.

However, there are some who, like birds, are tied by long and strong bonds of attachment to the I and the mine, bonds which arise from holding to the reality of the self. Such, though they have progressed far and commit no ill acts, are unable to go beyond being born into the three planes of exist-
358 ence and cannot reach the blissful city of *nirvāṇa* where there is neither old age nor death. Such are of the middle group of those who need guidance, and to them the illustrious Buddhas, in their desire to show favour to those who need guidance, have also taught the non-existence of self in order to weaken the attachment to the false view of the self and to awaken the longing for *nirvāṇa*.

And there are those who, thanks to their earlier discipline, have perfected their potential by adhering to the profound truth. To such superior followers, for whom *nirvāṇa* is near, who are free of attachment to a self, who are capable of penetrating to the hidden truth in the words of the foremost sage, the Buddhas, having seen the worthiness of these, have taught: 'No self whatsoever either exists or does not exist.' Even as the theory of self is not the truth of things, no more is the theory of non-self. That is why it is taught: 'There is no self whatsoever, nor is there any non-self whatsoever.'

As is said in the *Āryaratnakūṭa*: ' "There is a self", Kāśyapa, is one dogma. "There is no self" is the opposing dogma. What avoids these two dogmas is said to be without a specific nature, beyond proof, not related, invisible, without an abode, not to be known conceptually. It is, Kāśyapa, the middle way; it is the right way of regarding the true way of things.'

359 As is said in the *Āryaratnāvalī*: 'And so neither a self nor a non-self is perceived in the way things truly are. The great sage has eradicated false views stemming from self and non-self. What is seen and heard and otherwise perceived is not said by the sage to be either real or false. From one view would arise its opposite and neither would be true.'

[1] P. 36, 1.

As, in this way, the actual teaching of the truth by the illustrious Buddhas in repudiating self, not-self and both together, takes account of the various dispositions of those who are to be guided whether they are of the lesser, middle or superior category, therefore the Mādhyamikas are not at variance with the authoritative texts.

This is why the master Āryadeva said, 'The one who knows how, in the beginning, to ward off ill deed and, later, how to ward off the self and, after that, how to keep all things under control, he has achieved wisdom.' And Nāgārjuna said, 'Even as the grammarian would teach language, even so Buddha taught the Truth according to the capacity of those who were to be guided. To some he taught the Truth in order to lead them from ill deeds; to some for the sake of good deeds; to some for the sake of both. And, beyond both, he taught the
360 hidden Truth, terrifying to the timid, concealed in the absence of being and universal compassion; and to yet others he taught the realization of enlightenment.'[1]

There is another interpretation of the *kārikā*.[2] The Sāṁkhya school and others, after accepting the lack of a necessary connection between an act and its consequences in compound elements which are in constant flux, still talk about a self. And the naturalists (*lokāyatikas*), not seeing, in rigorous perception, a transmigrating self, talk about a non-self. They say, 'A person is absolutely nothing more than what is within the sensefields. O blessed one, what the learned talk about is but a faulty inference.'

Even as those not suffering from eye disease do not see the hairs and mosquitoes and such things which are perceived by those with eye disease, so the Buddhas in no way whatsoever see self and non-self as self-existing realities in the way ordinary people imagine them. ' "Neither self nor non-self exist" has been taught as well by the Buddhas.'

The limitation of language

364.1 Someone may object: If the illustrious Buddhas taught neither that the self exists nor that the self does not exist, what then did they teach? The reply is:

> 7 When the object of thought is no more there is nothing for language to refer to. The true nature of things neither arises nor perishes, as *nirvāṇa* does not.

[1] *Ratnāvalī*, IV, 94–6. [2] P. 175, 6.

This means that if there were something real (*vastu*) for language to refer to there could be didactic argument (*deśyeta*). When, however, what language refers to is no more, when there is no object (*viṣaya*) for utterances to refer to, then there is no didactic argument by the Buddhas whatever. Why does Nāgārjuna say there is nothing for language to refer to? Because 'The object of thought is no more.' Object of thought means what thought (*citta*) has as its object (*gocara*). Object means the object grasped in thought. If there were such an object of thought, then, by imputing a specific character (*nimitta*) to it, speech would be able to function. When, however, no object of thought exists, how can specific character be imputed by which speech would function? How it is that there is no object of thought Nāgārjuna explains when he says: 'The true nature of things (*dharmatā*) neither arises nor perishes, as *nirvāṇa* does not.'

As the true nature of things, understood as their inherent, self-existent nature, their ur-nature, does not arise nor perish, like *nirvāṇa*, so discursive thought cannot function with respect to it. And if thought does not function how can specific character be imputed to things? And if this is wanting how can speech function? That the illustrious Buddhas have didactically argued nothing whatever is therefore established beyond question.[1] That is why Nāgārjuna will say later, 'Beatitude is the coming to an end of taking things in their particularity, the coming to an end of the manifold of named things. No doctrine about anything at all has been taught by Buddha at any time.'[2]

365 Let it be so, you may say, but what of the earlier statement 'The manifold of named things comes to an end in the absence of being.' How can there be an end to named things in the absence of being (*śūnyatā*)? The reply is, 'because what language refers to has come to an end'; this should be understood here as it was earlier.

Well but what about the earlier statement 'It is the utter cessation of I-ing and mine-ing in both personal and non-personal regard through ceasing to take anything whatsoever, whether personal or non-personal, as real in its particularity that is for us the way things are really'? Is it possible to say more precisely what the way things are really (*tattvam*) is?

To the line 'When the object of thought is no more there is

[1] An incisive, if brief, essay on the natural limits of metaphysics.
[2] P. 262, 24.

nothing for language to refer to' should be added 'and that is the way things are really' (*tattvataḥ*).

And if, further, you ask: What is the reason why, in that real way of things, what language refers to is no more when the object of thought is no more? Nāgārjuna says 'because the true nature of things neither arises nor perishes, as *nirvāṇa*
366 does not'. The exposition given earlier fits here precisely.

As is said in the *Tathāgataguhya Sūtra*: 'O Śāntamati, in the night when the *Tathāgata*[1] became perfectly enlightened with the unsurpassable perfection of illumination, during the night when he attained perfect freedom, during this time the *Tathāgata* neither uttered nor enunciated even one syllable. The illustrious one taught the message in different ways to all beings who are to be guided, to gods, demons, men, *Kinnaras*, the saints, *Vidhyādharas* and serpents. By the utterance of one momentary cry he banishes the darkness from men's minds, he awakens the lotus of enlightenment in its many forms, he dries up the ocean of old age and death and he confounds the multitudinous rays of the seven suns which shine at the end of a
366.7 cosmic age.' And from the *Samādhirājasūtra*: 'When Buddha,
367.12 the sage, the king of truth, the revealer of all truths appears, the refrain is sounded from grass and bush and tree and plants, from the rocks and the mountains: all elements of existence are without being.'

'Howsoever far mere words reach in the world realm, all are without being, none is real; and so far resounds the call of the
367.16 realized one, the guide and teacher of all men.'

Mādhyamika is not nihilism

368.4 At this point some will insist that the Mādhyamikas are indistinguishable from nihilists (*nāstika*) because they hold that good and ill acts, responsible agents, the fruits of action and the entire world of personal existence are without self-existence. And the nihilists as well hold that 'Things have no permanent existence.' Therefore Mādhyamikas are indistinguishable from nihilists.

It is not so. Why? Because Mādhyamikas are exponents of the view that all things arise in dependence. Having grasped the significance of causal conditions they argue that everything in this life and in the next is lacking self-existent nature because it arises in dependence. The nihilists are naive realists

[1] Buddha.

and do not understand the non-existence of the next life and the other things as due to lack of self-existent nature in things because they arise in dependence. Rather, even though they take the things of this world to have self-existent natures, as they do not admit that one is born into this life from another or into another life from this, they deny that things such as are experienced in this life exist elsewhere.

You may say: But, as they hold that nothing exists as real in itself there is, in this respect, an identity of view. It is not so. Why? As Mādhyamikas accept things as real for purposes of the everyday world, the two views are not comparable. But are they not comparable in essentials? Even though comparable in the essential point of the unrealness of things they are not comparable because those putting the views into practice differ.

Suppose a man has committed a crime. Someone, who did not recognize the criminal beyond a doubt, urged by an enemy of the criminal, falsely gives witness that the crime was committed by a certain man. Someone else, an eye-witness of the
369 crime, accuses the same man. Now, even though there is no difference in objective content, none the less, because of the difference between the two witnesses, the one is said to speak falsely and the other to speak the truth. When the facts come to light the first one is worthy of disgrace and demerit, but not the other one.

So it is in this case. There is no identity of insight or of explanation between the Mādhyamikas who have fully realized the real nature of things as it is (*vastusvarūpa*) and who expound that, and the nihilists who have not fully realized the real nature of things as it is, even though there is no difference in their theory of the nature of things.

Just as, though a certain imperturbability is common to the ordinary man who has not achieved a tranquil mind and to the saint who has, there is a great difference; and just as, though there is something in common between a man blind from birth and one who can see, if both are lost in a difficult and precipitous region, there is a great difference; so there will be a great difference between the nihilists and the Mādhyamikas. Thus the teachers of earlier times. But enough of these arguments. We will continue our exposition.

The nature of the teaching of the Buddhas

You may object that, even though 'The true nature of things

neither arises nor perishes, as *nirvāṇa* does not', and that there can be no assertive use of speech (*vāc*) nor any discursive thought (*citta*) with respect to it, none the less this truth can certainly not be known if it is not didactically argued. In bringing this truth to those who need guidance there must necessarily be recourse at times to a graduated (*anupurvī*) teaching given in terms of everyday, unenlightened experience and so the truth will be expounded.

We reply. It should be realized that this graduated teaching of the illustrious Buddhas which penetrates to the way things are eternally is simply:

> 8 Everything in this world can be taken as real or not real;
> or both real and not real; or neither real nor not real.
> This is the Buddha's teaching.

370 To quote: 'Whatever is most familiar to one is most effective for him naturally. If one is bewildered how can one receive the truth? As it is not possible to make a foreigner understand by a language not his own, so the unenlightened person (*loka*) cannot be made to comprehend except by means of the everyday.'[1]

As the illustrious one said: 'The unenlightened person is at variance with me; I am not at variance with the unenlightened person. What is accepted by the unenlightened is accepted by me; what is not accepted by the unenlightened is not accepted by me.' Thus the scripture. The illustrious one always treated the elements of personal existence, the senses and their objects, and the types of consciousness as 'real' (*tathyam*). These are thought to be real when perceived by those who are to be guided – those suffering from the optical defect of primal ignorance – in whom has been aroused the desire to learn about the various natures of the things generally accepted as real. And this with an eye on the higher truth and with a view to arousing the faith of the ordinary man in himself.

'This holy man is aware of every last happening in the world,
371 he is omniscient and all-seeing; he possesses the knowledge of the inanimate world from the infinity of space to the coursing of the winds and he knows the uttermost limits of the world of beings; he knows incontrovertibly the many kinds of origin, existence and end, what is cause, what is effect, what is pleasurable, what is painful.'

So, after those who are to be guided have realized the

[1] Or, the World cannot be made to comprehend except in its own way.

omniscience of the illustrious one, at a later time it is explained that everything is not real (*na tathyam*) as naively taken. At this point what is real is what does not change. But all compounded things change in fact because they perish by the moment. Therefore, because of this fact of change, they are not real either. The word 'or' means 'and';[1] it is to be taken as joining the two views. That is: 'Everything in this world can be taken as real and as not real.'

For some it is explained that everything in the world is both real and not real at the same time. For the unenlightened everything in the world is real; for those who have started on the way everything is false because not perceived in its naive reality (*evam anupalambha*).

There are those however who, from long practice, see things the way they really are, who have eradicated the obstructions (*āvaraṇa*) virtually completely like the roots of a tree; for them it is explained that everything in the world is neither real nor not real. In order to remove what remains of the obstructions, both alternatives are rejected even as one rejects predicates like black and white for the son of a barren woman.

This is the teaching of the illustrious Buddhas. It leads men from byways and establishes them on the right way. In the interests of gradual instruction and of adapting to those who are to be led, the teaching is flexible.

372 All the teachings of the illustrious Buddhas, who are possessed of universal compassion, ultimate insight and practical wisdom, are intended to be a means of penetrating (*avatāra*) to the eternal way of things (*tattvāmṛta*). The perfectly realized ones have not uttered one word which was not in fact a means of penetrating to the eternal way of things. They administer medicine suited to the illness. They have the urge to succour those who need guidance and they teach the truth accordingly. To quote from the *Four Hundred Verses*: 'Things are real, things are not real, things are both real and not real: all this is said variously. Indeed all cures as such are cures for a specific desire.'

The true way of things

But, you ask, what is the nature of 'the way things really are' which the teachings of the revered ones are intended to penetrate to? This is explained in the verse 'When the object of

[1] Cf. *Kārikā* 8, p. 181.

thought is no more, there is nothing for language to refer to.'[1] When this obtains what further questions can there be? Though this is so, none the less the way things are really must be spoken of. This is done by speaking in a second sense (*samāropataḥ*). One accepts the everyday (*laukika*) terms 'real', 'not real' and so on which are drawn from the world of transactional discourse (*vyavahārasatya*).

Nāgārjuna expresses it this way.

> 9 Not dependent on anything other than itself, at peace, not manifested as named things, beyond thought construction, not of varying form – thus the way things are really is spoken of.[2]

373 'Not dependent on anything other than itself' (*aparapratyaya*) means that in the way things really are one is not dependent on anything; it is to be attained without mediation and not by the instruction of another. Those with an optical defect see hairs, gnats, bees and so on which do not exist. Even though instructed by those of sound vision they are incapable of realizing the true nature of the illusory hair as it is, that is, they are not capable of not seeing it even as those of sound vision do not see it. Rather they understand theoretically, from the instruction of those with sound vision, merely that such things are optical illusions. When, however, those suffering from the defect become people with the eye of wisdom, cured by the balm of unmediated seeing that such things are irrefragably without substance, then they realize directly and for themselves that it is the true nature of such things not to be seen at all. So much for the phrase 'Not dependent on anything other than itself.' The true nature of things (*svarūpa*) is the way things are truly (*tattvam*).

The true nature of 'at peace' (*śānta*) is to be entirely without self-existence like the illusory hairs not seen by those of sound vision.

And then the expression 'not manifested as named thing'.[3] 'Named thing' means that language gives rise to things with meanings. 'Not manifested as named thing' means inexpressible by verbal utterance.

374 'Beyond thought construction' (*nirvikalpa*). Thought construction is the innate activity of mind. To be free of that is the way things are beyond thought construction. As the *sūtra*

[1] P. 177, 7. [2] *tat tattvasya lakṣaṇam.*

[3] *prapañcair aprapañcita.* 'Inexpressible in verbal language' would be an alternate translation.

says: 'What is the higher truth? Where nothing is happening, not even knowledge, how could there be any utterance of words?' This is what 'beyond thought construction' means.

Something which is said to be 'of varying form' has different forms. This means that what is not of varying form (*anānārtha*) is invariable, does not have multiple, differing forms.

374.5 As is said in the *Satyadvayāvatāra Sūtra*: 'Mañjuśrī ex-
374.15 plained to Devaputra: In higher truth, all the putative elements of existence are of the same nature because in not being produced, in not being born in any sense at all, they are the same nature. Why is that? Because, in higher truth, all the elements
375 of existence become undifferentiated in *nirvāṇa* from not really arising in any sense at all. Even as, Devaputra, the space in a clay jar is the same as the space in a bejewelled jar, both being of the nature of space, in higher truth undifferentiated; similarly, Devaputra, afflicted existence, in higher truth, does not arise in any sense; nor does purification arise in any sense. The birth-death cycle itself is, in higher truth, one with non-arising. Even *nirvāṇa* is in higher truth absolutely the same as non-arising; in it in higher truth, there is no differentiable factor. Why is that? Because, in higher truth, all elements of existence are absolutely undifferentiable.'

In this sense is invariableness to be understood as a characterization of the way things really are. It is because the absence of a self-existent nature is essentially one in all things. Further such exposition can be had from the same source. So much for the way those wise ones, who have vanquished the cycle of birth, old age and death, speak of the way things really are.

The truth in the world of cause and effect

Concerning the characterization of the way things are in the world of everyday Nāgārjuna says:

> 10 What comes into existence dependent on something else cannot be that very thing; nor can it be wholly other either; therefore things neither perish completely nor are they everlasting.

376 Anything dependent on a cause comes to be as an effect. A rice sprout, for example, comes into existence in dependence on a rice seed and a complex of conditions like the soil, etc. But it cannot be said that the sprout is precisely the same thing as the seed, nor that the seed is precisely the same thing

as the sprout because of the absurd consequence that what is born and what gives birth would be one and the same: that father and son would be identical. If there is no difference one would take the seed to exist in the sprout phase, i.e. as sprout, and one would take the sprout as the seed. The seed would thus be eternal because imperishable. Because this entails the doctrine of eternalism it would result in a mass of grievous faults; it would follow that action and its consequences were not real. Therefore, it does not make sense to say that the seed is identical with the sprout. Nor is the one entirely other than the other; the sprout cannot be entirely other than the seed or it would follow that the sprout could sprout even apart from the seed. As Nāgārjuna says: 'If what is "other" is entirely other than "the other" it would be other without anything other.'[1] It would follow if the seed persists in the sprout that the seed would be imperishable. This would entail the logical fault of holding that the effect pre-exists in the cause. And so, to say 'Anything dependent on a cuase comes to be as an effect' does not mean 'the cause becomes the effect'. Nor again is the effect wholly other than the cause. Therefore, it is possible to conclude 'the cause is neither perishable nor eternal'.

As Āryadeva says:[2] 'From the fact that things function they are not nothing; from the fact that things cease function-
377 ing they are not eternal.' It is said in the *Lalitavistara*: 'If there is a seed there is a sprout, though the seed is not the sprout, nor is it wholly other. This is why the nature of things is neither perishable nor eternal.'

Immortality of the Buddhist teaching

So, in accordance with the account given:

> 11 Not of one form nor of various forms, not perishable nor eternal: such is the immortal teaching of the Buddhas, the lords of the world.

378.3 As the *Catuḥśataka* says, 'Even if one who has comprehended the real nature of things does not attain *nirvāṇa* in this life, he will achieve it necessarily, without further effort, in a future life as the just fruit of his acts.'[3]

More precisely:

> 12ab If the fully enlightened are no longer born, and the disciples have vanished;

[1] From a chapter not included in this translation.
[2] *Catuḥśataka*, X, 25. [3] VIII, 22.

there would be no realization of the eternal way of the Buddhist truth because of the lack of a beneficent friend to demonstrate the true and exalted path. None the less, from the force of hearing the truth of things in a previous life, in this world and without ordinary instruction, depending solely on recourse to complete solitude, the self-validating

> 12cd Insight of those who attain *nirvāṇa* for themselves is realized without help from others.

'Without help from others' means solitude in body and mind or not seeking out a beneficent friend. So it is that because ultimate insight is solitary, those seeking enlightenment for themselves even in an unenlightened age, can attain to the way of the Buddhist truth. This proves the effectiveness
379 of the cure – the eternal way of the truth of truths (*saddharmatvāmṛta*) – as administered by the great masters of healing, the fully enlightened ones.

This being so it is possible for the man of wisdom to turn his back on the everyday world and to go in search of the way of the truth of truths.

XV

Time

382 Some hold that the self-existence of things is a fact because it is the basis for our conceiving of time as three-phased (*kālatraya*). In this way of thinking the three time phases, as explained by the illustrious one, are (a) what is past (*atīta*); (b) what is not yet realized (*anāgata*);[1] (c) what is arising here and now (*pratyutpanna*);[2] and these have their basis in things. That is, a self-existent thing which has arisen and perished is said to be past; what has arisen but has not perished is existent; something which has not yet attained self-existence is said to be not yet realized, i.e. future. The three phases of time are explained in this way as dependent on the self-existence of things and are held to be real. It follows that what they are dependent on – the self-existence of things – is also real.

Past, present and future interdependent and so unreal

We reply that there would be self-existence of things, by reason of which we can conceive of the three phases of time, if these as conceived by you were themselves real. But they are not. How they are not real Nāgārjuna expounds in this way:

> 1 If what is arising here and now and what is not yet realized are dependent on what is past, what is arising here and now and what is not yet realized will be in past time.[3]

The thinking here is that if there were the existent (*vartamāna*) and the not yet realized they would be either dependent (*apekṣya*) on past time or they would not be (*anapekṣya*). In the first case, if their dependence on the past is established, they will necessarily be in past time. However, there can be no dependence of something on that which is non-existent. This

[1] The future. [2] The present.

[3] Paraphrase: If present and future are dependent on the past, present and future will be in the past.

would be like progeny issuing from a barren woman, or a flower from a garland in the sky, or sesame oil from a grain of sand. It will not do to argue that the dependence is reciprocal even as light depends on darkness – which is non-existent – and darkness depends on light, because this is a vitiated circle (*sādhyasamatva*). In this case if the existent and the not yet realized are considered to be in past time for the purpose of establishing their dependence in this way, these two would be
383 past as well because they exist in a real past time and are of the essence of the past. It follows that there would be no past either. Hence, as the past is what has passed beyond the existing state, the not yet realized cannot be realized. So long, however, as both the existent and the not yet realized are entirely impossible how could there be a past of anything whatsoever? It follows that there is no past either.

Now, wishing to avoid this faulty consequence:

> 2 If, on the other hand, arising here and now and being not yet realized are not based in the past how could arising here and now and being not yet realized be related to the past?

If it is imagined that the time phases of the existing and the not yet realized are not based in past time, then in this case as well, they cannot be related to the past because like the lotus blossom in the sky they do not exist in the past.

It may be further urged that for the proponents of time, time exists as fact (*vidyata eva*); what is the importance of dependence on the past? We reply, even here

> 3 The reality of these two cannot be established independently of the past; the time phases arising here and now and being not yet realized are, therefore, not real.

Because they are unrelated to the past, what is arising here and now and the not yet realized, like the horns of a donkey, are without reality (*asattva*). This is the way it is with what is arising here and now and the not yet realized. It should be understood that it follows that time is not real (*na vidyate*).

In so far as, in the way shown, what is arising here and now and the not yet realized cannot be proved either in relation to the past or without relation to it, in the same way the dependence or non-dependence of what is past and what is not yet realized on what is arising here and now cannot be shown, and the dependence or non-dependence of what is arising here and
384 now and what is past on what is not yet realized cannot be

shown. In precisely this sense, by the same proof used in the case of the dependence or non-dependence of what is arising here and now and what is not yet realized on what is past, Nāgārjuna points out exactly the same vitiating fault:

> 4 Precisely the same procedure applies to the remaining two divisions of time. It could be applied to such distinctions as high, low and middle as well as to unity, duality, and so on.

It could be done this way: If what is past and what is not yet realized are dependent on what is arising here and now, the times of past and the future will be based in what is arising here and now. If, on the other hand, past and future time are not based in what is arising here and now, how would past and future times be dependent on it? Again, these two cannot be established (*siddhi*) independently of what is arising here and now, hence what is called past and future time are not real. This much for the one division of time.

And for the second division of time: If what is past and what exists are dependent on what has not yet arisen, what is past and what exists will be based in the time of what has not yet arisen. If on the other hand what is past and what exists are not based in what has not yet arisen how could what is past and what exists be dependent on it? Again if these two are not dependent on what has not yet arisen they cannot be established. It follows that past time and present time are not real.

385 These were supplementary verses. The two divisions of time are to be understood in this way.

It follows, after this kind of investigation, that the three phases of time do not exist (*nāsti*). Time therefore, is not real (*na vidyate*); and because time is non-existent there is no true existence of things either. This is now established. And as the three phases of time have been investigated, in the same way 'It could be applied to high, low, middle and such distinctions, as well as to unity and so on.'

To be understood by the expression 'and such distinctions' in the line beginning 'high, low, middle' are all such triadic conceptualizations as good, not good, indefinable; arisal, existence, decay; beginning, end, middle; the realms of desire, of form, of the formless; correct, incorrect, neither correct nor incorrect. By the expression 'unity, duality and so on' should be understood unity, duality and plurality. It should be realized that by the exposition of the three phases of time, high, low and so on, as well as unity, plurality and so on have been expressly dealt with.

Time incomprehensible either as lived or as unchanging

One may object that time is real because it is measurable (*parimāṇavattva*). The thought here is that what *is* not, cannot in fact be measurable as the horns of a donkey cannot be, whereas time *is* measurable: in virtue of the distinctions of moment, minute, hour, night, day and night, fortnight, month, year and so on. It follows that because it is measurable time is real.

We reply that if there were something called time it would be measurable. But there is not.

> 5 Time cannot be comprehended as variable; there is no unchanging time which can be comprehended; how speak sensibly about a time which is incomprehensible?

386 The reasoning here is that if what we call time were invariable (*avasthita*), quite different from periods of time such as moments, minutes and so on, it could be understood as being measurable into such periods. But there is no such thing as invariable, unchanging time which could be understood in terms of periods such as moments and minutes. Hence variable (*asthita*) time cannot be understood; that is to say, it cannot be understood *in* its variableness.

It might be urged that what is called time is in its invariable essence imperishable but manifests (*abhivyajyate*) itself in time periods such as moments. It is said: 'Time transmutes the elements; time sustains being; time cares for the sleeping; time is insurmountable.' So in this sense the distinguishing characteristic of time is the essence of invariableness itself.

We reply that in this sense as well there is no invariable time which could be conceived of as manifesting itself in time periods such as moments and minutes. If you ask again why this means that time cannot be invariable, it is because time cannot be conceived of as something distinct from periods of time such as moments and minutes.

Furthermore, time will exist as either compounded or uncompounded by nature. Both alternatives are repudiated in the Chapter 'The Compounded'[1] in the *kārikā* 'If origination, existence and perishing are not established there can be no

[1] Not included in this translation.

compounded. If the compounded is not established how will the uncompounded be grounded?' So, in this way, there is no invariable time which could be comprehended.

Now to consider the time which cannot be comprehended
387 because it is its essential nature to be spoken of in terms of variableness; it is inconceivable how it can be spoken of sensibly in terms of time periods such as moments. As Nāgārjuna puts it, 'How speak sensibly about a time which is incomprehensible?' It follows that time simply is not.

Time is not merely an aspect of things

One might counter, saying that it is true that there is nothing called time which is imperishable, which is unrelated to objects and the other factors of personal existence and which has an essence of its own. None the less there is a time which in a practical way is conceived of (*prajñapta*) as resting on (*upādāya*) the factors of personal existence and on compound things and is spoken of in terms of time periods such as moments. So there is no fault in this.

We reply: Again,

> 6ab If time is dependent on things how can time be separate from things?

If, that is, one defines time as 'dependent on things' then in so far as things are not real, time, being based on them, is necessarily not real either. Nāgārjuna explains:

> 6c But no thing whatsoever is real.

This follows both from the arguments given earlier and from the refutations yet to be given. So long as, thus, it is the case that no thing whatsoever is real, then

> 6d How can there be time?

And because there is no time, there are no divisions of time such as moments, seconds and hours which are measurements of it. How therefore can time be grounded in its being measurable? From this it follows that things are definitely not self-existent.

XVI

The Perfectly Realized One

431 Some argue that the individual birth-death cycle (*bhavasaṁtati*) is fact because the perfectly realized one (*tathāgata*) is incontestable fact.

According to this view the illustrious one, endowed with great compassion and the twin achievements of perfect awareness (*prajñā*) and practical wisdom (*upāya*), single-mindedly devoted to ending the misery of existence for all creatures in the three worlds, attained the estate of omniscience, capable of discernment in every form. Throughout perhaps three or perhaps countless aeons, progressing uninterruptedly step by step through undertaking various unsurpassable and exceedingly splendid meritorious deeds out of love for the entire creation, a love surpassing even that for an only son, and obedient to his great compassion for the weal of the entire creation, and becoming in ways appropriate to the need of each, a healing tree for all living creatures in the great universe being like the universal elements earth, air, fire and water, he attained omniscience.

432 The one who thus attains this omniscience is the illustrious one. He is held to be the truth (*tattvam*) of all things (*dharmā-nām*) precisely because he is perfectly realized, because he is perfectly enlightened: the perfectly realized one. So, if there were no individual birth-death cycle there would be no perfectly realized one either. As it is not possible to attain perfect realization in one life, the individual birth-death cycle must be fact because the perfectly realized one is incontestable fact.

In reply we say that it is great ignorance which leads to this notion of an uninterrupted series of births throughout a great period of time. The darkness of a great mass of ignorance may be dispersed by many and various flashes of insight, like the autumn moon; however, if it increases in complexity because of dispositions acquired over a very long time, it is not to be dispersed nor rendered null.

If there were any such thing as a self-existent (*svabhāvataḥ*) perfectly realized one there would be a series of manifestations of such a one in different births throughout a great period of time. But no such thing as a self-existent perfectly realized one is ever directly experienced (*upalabhyate*). But if one's vision is afflicted by a great defect, one is in primal ignorance, and, like two moons and optically illusory hair and gnats, direct experience of the perfectly realized one as self-existent is illusory.

Why it is that the perfectly realized one is not self-existent, Nāgārjuna explains in this way:

> 1 The perfectly realized one is not identical with the factors of personal existence, nor other than them; he is not in them, nor they in him; and the perfectly realized one is not the possessor of the factors of personal existence. What then is the perfectly realized one?

If there were an entity called a perfectly realized one, pure and beyond all named things, then either he would be self-existent *as* the factors of personal existence, i.e., he would be self-existent *as* the five factors: body, feelings, ideation, dispositions and consciousness; or perhaps *as* the five states: morality,
433 meditation, wisdom, freedom and the intuition and knowledge of freedom. The other case is that he would be separate (*vyatirikta*) from them. The five factors of personal existence are adopted in this investigation because they are the reason for assuming individual beings. The five states are not universal and are included in the former.

On the other hand, the perfectly realized one might be entirely separate from the five factors of personal existence. In this case either the perfectly realized one would be based in the factors of personal existence; or the factors of personal existence would be based in the perfectly realized one; or the perfectly realized one would possess the factors of personal existence as Devadatta possesses wealth. On being thought through however, none of these ways is possible.

Why? To begin with, the perfectly realized one is not identical with the factors of personal existence. For what reason?

Because, as was argued: 'If fire is fuel that would be identity of agent and act.'[1] This verse is also relevant: 'If Buddha were identical with the factors of personal existence,[2] that would be identity of agent and act.'

Likewise, it is said: 'If the self were identical with the

[1] P. 132, 1. [2] *upādāna*: 'what is appropriated'.

factors of personal existence, it would itself arise and perish.'[1] And this is relevant here: 'If Buddha were identical with the factors of personal existence, he would be subject to arising and perishing.' Thus, in the first place, the perfectly realized one is not the factors of personal existence.

Nor is the perfectly realized one other than the factors of
434 personal existence. Why? Because, as was argued: 'If fire is wholly other than fuel then it could exist even without fuel.'[2] Again: 'Because it is unrelated to anything else, it is not caused by bursting into flame; as it burns forever it follows that it is pointless to kindle it again.'[3] The following is relevant here too: 'If Buddha were other than the factors of personal existence he would exist apart from them.' Again: 'Not being dependent on anything else, the Buddha would not be influenced by the factors of personal existence. Moreover every spiritual act being thus futile, the Buddha would be ineffectual.' Again: 'If he were other than the factors of personal existence he could not be characterized in their terms.'

Because the perfectly realized one is not other than the factors of personal existence he cannot logically exist in the factors of personal existence nor they in him.

In the *Madhyamakāvatāra* these two theses are expounded in this way:[4] 'The self does not exist *in* the factors of personal existence nor are these *in* the self. If these two were other than each other this conception would be plausible; but as they are not other it is an empty hypothesis.'

And how it is that the perfectly realized one cannot possess the factors of personal existence is argued in the same place: 'The self is not to be thought of as possessing a body because the self does not exist; the idea of possession cannot therefore
435 obtain. In the case of the possessor of cattle there is a difference but in the case of what has a body there can be no distinction between possessor and possessed; the dichotomy of identity and otherness does not obtain in this case as the self has no bodily form.'

It should be understood that all five theses[5] are really included in the thesis concerning identity and otherness. Nāgārjuna deals with all five theses because the problem of the perfectly realized one is cognate with that of the permanent personal self. In what other base can the perfectly realized one exist who, on thorough investigation, is not based in the factors of personal existence? A perfectly realized one is logically and

[1] P. 166, 1. [2] P. 132, 1. [3] P. 133, 3.
[4] VI, 142, 143. [5] Cf. p. 192, 1.

factually impossible[1] in every respect. Not discovering him as self-existent the venerable teacher, Nāgārjuna, said, 'What then *is* a perfectly realized one?' He means that there is nothing ontic (*vastu*) in all the three worlds which can be truly discerned as self-existent.

Because the perfectly realized one is ontically non-existent, it is established that the birth–death cycle as a round of real entities does not exist.

At this point some will interject: We do not say that the perfectly realized one is identical with the factors of personal existence because of the faulty consequence pointed out; nor that he is entirely separate from them. Nor do we say that the purified factors of personal existence are in the perfectly realized one as a group of trees is on a snowy mountain, nor that he is in the factors of personal existence as a lion is in a clump of trees; nor do we say that he possesses the factors of
436 personal existence as the universal monarch possesses his qualities, because we do not agree that he must be either identical with or different from them. But we definitely affirm that the perfectly realized one is based on (*upādāya*) purified factors of personal existence and is indefinable in respect to identity and difference.[2] Therefore your logic does not dispose of our point of view. To this it is rejoined:

> 2 If the Buddha is based in the factors of personal existence he is not self-existent; and how can anything exist in dependence on another if it does not exist in itself?

If the Buddha is understood as based in purified factors of personal existence though it is impossible to say if he is identical with or other than them, then it is obvious that he is not self-existent because he is understood as dependent, like a reflection. How can one who is not self-existent in the sense that he does not have a substance (*svarūpa*) of his own (*ātmīya*) – one who, in fact, is not self-existent – have his existence in dependence on the factors of personal existence? It does not make sense that a factually non-existent son of a barren woman could exist in dependence on the existence of another.

Let it be so, you may interject. In that case he will be like a reflection, which, though it does not exist as a reality in itself, does exist in dependence on other factors such as the face, the

[1] *na saṁbhavati.* Though the words 'logically' and 'factually' are not separate words in the Sanskrit, the verb *saṁbhavati* implies both.

[2] This refers to the concept of the *dharmakāya*: Buddha as the embodiment of truth.

mirror and so on. And so the perfectly realized one too, though not in fact self-existent, will have being in dependence on other factors through being based in the five purified factors of personal existence.

However:

437 3 One who is dependent on another's being, is, it follows, without a self; and how can one who is without a self become a perfectly realized one?

If the perfectly realized one is thought of as dependent on other factors, as is a reflection, then in so far as he is like a reflection, it follows that he is without a self; it would not make sense that he would have a being of his own. The term self is a synonym for the term self-existent. How can one who is without self, without a being of his own, exactly as is a reflection, be a self-existing, concrete, perfectly realized one? The thought is that he cannot be one who has followed the veritable way.[1]

Furthermore, if there were any self-existence of the perfectly realized one, then, with regard to that self-existence, the self-existence of the factors of personal existence would constitute other being and the perfectly realized one would be dependent on it; as however, there is no self-existence in the perfectly realized one how could there be otherness in the factors of personal existence?

Nāgārjuna expounded this when he said

4ab If there is no self-existence how can there be other-existence?

As thus there is neither self-existence nor other-existence[2] so:

4cd What perfectly realized one can there be apart from self-existence and other-existence?

Any existing thing is either self-existent or other-existent. The conclusion is that apart from these two possibilities what other thing could a perfectly realized one be? Therefore the perfectly realized one is not self-existent.

438 Furthermore:

5 If a perfectly realized one existed without being based in the factors of personal existence, at some point he would appropriate them[3] and thus be based in them.

[1] *aviparītamārgagata*; a play on the term *tathāgata*.
[2] I.e. existence as other; or existence-through-another.
[3] *upādayāt*: enter into a concrete personal existence.

If you think a perfectly realized one, because it cannot be said whether he is identical with or other than the factors of personal existence, is to be understood as not based in them, that could hardly make sense. If there were a perfectly realized one who was not based in the factors of personal existence, not having taken possession of them, he would at some point have to make them his own (*upādayāt*). As Devadatta, in a prior state is wholly separate from his wealth, he must at some point take possession of it; so if a perfectly realized one were not based in the factors of personal existence he would at some point have to take possession of them as his own. Therefore he could be said to be based in the factors of personal existence. From this investigation it follows

6ab There is no perfectly realized one not based in the factors of personal existence;

because that would mean he was beyond causation.

6cd How can one who, not being based in the factors of personal existence, does not exist, take possession of them?

Because he would be factually non-existent, is meant. Thus, as there is nothing which enters into possession it does not make sense that a perfectly realized one could take possession of, or be based in, the factors of personal existence.[1]

As, thus, a perfectly realized one prior to the factors of personal existence cannot enter into possession of anything, because he does not factually exist, so it is not possible that there can be possession of factors of personal existence which have not been taken possession of by any one at all.

Nāgārjuna explains this:

439 7ab There can be no factors of personal existence whatever which have not been taken possession of;

as factors of personal existence which have not been appropriated by anyone are not factors of personal existence. So, if nothing is appropriated there is no one who appropriates.

[1] That is, they cannot be what they are supposed to be. The play on words here defies translation. The word for the factors of personal existence – *upādānam* – means 'that which is appropriated'. Hence the inconceivability of the factors of personal existence without one who appropriates them. The argument is more self-evident in Sanskrit than it is in English.

7cd In no way can there be a perfectly realized one who is without appropriated factors of personal existence.

So, according to the logic developed:

8 How can someone who, after the fivefold enquiry, is neither identical with factors of personal existence nor other than them, be comprehended as a perfectly realized one in terms of the factors of personal existence?

The perfectly realized one, on being critically thought about, exists neither in virtue of identity, that is, oneness with the factors of personal existence, nor in virtue of otherness, that is, separateness from them. How can one who, after the enquiry into the five theories – identity, otherness, non-existence, base and quality – does not exist, be capable of being taken as a perfectly realized one, one who is completely non-existent in fact? Therefore the perfectly realized one is not self-existent.

It is not only a perfectly realized one who according to this line of thought does not exist.

9ab The factors of personal existence[1] as well are not self-existent.

440 What is appropriated – the fivefold factors of personal existence: body, feelings, ideation, disposition and consciousness – does not exist as real in itself, because it arises in dependence and because of the detailed refutation given in the Chapter on the factors of personal existence.[2] Again it might be thought that the factors of personal existence, though not self-existent, exist in dependence on something else, because this is the nature of causal dependence. Nāgārjuna explains that that is not logically possible.

9cd How can something which does not exist in itself, exist in virtue of something else?

How can the son of a barren woman, totally non-existent in itself, be made sense out of (*prajñapayitum*) in virtue of being dependent on something else? Therefore the factors of personal existence do not exist. Or, as it is put: 'The factors of personal existence as well are not self-existent.'

As there are no appropriated factors of personal existence unrelated to someone appropriating them because they are

[1] I.e. what is appropriated (*upādānam*). [2] Chapter VI.

inherently dependent on an appropriator, the self-existence of the factors of personal existence has not been established. But, if you say: It is not possible to establish the self-existence of the factors of personal existence unrelated to an appropriator, so let them exist in dependence on him, the reply is, 'How can something which does not exist in itself, exist in virtue of something else?' How can appropriated factors of personal existence which are not self-existent, that is, which are not real, exist in dependence on someone who appropriates them? It follows that the factors of personal existence do not exist.

And now, to show what has been demonstrated, Nāgārjuna says

> 10ab Thus, in every respect, both the appropriated factors of personal existence and the one appropriating them are devoid of being.

The factors of personal existence, having been investigated from every angle, are devoid of being. That is, they do not have their being in themselves; and the appropriator is devoid of being, that is, he is without self existence.

441 10cd How can a perfectly realized one, himself devoid of being, be comprehended in terms of what is itself devoid?

In terms of the factors of personal existence, that is. It is in no way possible that a non-existing perfectly realized one could be made sense of by means of what itself is non-existent. Therefore it is not logically possible to make sense of (*prajñapyate*) the perfectly realized one as based in the factors of personal existence.

At this point some would object. Our aspirations are destroyed by you. We have had to give up the pleasures we had in refuting the heresies of the Vaiśesikas, Akṣapāda, the Jains, Jaimini, the Naiyāyikas and the others, who are as if firmly entangled in the vines of the harmful, vain conjectures of their own imaginations, who are denied walking the veritable path which leads to the city of *nirvāṇa*, who have not penetrated the forests and jungles and dangers of this world and who misunderstand the teaching about the veritable path which leads to heaven and final beatitude.

Aspiring to freedom and to supreme and perfect enlightenment for the sake of dispersing the darkness of ignorance, we have taken refuge in the illumination of the perfectly realized

one who destroys the darkness spread by the heretical views, who points out the veritable path leading to heaven and final beatitude, who has filled all the worlds with effulgent rays and his teaching of the Truth, who has devoted himself to arousing the petals of the lotus – the spirits of the different peoples to be freed – who is the sole and pure eye for those capable of understanding the truth of the nature of reality, who is the sole refuge of all men, whose halo is formed of the Buddha's
442 own true properties – the ten powers, the four assurances and so on – who is the best guide and leader of the Mahāyāna, who is endowed with swiftness of mind and foot – the seven-membered enlightenment – who dries up for men of all the three worlds the rivers in the forest of the cycle of birth, old age and death, who conquers his foes – the four incomparable Māras – with arrows and who confounds the evil demons, Rāhu, Vigraha and Udgraha in all the three worlds. You have destroyed our hope for freedom and our aspiration to supreme, perfect enlightenment by declaring, 'Thus, in every respect, both the appropriated factors of personal existence and the one appropriating them are devoid of being. How can a perfectly realized one, himself devoid of being, be comprehended in terms of what is itself devoid?'

So by your proclaiming that nothing has its being in itself you destroy our hope for freedom and our aspiration for the attainment of the unsurpassable perfect enlightenment. You have succeeded in obscuring the great, luminous orb of the perfectly realized one by improperly generating a succession of clouds not unlike the ignorance of the world.

Our reply is that we have destroyed the hope only of people who, like you, have been unable to bear the supremely profound lion's roar of the truth that there is no self, a truth absent from all heretical systems. You have, indeed, desiring freedom, abandoned the systems of the heretics and have followed the way of the supreme and incontrovertible Teacher, the perfectly realized one; but, because of the weakness of
443 your aspiration you err about like antelopes on the evil paths of this forest, of this jungle, of this prison – this ineluctable cycle of birth and death – paths full of the pitfalls of faulty views which those astray follow. The perfectly realized ones never teach the reality of the factors of personal existence or of the self.

As it is said in the *Bhagavatī*, 'Buddha himself, venerable Subhūti, is like *māyā* or a dream; and the essential qualities of Buddha are like *māyā* and a dream.' Again, 'The Truth, properly understood, is devoid of an existence of its own; enlightenment, properly understood, is devoid of an existence of its own; and one who would enter the way is also devoid of self-existence. So think the wise though not the foolish.'

But we are not urging that the perfectly realized ones who are beyond all named things do not exist in any sense at all; to deny that they do would be an error on our part. A wise and saintly one, explaining that the perfectly realized one is without self-existence, and desiring to speak the unerring truth (*aviparītārtha*), might say

444 11abc The terms 'devoid', 'non-devoid', 'both' and 'neither' should not be asserted as predicates;

we should not assert these terms as predicates in any of the four modes (*sarvam etan na vaktavyam*).

One cannot, however, enter into a comprehension of the true nature of a perfectly realized one as it really is without using words (*anukte*). That is why we employ the term 'devoid of being' in a special and secondary sense (*āropataḥ*). We base ourselves wholly in the transactional reality of the everyday (*vyavahārasatya*) in an everyday transactional way as it suits those who are to be guided. We employ as well, the terms 'non-devoid', 'both-devoid-and-non-devoid' and 'neither-devoid-nor-non-devoid'.

So Nāgārjuna says:

11d But such terms are used to teach the truth.[1]

To quote the words of the illustrious one: 'All elements of existence are devoid because without self-being, all elements of existence are uncaused being based in causelessness; all elements of existence are unattainable being unthinkable; all elements of existence are translucent by nature because of the utter purity of the surpassing awareness.'

Elsewhere non-devoidness has been taught: 'If, o monks, a past body does not exist in the future, the noble learned disciple will not acknowledge his past body. But as the past body exists, the noble learned disciple acknowledges his past body. If, o monks, a future body' and so on, up to, 'If, o monks, past consciousness is not real in the future' and so on as before.

In the thought of the Sautrāntikas the past and the future are devoid of being but everything else is non-devoid; non-

[1] *Prajñaptyartham*. *Kārikā* 11 and its commentary are seminal for Mādhyamika thought.

445 veridical mental acts are devoid. In the Vijñanavāda school mental constructs are devoid of self-existence because they do not arise causally; they are like such things as the two moons seen by the ophthalmic.

'Therefore all things are not to be taken either as devoid of being or as non-devoid; individuals are neither real beings nor unreal beings; this is the middle way.' One wishing to know for what purpose devoidness and the other concepts are taught may be enlightened by the Enquiry into the Self.[1]

To quote the *sūtra*, 'This world is like magician's work, you say, illustrious one, like the pretence of an actor or a vision in a dream. There is no self, no real person, no birth. The elements of existence are like a mirage, like a moon reflected; this world is devoid of being, at peace, unborn and without ground.

'By your compassion you will save by many means, in many ways, and by many teachings. You contemplate this world in perpetual turmoil from countless passions and ills; you move on earth as the incomparable healer. Oh Sugata,[2]
446 bring deliverance to the countless creatures. The entire world revolves like the wheel of a chariot; you reveal the supreme way to those fallen among animals, wickedness and hell fires, who are ignorant and without teacher or guide.'

But none of these terms holds good for the perfectly realized one who is not of the nature of a named thing. And it is not only the four assertions concerning devoidness which do not hold good for the perfectly realized one, but:

> 12 How could the four assertions concerning the eternal and the non-eternal be made of what is at peace?[3] How could the four assertions concerning the finite and the infinite be made of what is at peace?

The fourteen questions on which no stand may be taken (*avyākṛtavastūni*) are given by the revered one in the following way. Existence (*loka*)[4] is eternal;[5] existence is non-eternal; existence is both eternal and non-eternal; existence is neither eternal nor non-eternal. Thus the first tetralemna. Existence has an end;[6] existence is without end; existence both has and has not an end; existence neither has nor has not an end. Thus the second tetralemna. The perfectly realized one exists after

[1] Chapter XIV. [2] Buddha.
[3] *Sānta*, what is not subject to determination in time and space.
[4] 'World', but understood as personal world, or existence. This is not so much a cosmological problem, as an existential one.
[5] Without beginning. [6] In time.

his decease; the perfectly realized one does not exist after his decease; the perfectly realized one both exists and does not exist after his decease; the perfectly realized one neither exists nor does not exist after his decease. Thus the third tetralemna. The living person (*jīva*) is identical with the body; the living person is one thing and the body another.[1]

These fourteen topics are called the fourteen unresolved questions because they are by nature unresolvable. According to the argument already given, none of the four assertions concerning devoidness has any relevance[2] for the perfectly realized one who is without ontic existence and who is by nature at peace. Similarly the four assertions concerning the eternal and the non-eternal have no relevance; because they are
447 without relevance, as the predicates 'light' and 'dark' are without relevance for the son of a barren woman, the illustrious one did not resolve, did not take a stand (*na vyākṛta*) on the four questions concerning existence. In the same way the four assertions are without relevance for the perfectly realized one. Thus the four assertions concerning an end or no end to existence are not relevant to the perfectly realized one, who is at peace (*śānta*).[3]

And now Nāgārjuna proclaims the effective irrelevance of the four possibilities 'the perfectly realized one exists after death' and so on.

> 13 One who holds the crude notion that the perfectly
> realized one 'exists', must speculate, 'he does not exist'
> after his enlightenment.

One who holds to the very crude notion – an illusory conjecture – 'the perfectly realized one exists' must imagine that the perfectly realized one does not persist in final enlightenment after his death; that is, the perfectly realized one, being destroyed, does not persist in the time following his death, as he has ceased to exist in any sense. One so speculating would be forming a false view.

However, one for whom the perfectly realized one neither exists nor does not exist in any definite state (*avasthā*), because he is devoid of self-existence will think:

> 14 As he is by nature devoid it is not intelligible to say,
> 'After his death the Buddha exists or does not exist.'

[1] There is no formal reason why the fourth tetralemna is incomplete, but, traditionally, it is.

[2] *na saṁbhavati*: logically and really impossible.

[3] Cf. note 3, p. 202.

Nāgārjuna means that this is an illusory attribution (*kalpanā*)
448 like the illusory attribution of colours to the sky. As the perfectly realized one is beyond all named things, is without self-existence and is by nature at peace, it is thinking of but feeble insight which speculates 'he is eternal', 'he is not eternal', etc., 'he is imperishable', 'he is perishable', 'he exists', 'he does not exist', 'he is devoid', 'he is not devoid', 'he is omniscient', 'he is not omniscient', and so on.

> 15 Those who assert names of the Buddha – who is beyond named things and is unchanging – are all victims of their own naming and do not see the perfectly realized one.

Because names (*prapañca*) are bound to objects and the perfectly realized one is not an object, how could naming be efficacious? Therefore the perfectly realized one surpasses names. And, as he is by nature not causally produced and does not alter his nature, he is unchanging.

As this is the character of the perfectly realized one, those who discourse speculatively about the illustrious Buddha by means of various fancied non-existent distinctions stemming from the conceit of tainted and impure imagination and from self-induced error, such victims of their own discourse are turned away from and completely lose sight of the true characteristics of the perfectly realized one. So, like dead creatures, those of this school do not see the perfectly realized one as those blind from birth do not see the sun.

This is why the illustrious one said: 'Those who saw me in the body and who hung on my voice, such people, committed to erroneous notions, do not see me. Buddhas are to be seen as the truth of things; for they are of the substance of truth (*dharmakāya*); but the truth is not to be sought intellectually for it is incapable of being known intellectually.'

Here, in this enquiry into the perfectly realized one, the entire world of living creatures – gods, demons and men – has been investigated; and even as it is without a being of its own, so the inanimate world – from the wind and the sun to the great palace of Akaniṣta – is also without being of its own.

Nāgārjuna expounded this saying:

> 16ab The self-existence of a perfectly realized one is the self-existence of this very cosmos.

449 'Cosmos' means the universe without living beings. In what

sense the perfectly realized one is self-existent Nāgārjuna explains:

> 16cd The perfectly realized one is without a self-existent nature; the cosmos too is without a self-existent nature.

In what way the cosmos is without a nature of its own has been dealt with in the enquiry into causality and other chapters.

This is why it can be said in the *sūtra*: 'The perfectly realized one is ever independent of the elements of existence; all elements of existence are akin to the perfectly realized one; those of puerile intellect are subject to the notion of cause, and err about in the world among putative elements of existence, which are unreal. The perfectly realized one is of the nature of a reflection; he is of pure elements which cause no harm; here there is no perfection and no perfectly realized one; he is beheld in all the worlds as a reflection.'

To quote the illustrious *Prajñāpāramitā*: 'The sons of the gods said to venerable, revered Subhūti, "O noble Subhūti, are all beings not like magic (*māyopama*), are they not magic?" On this being said the venerable Subhūti said to the son of the gods, "All beings are like magic, all beings are like a dream (*svapnopama*); magic and beings are not two things, they are not by nature different; because dreams and beings are not two things; they are not by nature different. All the elements of existence, o sons of the gods, are like magic, like a dream. The one on his way to *nirvāṇa* is like magic and a dream. The spiritual achievement of one on the way to *nirvāṇa* is like a magic and a dream. And so too one to be born only once more
450 and his spiritual achievement are like magic and a dream; so too one who is not to be born again and his spiritual achievement; the realized saint as well is like magic and a dream; the spiritual achievement of sainthood is like magic and a dream; the perfectly enlightened individual is like magic and a dream; perfect individual enlightenment itself is like magic and a dream. Even the ultimate Buddha is like magic and a dream as is ultimate Buddhahood like magic and a dream. Thus I say." '

Thereupon the sons of the gods said to venerable Subhūti, 'You say, o noble Subhūti, that the perfectly enlightened individual is like magic and a dream and that even perfect enlightenment itself is like magic and a dream.' Subhūti replied, 'Even *nirvāṇa* is like magic and a dream; how much more other truths.'

The sons of the gods said, 'You say, o noble Subhūti, that even *nirvāṇa* is like magic and a dream.' Subhūti replied, 'Whatever other truth there might be even more excellent than *nirvāṇa* that also I would say was like magic and a dream, because *nirvāṇa* and magic are not two things, they are not by nature different.'

XVII

The Basic Afflictions and the Four Misbeliefs

Relation of affliction and misbelief

451 Some argue that the round of birth and death (*bhavasaṁtati*)[1] exists in fact because its cause exists in fact. They argue, that is, that action (*karma*) proceeds from the basic afflictions, and that the unbroken succession of birth and death follows as the effect of action which arises from the basic afflictions. This unbroken succession of birth and death is what is meant by the round of birth and death. The basic afflictions are the factual, material cause (*pradhānaṁ kāraṇam*) of this because the round of birth and death ceases when they have been eradicated. But the basic afflictions – desire and the rest – are fact. Therefore the unbroken succession of birth and death, the round of birth and death, being the factual effect (*kāryabhūta*), will, by virtue of the necessary connection, exist also.

We reply. There would be the round of birth and death if the basic afflictions, as its cause, existed. But they do not. How is that? The illustrious Buddhas, who destroy their enemy, the afflictions of beings in all the three worlds, and who emerge triumphant from the struggle with their adversaries, the four Māras,

> 1 Explain that desire, aversion and illusion are born of volitive thought and that they arise in dependence on the 'good', the 'bad' and misbelief.

'Volitive thought' (*saṁkalpa*) means conceptual activity (*vitarka*); 'born of' means arising directly from. As the verse expresses it, 'O desire I know thy roots, thou art born of volitive thought. I will not will thee in my thought and thou willst exist no more for me.' 'Desire (*rāga*), aversion (*dveṣa*) and

452 illusion (*moha*) are said to be born of volitive thought.' Only

[1] A synonym for *saṁsāra*.

these three afflictions are named because they are the roots of the others and are primary. 'And these three basic afflictions arise in dependence on the "good" (*śubha*) the "bad" (*aśubha*)[1] and misbelief (*viparyāsa*).' That is, desire arises in direct dependence on what takes the form of the 'good'; aversion is dependent on the 'bad'; and illusion arises in direct dependence on misbelief. However, volitive thought is the common cause of these three arising.

How is it that illusion is born of volitive thought? We explain. The illustrious one said in the *Pratītyasamutpāda Sūtra*, 'Even primal ignorance, o monks, has its reason, its conditions, its cause. What is the cause of ignorance? A groundless act of consciousness, o monks, is the cause of ignorance. A confused act of consciousness, born of illusion, is the cause of ignorance.' Thus ignorance comes into being born of volitive thought.[2]

453 2 What arises in dependence on the 'good', the 'bad' and misbelief cannot be self-existent; therefore the basic afflictions do not exist in truth.

If desire and the other afflictions were, indeed, self-existent they would not arise in dependence on the 'good', the 'bad' and misbelief, because what is self-existent is neither created nor related to anything other than itself. But they do arise in dependence on the 'good', the 'bad' and misbelief; they are therefore wholly lacking in self-existence and are not real in truth (*tattvataḥ*). That is, they do not exist in the higher sense (*paramārthataḥ*), in the sense of self-existence.

Afflictions of a self are unintelligible

What is more,

3 The existence or non-existence of the personal self has not been established in any way at all; but, without a self, how can the existence or non-existence of the basic afflictions be established?

In what way the existence or non-existence of a personal

[1] The 'bad' is the 'not-good'.

[2] This is not quite lucid. It appears that the 'good', the 'bad' and the four misbeliefs (cf. p. 214) are posited and that conceptual activity carried by volition then results in desire, aversion and illusion or ignorance, respectively. In Buddhist thought, however, good, bad and misbelief themselves presuppose ignorance. The circle is obvious and quite acceptable to Mādhyamika which abjures lineal explanation.

self (*ātman*) is not established has been explained in detail.[1] That being so, how can there be existence or non-existence of a putative element of existence which presupposes a self?

If someone says: Let it be agreed that the existence and non-existence of a personal self are not established, what is the consequence for the afflictions, as their existence or non-existence have not been established?

Nāgārjuna's reply:

> 4 The afflictions must afflict someone, but this someone has not been proved to exist. Without someone as subject surely the afflictions cannot afflict anyone.

454 It is commonly thought that desire and the other basic afflictions arise in dependence on a substrate, as a mural painting depends on a wall or ripeness and such qualities depend on a fruit. That is, they are the afflictions of someone and cannot be without someone as a substrate. This substrate is conjectured to be either a personal self or consciousness (*citta*). There is no such substrate of the afflictions, however, as it was rejected earlier. Without a substrate, personal or impersonal, who or what would the afflictions afflict? They belong to no one, because no one exists in fact. As the *kārikā* put it, 'Without someone as subject, surely the afflictions cannot afflict anyone.'

Some may object: We do not suppose there is any pre-existing substrate of the afflictions. There is nothing called a personal self which can be determined as the substrate because such is without causal efficacy like a mango tree in the sky. Nevertheless the afflictions supervene in dependence on an afflicted consciousness; that consciousness is born simultaneously with the afflictions.

Nāgārjuna says that that does not make sense either.

> 5 As with the problem of the permanent personal self, the basic afflictions cannot exist in what is afflicted in any of the five possible ways,[2] nor can what is afflicted exist in the afflictions in any of the five ways.

The designation 'permanent personal self' refers to the factors of personal existence, body, feelings, dispositions and so on. The theory of the permanent personal self is the view that the factors of personal existence are the self; this theory takes the form of the persistent belief in the reality of the 'mine'.

[1] Chapter XIV.

[2] They cannot be identical with it, nor other than it; they cannot be in it, nor it in them; and they cannot possess it. See p. 166.

That this personal self, on being thought through in the five ways, is not possible in terms of the factors of personal existence, Nāgārjuna said earlier. 'The perfectly realized one is not identical with the factors of personal existence, nor other than them; he is not in them, nor they in him; and the perfectly realized one is not the possessor of the factors of personal existence. What then is the perfectly realized one?'[1]

455 Similarly, the afflictions, on being examined critically in the fivefold way, cannot exist in the afflicted consciousness, because the afflictions afflict, and the afflicted consciousness is afflicted. In that case the very thing afflicted would be the afflictions. This makes no sense because it involves the identity of the agent of burning and the fuel. That the afflicted consciousness is one thing and the afflictions another makes no sense, because, being separate and unrelated to each other, it involves an affliction which does not afflict anything. Therefore, because neither their identity nor their difference holds, and because neither can be subject or attribute to the other, what is afflicted (*kliṣṭa*) is not based in the afflictions. Nor are the afflictions based in what is afflicted. Nor is what is afflicted the possessor of the afflictions. Thus, after critical examination of the five possibilities, the afflictions cannot possibly be based in what is afflicted.

Similarly the afflictions cannot possibly be the cause of what is afflicted. And, critically examined in the five ways, what is afflicted, taken as the cause of the afflictions, cannot possibly be based in the afflictions.

What is afflicted cannot be the afflictions, because that would entail the identity of doer and deed; nor can the afflicted be one thing and the afflictions another because that would entail that they were unrelated (*niṛapekṣakatva*); nor can what is afflicted be based in the afflictions nor these in that; nor is what is afflicted possessed by the afflictions. Thus, analogously to the personal self, what is afflicted is not based in the afflictions in any of the five ways. From this it follows that neither what is afflicted nor the afflictions can be established by reciprocal reference (*parasparāpekṣa*).[2]

The afflictions have no objective basis

You may object: Even though you have refuted the afflictions, none the less the 'good', the 'bad', and the misbeliefs, which

[1] P. 193, 1.
[2] Cf. Chapter VIII, 'Desire and the Other Afflictions'.

cause the afflictions, exist and because they are solid fact, the afflictions exist.

Our reply is: The afflictions would exist if the 'good', the 'bad' and the misbeliefs existed. However,

> 6ab The 'good', the 'bad' and the misbeliefs are not self-existent;

that is because of the dependent arising of all things and because of the refutation to follow. As, however, they are not self-existent,

> 6cd On which 'good', 'bad' and misbelief could the afflictions be dependent?

456 You may object: The afflictions *do* exist because their objective basis (*ālambana*) is fact. The assumption is that what does not exist has no objective basis, like the son of a barren woman. But the sixfold objective basis – sights, sounds, smells, tastes, touches and mind objects (*dharmas*) – does exist. So because the objective basis exists the afflictions exist as well.

Our reply is: Your theory is as follows:

> 7 Sights, sounds, touches, smells, tastes and mind objects are conceived of as the sixfold external reality of the afflictions – desire, aversion and illusion.

'External reality' (*vastu*) stands for 'objective basis', that is, desire and the other afflictions are based in it when they arise. And that objective basis is sixfold, according to the distinctive perceptual judgments of the six senses, namely sights, sounds, tastes, touches, smells and mind objects.

Sight determines 'here' and 'there' and is a resort in proof. Sound is that by virtue of which things are named and revealed. Smells are smelled or suffered by being perceived elsewhere than where they have come from. Tastes are tasted or savoured
457 immediately. Touch is what is touched; mind objects are so called because based in the putative elements of existence from *nirvāṇa* on down and because they are self-defining. That is what is meant by the sixfold objective reality or basis.

But the basis of what? Of desire, aversion and illusion. Desire is the act of desiring, it is liking and actualized effort; it is also the desirous state of mind. Aversion is vitiating, it is the annihilation of either creatures or things; again, it is a vitiated state of mind. Illusion is the being deluded, it is befuddlement (*saṁmoha*), it is the faulty understanding of the true nature of things; again, illusion is a deluded state of mind.

Thus are sights, sounds, and so on, the sixfold objective basis of the afflictions. Desire supervenes by the gratuitous projection (*adhyāropa*) of the quality of 'good' onto them; aversion by the gratuitous projection of the quality of 'bad'; the misbeliefs arise from the gratuitous projection of the imperishability of things and of the permanence of the personal self, and so on. This sixfold objective basis is considered by the simple-minded to be reality (*satyam*). Its true nature (*svabhāva sattā*) is that it is non-self-existent (*avidyamāna*); but it is erroneously considered by you to be the objective basis of desire and the other afflictions, as those with an optical defect erroneously imagine hairs, mosquitoes, flies, double moons, and so on.

Nāgārjuna expounds:

> 8ab Sights, sounds, tastes, touches, smells and mind objects are abstractions;

by 'abstractions' (*kevala*) he means they are mere thought constructs, lacking self-existence. But if they lack self-existence, how is it they are taken to be objects (*upalabhyante*). He answers:

> 8cd They manifest themselves as does a fabled city, they are like a mirage, a dream.

They are perceived as objects; yet only in misbelief (*viparyāsa*), as is a fabled city and so on.

Desire and aversion are not based in good and bad

So,

458

> 9 How can 'good' or 'bad' be based in such, which are analogous to a man created by magical power or are like a reflection?

From this it follows that, because 'good' and 'bad' arise from an illusory basis (*mithyāśraya*), they are utterly false (*mṛṣatvam eva*) if taken as objective. To quote from the *Ratnāvalī*: 'The factors of personal existence arise from the sense of "I", but this "I" is, in truth, false. If the seed of something is false how can the resulting thing itself be true? Having seen that the factors of personal existence are unreal the sense of

"I" is expelled. When the sense of "I" has been abandoned the factors of personal existence are no longer possible.'

Not only because 'good' and 'bad' have an illusory basis are they illusory taken as objective, but they are illusory for the following reason, as Nāgārjuna expounds it:

> 10 Without relation to 'good' there is no 'bad', in dependence on which we form the idea of 'good'. Therefore 'good' is unintelligible.

That is, if there were anything called 'good' (*śubha*), 'bad' (*aśubha*) would necessarily be related to it. It is like the near and the far, the seed and the seedling or the long and the short. Because 'good' is dependent on a relation to something outside
459 itself, and as that on which it is to be dependent, the 'not-good' – the 'bad' – does not exist apart from it, there is no 'not-good' unrelated to 'good'. The thought is that 'not-good' cannot stand outside of all relationship to 'good'. The good we conceive of and determine is dependent on and related to what is not-good. In the *kārikā* the word 'which' refers to the word 'not-good' which precedes it; the expression 'form the idea of' refers to 'good' which follows it. It follows that there is no other category of thing, the not-good, to which the idea of good would have to relate, as a relation to something other than itself. The good, therefore, is unintelligible, even as the long and the farther shore are unintelligible because of the impossibility of the short and the near shore. This is the idea.

And now Nāgārjuna expounds how the not-good – the bad – as well, is not possible:

> 11 There is no 'good' unrelated to 'bad'; yet we form our idea of 'bad' in dependence on it. There is therefore, no 'bad'.

That is, if there were something called 'bad' – 'not-good' – it would necessarily be correlated to the good, as the far shore is correlated to the near shore and the long to the short. It is because the not-good is dependent on a correlation with a different category of thing. And that, too, the good on which it is to be dependent, would not exist in the absence of the not-good. The good does not exist unrelated to the not-good. The idea is that the good is not possible out of all relationship to the not-good. We form our idea of the not-good and define it in correlation with and dependence on what is good. In the *kārikā* the word 'it' designates the word 'good' in the first line; the verb 'form an idea' is connected with the following word, 'bad'. It follows that there is no other category of thing, the good, to which the idea of not-good would have to relate, as a relation to something other than itself. It follows that the not-good cannot exist. Thus neither good nor not-good is possible.

So:

> 12 As 'good' is non-existent how can there be desire? As 'bad' is non-existent how can there be aversion?

460 The thought is that desire and aversion, which are evoked by the good and the not-good, are not possible if the good and the not-good as what evokes them, do not exist, because then they would be without cause.

The four misbeliefs are unintelligible

Even as the non-existence of desire and aversion is established by the non-existence of what evokes them – the good and the bad – so now Nāgārjuna expounds that illusion (*moha*) too is non-existent as such (*svabhāvābhāva*) by showing that misbelief (*viparyāsa*) does not exist as such.

> 13 If the belief that the imperishable is immanent in the perishable is held to be a misbelief, but there is nothing perishable in the absence of being, how can this belief be a misbelief?

The assumption here is that there are four misbeliefs. First, the belief that there is something imperishable (*nitya*) in the five perishable (*anitya*) factors of personal existence which undergo destruction in every moment, is a misbelief.

Second, 'The very nature of whatever is perishable is suffering: that is not happiness; so everything that is perishable is afflicted existence.'[1] According to this argument what is perishable is afflicted existence and all compounded things as such are perishable. So the perverted belief (*viparīta grāha*) in happiness (*sukham*) within the five factors of personal existence whose very nature is afflicted existence, is another misbelief.

461.3 Further, 'You, who know well that the seed of the body is blood and sperm, that it grows by voiding urine and excrement, that it is like faeces, how could desire attract you to it?' The body is, in its ownmost nature, and in every respect, the quintessence of impurity. It is the idea, born of illusion, that the

[1] *Catuḥśataka*, II, 25.

body is pure (*śuchi*) and the persistent belief in this, that constitutes the third misbelief.

Again, one distinguishes an enduring self among the five factors of personal existence, which are lacking in substance and are devoid of a person who exists as such because they are in constant change and because it is their nature to arise and to vanish. In this case it is the idea of an enduring self (*ātman*) and the persistent belief in it – that is the persistent belief in an enduring self in what does not endure – that is the fourth misbelief.

These four misbeliefs are the root causes of complete illusion.[1]

And now an analysis of this. If we define the theory or the belief (*grāha*) that the imperishable exists in what is devoid of self-existence, as a misbelief, it is equally true that there can be nothing perishable in the factors of personal existence, which are devoid of self-existence, either. 'There is nothing perishable in the absence of being; how can this view be a misbelief.' Imperishability is defined as a misbelief in relation to its opposite, the perishable; however, the perishable does not exist in the absence of being. But if there is no imperishability how could its opposite, perishability, exist and how could the theory of the imperishable exist as a perverted belief? It follows that this is not a misbelief.

As the perishable is not possible in the absence of being, that is, where self-existence is lacking, where nothing arises as self-existent, so afflicted existence is not possible either, nor is there impurity nor absence of self. If these, lacking self-existence, do not exist, how can there be misbeliefs in imperishability, happiness, purity and enduring self, as they are the counter-concepts to these? It follows that misbeliefs do not truly exist (*svarūpataḥ*). But if they do not exist how can there be primal ignorance, as it will have no cause?

462 As the illustrious one said: 'There has never been primal ignorance nor anything dependent on it; it does not exist as such anywhere in the world; and for this reason I have called it primal ignorance.' Again Mañjuśrī asks, 'What, o illustrious one, is illusion in the mystical verse?' The illustrious one answered: 'Illusion, Mañjuśrī, is to be utterly lost; which is why it is called illusion.' In this and the following passages misbelief is defined.

Let it be so, you may say, that it is not tenable that what

[1] Thus far the orthodox view of the four misbeliefs.

is perishable can be in something which is not self-existent; but why is that not just what is meant by misbelief? Nāgārjuna expounds:

> 14 If the view that the imperishable is in the perishable is held to be a misbelief; why is the view that the perishable exists in what is devoid of being not also a misbelief?[1]

As the imperishable and the perishable are exclusive contrary terms, there is no third term, apart from them, which would not be a misbelief. As nothing is free of misbelief, in relation to what would misbelief exist? According to this reasoning as well, then, there can be no misbelief.[2] Because there is no misbelief there can be, in truth, no primal ignorance. As the misbelief consisting of the view that the imperishable is in the perishable is not possible, it will follow that, in the same sense, the other misbeliefs are not possible either.

That is exactly why the illustrious one said, in the *Dṛḍhāśayaparipṛcchā*, 'It is thus, worthy youth, for one search-
463 ing for an end to the birth-death cycle on the Buddhist way. Even though the realized one has abandoned the appropriative elements of existence he does not teach a theory of the annihilation of aversion or illusion. Why does he not? The realized ones, o worthy youth, do not teach the truth for the sake of getting rid of or acquiring any elements of existence at all, nor for the sake of the clear knowledge of afflicted existence, its overcoming, and the final realization, nor for the sake of clear understanding nor for escaping from the birth-death cycle nor for the sake of the way to *nirvāṇa*, nor for the sake of casting out nor discrimination. Because, o worthy youth, the true nature of a realized one is to be free of the dominance of duality. Those who live in dualities are said not to strive in the correct way, but to strive mistakenly. What, o worthy son, is meant by duality? It is duality when one says, "I will annihilate desire"; it is duality when one says, "I will annihilate aversion"; it is duality when one says, "I will annihilate illusion". Those who strive in this way, it should be realized, are
463.9 not striving in the correct way, but are striving mistakenly.'

Belief is unintelligible

464.21 Someone may object: Although the perverted belief (*grāho*

[1] This, of course, confounds the orthodox view.
[2] If no truth, no falsehood.

viparyaya) consisting of the belief that the imperishable is in the perishable does not in the end make sense (*na saṁbhavati*), none the less the belief itself is a fact. What is called belief is
465 the act of believing and this is an existent thing. There must necessarily be an appropriate element, for example imperishability, which is the effective basis of believing, also an independent agent, either a permanent self or a mind. There must be, further, an act of the agent, and an external or internal object immediately intended. If the object, the agent, the act and the effectuating basis are accepted as facts, then everything we wished to establish is established.

We reply. This is an illusory hope. According to the reasoning we have given,

> 15 The effectuating basis, the believing itself, the believer and an external reality are all unreal; therefore belief itself does not exist.

The assumption here is that there is a believing agent, who believes there is an object of action – an external reality consisting of sights, sounds, and so on; and an effectuating basis of his belief – imperishability and the other misbeliefs.

How this is not possible was expounded earlier in the *kārikā* beginning 'If the belief that the imperishable is immanent in the perishable is a misbelief'.[1] It was shown that imperishability, and the others as effectuating bases are not possible. And that there is no one who believes was expounded in the *kārikā* 'The existence or non-existence of the personal self has not been established in any way at all.'[2] And that the object of belief does not exist was expounded in the *kārikā* 'Sights, sounds, tastes, touches, smells and mind objects are abstrac-
466 tions.'[3] If, however, in this way, the believer, the effectuating basis of belief and the object of belief are not established, how can there be belief itself, which would lack all basis in reason (*nirhetuka*)?

Hence: 'The effectuating basis of belief, the believing itself, the believer and an external reality are all unreal.' The meaning is that all these are nought because they do not arise in self-existence. This is exactly why 'Therefore belief itself does not exist.'

Or again, in the chapter inquiring into causes and those following, it has been expounded that in no respect do means, agent and object arise in time. So, all such things, because they

[1] P. 214, 13. [2] P. 208, 3. [3] P. 212, 8ab.

lack existence in their own right, are not real. And so there is no such thing as belief.

You may object: Misbeliefs do exist because of the factual existence of the one who believes amiss. That is, someone named Devadatta who persists in misbelief, exists. One who persists in misbelief is not possible if there are no misbeliefs. Therefore misbeliefs exist because of the factual existence of the one who believes amiss.

Misbelief presupposes right belief which is impossible

We reply. We have explained that there is no belief itself because there is no effectuating basis, no agent and no object. And so,

> 16 As there is no belief, whether false or true, whose could be the misbelief, whose could be the non-misbelief?

If there is no belief, true or false, in anything, by anyone, how could there be perverted belief or non-perverted belief? There are thus, no misbeliefs.

Moreover, these misbeliefs considered to be of a subject would be conceived to be of someone who either is in error or is not in error or who is erring.

Nāgārjuna shows that in every respect such ideas are not logically possible, saying

467

> 17 Misbeliefs are not possible for one who is in error, nor are they possible for one who is not in error.
>
> 18 Misbeliefs are not possible for one who is just erring. Consider it yourself; to whom could misbeliefs possibly belong?

In the first place misbeliefs are not possible in one who is in error (*viparīta*). Why not? Because the one who is in error has already erred;[1] why would there be, once again, meaningless involvement in error? Nor do misbeliefs make sense attributed to one who has not erred (*aviparīta*). Because it would follow that the Buddhas – those who realize the mind of enlightenment by bringing ignorance and blindness of the mind to an end – could be in error. Similarly, there are no misbeliefs in one who is just erring (*viparyasyamāna*). Because such a one does not exist. Who would this third category – the

[1] Misbelief is an 'act'.

one who is just erring – be, utterly other than the one who is in error and the one who is not? Do you say the one just erring is half in error? And that one such believes some things amiss and some things not amiss? In such a case, what constitutes the misbelief is not made into an error by himself because it is already an error; nor is what constitutes the non-misbelief made into an error by him, because it is not error. It follows that misbeliefs are not possible for one who is in the act of erring. In this way, then, neither the man in error nor the man not in error is possible, nor the one who is just erring. Now considering this for oneself, by one's own insight adopting a middle position: Who could be the subject of the misbeliefs? Thus, because of a lack of any base for them, there are no misbeliefs.

Further,

> 19 How can there be misbeliefs if they do not arise? If
> 468 misbeliefs are unborn how can one commit them?

And,

> 20 A thing arises neither from itself nor from another; not arising either from himself nor from another, how can there be one who believes amiss?

The meaning is, how could there be one in error? And so, as stated, it does not make sense to say that the misbeliefs exist because the one who misbelieves is a fact.

Further, even for the one who accepts the existence of the four misbeliefs it is impossible to determine the nature of misbelief. Why is that? Because:

> 21 If there is self, purity, imperishability and happiness, then self, purity, imperishability and happiness are not misbeliefs.

If self, purity, imperishability and happiness are defined as misbeliefs do they exist or not? If they exist, they are hardly misbeliefs, as they are factually true in the same way that the absence of self, perishability, and so on are. If they do not exist, then, not only is there no misbelief, because they are not factual, but the non-misbeliefs – absence of self, perishability and the others – are not factual because their opposites, the misbeliefs, do not exist. Nāgārjuna expounds:

> 22 If there is no self, no purity, no imperishability and no happiness, then there is no non-self, no impurity, no perishability and no afflicted existence.

If you think self, purity and imperishability do not exist because of the impossibility of holding something to be false if it exists and that non-self, impurity and so on are not to be understood as misbeliefs because they are true; this should be rejected as, there being no opposite, there is nothing to be negated. As, thus, non-self and so on are not possible, why should non-self not be a misbelief, because it does not exist as such even as self and the others do not exist as such? Therefore all these eight misbeliefs[1] are to be rejected by those desiring freedom from their fetters in the prison of endless coursing through birth, old age and death. Nāgārjuna expounds the great value of the analysis of misbelief given as a means of destroying ignorance and the afflictions.

Banishing misbelief eliminates the afflictions

> 23 Thus by eliminating misbelief, ignorance is destroyed; ignorance being destroyed, personal dispositions and the other causes are destroyed.

When the wise one does not hold to the misbeliefs in the sense we have explained, then, no longer believing amiss, ignorance, which is caused by misbelief, is got rid of and because of the destruction of ignorance all the putative causal factors (*dharma*)[2] which result from ignorance, from personal dispositions to old age and death which are accompanied by sorrow, lamentation and despair, are done away with. For ignorance is the root cause of afflicted existence, of the entire conglomerate of afflictions from birth on. Even as all sense organs derive from a central awareness, and the central awareness being
470 eliminated they too are removed; so all the causes in the round of existence from personal dispositions on, function with ignorance as root cause; necessarily then, if ignorance is removed they are eliminated. Nāgārjuna expounds this, when he says, 'Ignorance being destroyed, personal dispositions and the other causes are destroyed.'

Someone may object: If, from the elimination of the misbeliefs, primal ignorance is removed, then, in that case, the removal of this primal ignorance, which follows from the elimination of the misbeliefs, really happens; for one does not search for the effective ways to remove a non-existent dryad

[1] To label four key beliefs, misbelief, i.e. heresy, is a stinging challenge to Buddhist orthodoxy.

[2] The twelvefold cycle of birth and death: *saṁsāra*.

in the sky. Therefore primal ignorance is, in fact, real; because, in fact, one does search for effective ways of removing it. It follows that the basic afflictions, desire and the rest, which spring from primal ignorance, are fact. Because the basic afflictions are fact, the round of existence, the coursing through births and deaths, is indeed real.

We reply. This is, in truth, the utmost in perverse learning. There are saintly persons who gird up their loins and, with their whole heart, for the sake of others, issue forth into the unredeemed world of passions, afflictions and infinite sorrows – that poisonous growth so rich and thick with fruit; and they attempt to uproot it by the power of their wisdom, their skill in means and their secret knowledge. But you not only do not support them but are stolidly opposed to them as one ensconced on the rock of realism. You oppose those who, by the power of secret knowledge, are uprooting that tree which is poisonous with afflictions, whose sole fruits are ill – a flood of grief, birth, old age and death. You, in your obduracy, are devoting yourself to making that tree flourish by your stubborn belief in the reality of things.

What is more, if it were possible to eliminate primal ignorance and the other afflictions then there could be a search for a way to eliminate them. But their elimination (*prahāṇa*) is not possible.[1] If it were, then it would be the elimination of afflictions whose nature it was either to exist in very truth or not to
471 so exist. What follows from that?

In the first alternative, if one thinks of eliminating afflictions whose nature it is to exist in very truth, that would not be logically possible. Why? Because,

> 24 If there were self-existent afflictions of someone, how could they be overcome? Who can vanquish the self-existent?

It is not possible to bring to nought the self-existence of things whose self-nature it is to exist. The self-nature of earth – solidity – and of the other elements is not nullified. So, if there were afflictions – ignorance and the rest – whose self-nature it was to exist, and they belong to some person, how could they be overcome? They will not be overcome by anyone, in any way at all. Why are they not overcome? Nāgārjuna says, 'Who can vanquish the self-existent?' It is because it is impossible to bring what is self-existent to nought. The openness of space, for example, cannot be nullified.

[1] In the sense of the quotation on p. 216.

In the second alternative the afflictions are conceived to be by nature non-existent. Nāgārjuna says the elimination of afflictions is impossible in this way as well.

> 25 If there were non-self-existent afflictions of someone how could they be overcome? Who can vanquish the non-existent?

It is equally impossible to vanquish non-existent afflictions whose very nature it is not to exist. It is not possible to nullify the non-existent coldness of fire. Who can vanquish afflictions which by their very nature do not exist? No one at all can vanquish them.

In sum, as in neither alternative is there a possibility of elimination, afflictions cannot be eliminated. As there is no elimination, how can there be a search for the effective means of eliminating the afflictions?

472 Therefore the claim that the afflictions – ignorance and the others – do exist in fact because of the endeavour to find a means of removing them, does not make sense.

As is said in the *Samādhirāja Sūtra*, 'An existential element "desire" would be roused by something in someone; an existential element "aversion" would be aversion in someone to something; an existential element "illusion" would be illusion in someone concerning something.' Such an element of existence one cannot discover in thought nor perceive in fact. One who does not discover such an existential element in thought nor perceive it in fact is said to be free of desire, aversion and illusion, to have a mind free of misbelief, to be composed in spirit. He is said to have crossed to the other side, to
472.6 have penetrated deeply, to have attained peace.

XVIII

The Four Buddhist Truths

The nihilistic consequences of devoidness

475 At this point some object:

> 1 If the entire everyday is devoid of self-existence, nothing can come to be nor cease to be. It follows inexorably that, for you, the four Buddhist truths do not hold.

If, in point of logical argument the entire everyday (*sarvam idam*) – everything temporal both inner and outer – does not arise, that is lacks being (*śūnya*), and this is your teaching, then many and great are the difficulties which descend upon you. Why? Because if all things were devoid of being then what is so devoid cannot be said to really be and what cannot be said to be can, like the son of a barren woman, neither come to be nor cease to be, because it does not exist (*avidyamānatva*); so nothing whatsoever would come to be or cease to be. As there is no coming to be nor ceasing to be it follows inexorably for you, who hold that things lack being, that there are no four Buddhist truths[1] (*āryasatya*).

Why? Because it is Buddhist doctrine that the five appropriative factors of personal existence (*skandhas*), which are interdependent and arise from causes in time are designated afflicted existence (*duḥkha*) in virtue of existence itself being essentially afflicted, because all change is affliction, because all things that come to be in time are afflicted and because of the perversity and essential anguish of existence. Only the wise,
476 whose misbeliefs have been destroyed, fully comprehend afflicted existence. The unwise do not, being in the grip of

[1] These are the founding insights of earliest Buddhism and remain bedrock for all schools. They are: (1) existence is afflicted (*duḥkha*); (2) afflicted existence has an origin; (3) afflicted existence has an end; (4) there is a path leading to the end. These are the *āryan* truths, often translated as the noble or holy truths. For Nāgārjuna they are truths of the wise, i.e. truths for those who have penetrated Buddhism.

misbelief: the fixed view that things have self-existent natures even as they appear to have. Just as impaired sense organs, because of old age, sickness or disease perceive sugar and such things as bitter, though their true nature is sweet, and in this cognition bitterness, not sweetness is taken as the truth because the true nature of the object is not perceived, so it is in this matter. Even though the five appropriative factors of personal existence are by nature afflicted, still only those who clearly see the personal factors to be afflicted truly understand existence as afflicted; not those who perceive things otherwise than they are because they are in the grip of misbelief. As it is only for the wise (*ārya*) that the personal factors are afflicted by nature, the truth of afflicted existence (*duḥkhasatya*) is said to be a truth for the wise (*āryasatya*).

But are not painful feelings defined as afflictions by those who are not wise? How is it then that afflicted existence is a truth only for the wise? Because the truth is that not only painful feelings are afflictions but that all five appropriative personal factors are. As, therefore, only for the wise is that the truth it is called a truth of the wise.

It is said, 'One does not feel a piece of wool in the palm of the hand but if it gets into the eye it causes discomfort and torment. So the immature man, like the hand, does not know that existence is afflicted; but the wise man, like the eye, alone trembles at the torment.' Because, that existence is by nature afflicted is the truth only for the wise, it is known as a wise truth.

But if the wise truth of affliction is to make sense, things must come to be and cease to be. If, however, because all things are devoid of self-existence, nothing comes to be nor ceases to be, there can be no affliction. And if there is no affliction how can there be a truth about its origin (*samudaya-satya*)? The cause from which afflicted existence issues and springs is called its origin and is understood as the afflictions (*kleśa*) arising from actions which originate in the thirst for existence (*tṛṣṇa*) conceived as cause. If, however, there is no affliction which is of the nature of an effect, then there is no origin of it because a cause without an effect is illogical.

477 When afflicted existence disappears never again to arise, that is known as cessation. If, however, there is no affliction, of what would there be cessation? So the cessation of affliction is not possible either. Thus if there is no affliction (*duḥkha*) there can be no truth of its cessation (*nirodhasatya*). If there is no cessation of afflicted existence how will there be

a way which follows the Buddhist eightfold path leading to the cessation of afflicted existence. Thus the truth of the path (*mārgasatya*) does not hold either.

Accordingly, if one declares all things to be devoid of a self-existent nature, it follows inexorably that the four Buddhist truths do not hold. And what harm results from that?

Nāgārjuna says,[1]

> 2 Because the four Buddhist truths do not hold, the clear knowledge of afflicted existence becomes unintelligible as do its overcoming, the inner acceptance of the way to its overcoming and the final intuitive realization.

Given the consequence that the four Buddhist truths do not hold it becomes logically impossible that there should be (1) clear knowledge (*parijñāna*) of the truth of afflicted existence as the transience, substancelessness and ill of all things, or (2) overcoming (*prahāṇa*) of the source of affliction, or (3) the inner acceptance of a way (*bhāvanā*) leading to the cessation of affliction, or (4) the final realization (*sākṣātkaraṇa*) of its cessation.[2]

And if, because the four Buddhist truths do not hold, there is no clear knowledge of affliction and the other stages, what follows from that?

Nāgārjuna says,[3]

> 3 If these are nothing, then the four Buddhist spiritual attainments[4] are nothing; if they are nothing, then no one can either exist in any attainment nor be on the way to it.
>
> 478 4 If the eight spiritual categories[5] do not exist, there can be no Buddhist community of monks. Because the four Buddhist truths are nothing there can be no Buddhist Truth.
>
> 5ab If neither the community of monks exists nor the Buddhist Truth, how can there be an enlightened one?

As, in this way, there is no clear knowledge of afflicted existence, no overcoming of it, and so, these being non-existent, the four categories: stream-winner, once-returner,

[1] Still putting the opponent's objection.

[2] These four stages constitute the structure of the Buddhist path.

[3] Still putting the opponent's objection.

[4] The categories of Buddhist initiates; these are (a) the 'stream-winner', (b) the 'once-returner', (c) the 'non-returner', (d) the *arhant* (saint).

[5] The four attainments and the four states of being on the way to them.

non-returner and *arhant* are unintelligible. Why? It is the re-
479 moval of the afflictions which are considered to be the index of these categories.

480 The four categories with their correlated attainments and fruits are defined precisely in terms of the progressive elimination of afflictive attachments (*kleśa*) in all three worlds – the world of desire, the world of form and the world of the formless. There are exactly fifteen moments of realization on the way. But the pre-requisite for this process is the possibility of the four achievements – clear knowledge that existence is afflicted, overcoming the origin of afflicted existence, inner realization of the way to overcome it and the final realization. Without these there can be no wise one secure in any of the four attainments or on the way to them.

487.5 If neither the four Buddhist truths hold nor the four achievements – clear knowledge and so on – then, because the attainments in which, by inner acceptance and direct vision, these truths are to be grasped, do not obtain, the persons who would be progressing through these stages and realizing them, do not exist; so the Buddhist community of monks does not exist. The community of monks, which exists by virtue of penetration to the truth, and by virtue of the immediate experience of the ultimate truth due to not being sundered from the illustrious Buddha even by all the demons, and by virtue of its enjoying utterly clarified knowledge, would not exist if the eight spiritual categories of person did not exist.

If the four Buddhist truths are nothing, there can be no Buddhist Truth (*saddharma*) either. What is true for the truly wise Buddhists constitutes the Buddhist Truth.

488 The truth of the cessation of affliction is the doctrine of the attainments, whereas the truth of the path to end affliction is the doctrine of the conduct leading to the attainments; this is the doctrine of final attainment; the explanation which clarifies it perfectly is the doctrine of the scriptures. If the four Buddhist truths are nothing, all this is nothing. 'If the Buddhist truths are nothing, all this is nothing.' 'If the Buddhist truths are nothing there will be no Buddhist Truth; if the Truth and the community of monks do not exist how can there be an enlightened one?'

If the doctrine as expounded here[1] is true, then it is reasonable that there could be one who was utterly enlightened

[1] That is, the orthodox view opposed to Nāgārjuna.

concerning every mode of every aspect of things because he had realized both the basic truth and its applications. And if the community of monks is real then by its teachings there will be an accumulated store of knowledge, and by taking refuge in it and by reverence toward it and generosity there will be an accumulated store of merit and so, step by step, one can become enlightened.

Further, if there were no community of monks there would be no candidate for the attainments of stream-winner, once-returner, and so on. And if no one progresses through the various attainments no one can achieve enlightenment. For a revered one must necessarily have achieved the prior stage. Having attained the prior stage, which is by definition to be within the community, a revered one comes to be. If there is no community it follows that there will be no revered Buddha. Again, even a revered one belongs to the community, because he is no longer a learner. And there are those who explain that a revered one belongs to the community because of the saying 'the community of monks with a Buddha at its head'. In the opinion of these it is clarity itself to say, 'If the Buddhist Truth and the community do not exist, how can there be an enlightened one?'

489 The Madhyadeśikas, because of the system of stages[1] given in the *Mahāvastu*, maintain that a *bodhisattva*, as one who is secure in the first stage, having achieved the way of insight, is held to be included in the community of monks. But if the community does not exist there is no *bodhisattva* either. How then will there be an enlightened one? This is clarity itself. So,

> 5cd By declaring that all things lack self-existence you reject the three jewels.

That is, by arguing for the absence of being in things you are rejecting Buddha, the Buddhist Truth and the community, which are called the three jewels, because they are difficult to attain, arise only seldom, are not fully realized by those of lesser worth and because they are of great value. Further,

> 6 Through the lack of self-existence in things you reject the reality of the attainments, the distinction between truth and untruth, and even transactions in the everyday world.

[1] The ten stages of the *bodhisattva*, who becomes the ideal realized saint of Mahāyāna Buddhism; he is analogous to the earlier ideal of the *arhant*.

490 The words 'arguing for' should be understood before 'lack of self-existence'. If all things are devoid of self-existent natures (*śūnya*), if, that is, literally everything does not exist (*nāsti*),[1] then right and wrong action, together with the resulting fruits, desired or undesired, will not be possible as they are included in 'all things'. All those everyday action expressions such as 'do it', 'cook', 'eat', 'stay', 'go', 'come', are included in 'all things', and, as all the putative elements of existence are devoid of self-existent natures, they do not make any sense at all. It follows that the argument for the absence of being in things, as given, cannot stand.[2]

The Mādhyamika rejoinder

> 7 In our turn we declare that you do not know the purpose of devoidness, nor devoidness itself, nor its meaning. And so you torment yourself in this way.

You, solely by your own speculations, mistakenly foist onto us the view that the meaning of the absence of being (*śūnyatārtha*) is unreality (*nāstitva*), you calumniate us with such arguments as 'If all things are devoid of self-existence, there is no coming to be and no ceasing to be';[3] you fall into great distress and torment yourself excessively. You torment yourself by diverse unfounded speculations, is what is meant.

However, the meaning of the absence of being which we carefully delineate in this treatise is not the meaning you adopt. Not understanding the meaning of absence of being, you do not understand this absence itself; nor do you understand its purpose (*prayojana*). Because you have not comprehended the true nature of things as they are in themselves (*yathāvasthitavastusvarūpa*) your account makes no sense at all and is unrelated to our own explanation.

Well, what *is* the purpose of the absence of being or self-existence, in things? It is given in the Chapter on 'Self and the Way Things Really Are'. 'From the wasting away of the afflictions and karmic action there is freedom; the afflictions and karmic action arise from hypostatizing thought and this from

[1] The equation of *śūnya* and non-existence is the cardinal error of the opponent.

[2] Failing to make sense out of the everyday must be the most serious charge against any philosophy.

[3] P. 223, 1.

the manifold of named things. Named things come to an end in the absence of being.'[1]

491 This means that the absence of being is taught for the purpose of bringing the manifold of named things (*prapañca*), without exception, to perfect rest (*upaśama*). That is, the purpose of the absence of self-existence in things is to bring the entire manifold of named things to perfect rest.[2] You, however, in erroneously speculating that the meaning of absence is unreality, actually strengthen entanglement in the world of named things; you do not understand the purpose of the absence of being.

And now, what is the absence of being itself? This too was expounded in the Chapter on 'Self and the Way Things Really Are'. 'Not dependent on anything other than itself, at peace, not manifested as named things, beyond thought construction, not of varying form – thus is the way things are really spoken of.'[3] How can absence of being, whose very nature is the repose of named things, be unreal? You do not understand the absence of being itself either. We expound later in this very Chapter from what base of meaning the expression 'absence of being' derives its validity. 'It is the dependent arising of things which we interpret as the absence of being in them. Absence of being is a non-cognitive, guiding notion presupposing the everyday. It is the middle way itself.'[4]

As is said in the verse by the illustrious one, 'Whatever is born of conditions, that is not born; it does not come to be in self-existence. Whatever is dependent on conditions is said to be devoid of a self-existent nature. Whoever understands the absence of self-existence is wise.'

Thus the meaning of the term 'dependent arising' is the same as the meaning of the term 'absence of being'. But the meaning of the term 'non-existence' is not the meaning of the term 'absence of being'. By foisting on us the view that the meaning of the term 'absence of being' is the meaning of the term 'non-existence', you calumniate us. It is clear that you do not understand the meaning of the absence of being either. Not understanding and calumniating us in this way, you necessarily torment yourself.

[1] P. 171, 5.
[2] The philosophy of the *Prasannapadā* turns on this thought.
[3] P. 183, 9. [4] P. 238, 18.

The two truths

And who is it who calumniates us in this way? Whoever does
492 not understand the incontrovertible distinction between the two truths (*satyadvaya*) as taught in the sayings of the illustrious one, but who is given to reading the traditional texts literally. That is why Nāgārjuna, out of compassion for his adversary and with a view to refuting the false exposition of the doctrine, said, in clarification of the incontrovertible two truths as taught in the sayings of the illustrious one,

> 8 The teaching of the Buddhas is wholly based on there being two truths: that of a personal everyday world and a higher truth which surpasses it.

That is, the teaching of the illustrious Buddha in this world is effective and valid only as based on the twofoldness of truth. Which twofoldness? The truth of a personal everyday world (*lokasaṁvṛtisatya*) and a higher truth which surpasses it (*paramārthasatya*).

There is the saying, 'A permanent self among the factors of personal existence is known as a "world" (*loka*) because world is founded on such a belief.' The ordinary person is called a 'world' in so far as he is understood to be based on the five factors of personal existence.

'The everyday' (*saṁvṛti*) means being utterly obscured. Again, ignorance arising from the utter obscuring of the true nature of things is called the everyday. Again, to be reciprocally dependent in existence, that is, for things to be based on each other in utter reciprocity, is to be everyday. Again, the everyday means social convention, that is, the world of ordinary language and of transactions between individuals which is characterized by the distinction between knowing and the thing known, naming and the thing named, and so on.

493 It is everyday convention and obscurement for a person which is the personal everyday (*lokasaṁvṛti*). What would a non-worldly or non-personal everyday be from which we distinguish the personal or worldly everyday? This question is superfluous at this juncture and a reply would be a repetition of what has already been settled. Those who persistently perceive things mistakenly because of impaired senses, defective vision or jaundice for example, are without a world (*aloka*), or are non-persons. What they take to hold for the world holds for a non-world. The truth of the everyday world is distinguished from this. The *Madhyamakāvatāra* deals with this in

some detail and it can be studied there. What is true in and for a personal everyday world is personal everyday truth (*loka-saṁvṛtisatya*). The exhaustive totality of words and transactions which are based on the distinction between knowing and the thing known, naming and the thing named and so on, is what is meant by the truth of the everyday personal world. Such a world could not exist in a higher or surpassing sense (*paramārthataḥ*). Because 'When the object of thought is no more, there is nothing for language to refer to. The true nature of things neither arises nor perishes, as *nirvāṇa* does not.'[1] This being so how could verbal utterances (*vāc*) or acts of knowledge (*jñāna*) be effective and valid (*pravṛtti*) in the higher or surpassing sense? Because what is higher or surpassing is not dependent on anything other than itself, it is at peace, it is known in and through itself by the wise; it is beyond the world of named things as such; it cannot be demonstrated nor even cognized. As was said earlier, 'Not dependent on anything other than itself, at peace, not manifested as named things, beyond thought construction, not of varying form – thus is the way things really are spoken of.'[2]

494 What both makes sense (*artha*) and is surpassing (*parama*) is the higher or surpassing sense. That alone, taken as the truth, is truth in the higher or surpassing sense (*paramārthasatya*).

The due distinction between these two truths can be understood in detail from the *Madhyamakāvatāra*. The teaching of the Truth by the illustrious Buddhas is effective and valid in so far as it is based on this twofoldness of truth. The structure of the teaching being determined in this way, it follows:

> 9 Those who do not clearly know the due distinction between the two truths cannot clearly know the hidden depths of the Buddha's teaching.

Some may object: Let it be that the surpassing sense is inherently not of the nature of named things. What then is the purpose of the inferior teaching which has to do with the factors of personal existence, the elements, the senses and sense fields, the Buddhist truths, dependent arising and so on, and which has nothing to do with a higher sense? Surely what is untrue should be rejected; and why should that which is to be rejected, be taught?

We reply. That is indeed true. However, unless the everyday world of verbalized transactions (*laukika vyavahāra*) – that is,

[1] P. 177, 7. [2] P. 183, 9.

the realm of naming and the thing named, knowing and the thing known, and so on – has been accepted as a base (*abhyupagamya*) it is impossible to point out, or to teach (*deśayitum*) the surpassing sense. And if it is not pointed out, it cannot be comprehended; if the surpassing sense is not realized *nirvāṇa* cannot be attained. Nāgārjuna expounds it this way:

> 10 Unless the transactional realm is accepted as a base, the surpassing sense cannot be pointed out; if the surpassing sense is not comprehended *nirvāṇa* cannot be attained.

This is why the everyday world (*saṁvṛti*), as we have defined it, because it is the means to the attainment of *nirvāṇa*, must, at the outset, necessarily be accepted. It is like a container for someone who wants water. This being so, whoever gives an account of the absence of being in things, ignoring our definition of the twofoldness of truth as that of the personal everyday world and that of the higher sense, such a man,

495
> 11 Being feeble-minded is destroyed by the misunderstood doctrine of the absence of being in things, as by a snake ineptly seized or some secret knowledge wrongly applied.

The wise one on the way (*yogī*), having awakened to the fact that the personal world of the everyday arises solely from ignorance and is devoid of self-existence, and who understands that devoidness of self-existence is the higher truth of the everyday, does not fall into the extremes of dualism. He does not recoil to the belief that things are unreal because he has found no self-existence in them, thinking 'what once was, now is not'. He does not reject (*na bādhate*) the personal everyday world, which assumes the form of a reflection, outright, and so he does not reject outright actions and their moral consequences, the distinction between right and wrong, and so on. Nor, on the other hand, does he wrongly impute self-existence to everyday things in the higher sense; because he experiences such things as actions and their moral consequences as not self-existent; and because he does not experience them as self-existent.

However, one who, not seeing the due distinction between the two truths in this way, grasps at the lack of self-existence in all composite things and dwells on it, eager for liberation, either he imagines that all composite things do not truly exist or that the absence of self-existence in them itself exists like a thing (*kāṁcid bhāvataḥ*), in which case he imagines a self-existent reality of the nature of devoidness. In either case the doctrine of devoidness, wrongly understood, would inevitably destroy such a one. Why? Because if he imagines that just because the entire realm of things is devoid of self-existence it does not exist in any sense, then a serious heresy has taken hold of him.

The dangers of misconceiving the absence of being

496 To quote: 'This teaching, wrongly grasped, destroys the unwise man; he drowns in the quagmire of the view that all things are unreal.'[1] On the other hand, if one does not wish to deny the reality of all things one must reject the absence of being in things. How can things be devoid of self-existence when they are perceived by all the world of gods, demons and men? Therefore, having rejected the view that devoidness means only that everyday things are not self-existent, he will inevitably proceed to calamities as a result of inauspicious deeds tending to undermine the true doctrine.

It is said in the *Ratnāvalī*: 'A foolish and intellectually conceited person, because he misunderstands devoidness, destroys his own person by rejecting it and plunges headfirst into the hell of Avīci.'[2]

Thus, devoidness destroys the one who takes it to mean the non-existence of things. However, if one wrongly conceives devoidness itself to be an ontic existent (*bhāvena*) and imagines that the reality of everyday things is based on it, then the absence of being in things, being ill-suited to the way leading to *nirvāṇa*, becomes fruitless. This is why devoidness destroys the one taking it to be something of the nature of an ontic existent (*bhāvarūpeṇa*).

497 You may object that something which is beneficial will be useless if ineptly applied; but how could it destroy? Seed, improperly sown, does not destroy the one seeding. Nāgārjuna gives an example to clarify his point: 'like a snake ineptly seized or some secret knowledge wrongly applied'. A snake, aptly seized, brings a great treasure of riches from taking possession of the crest jewel because it conduces to the livelihood of the snake charmers. But the snake destroys one who seizes him not observing the prescribed rules. Secret knowledge, too, treated according to the rules, favours the magician but

[1] *Ratnāvalī*, II, 19. [2] II, 20.

destroys him if it is put into practice in neglect of the rules. So
in this matter. The absence of being as taught here is a great
esoteric wisdom, and realized in practice and fully grasped,
that is, without recourse to the ideas of existence and non-
existence, but as the middle way (*madhyamā pratipad*), can
lead to full enlightenment. It does this by extinguishing the
sacrificial fire of existence consisting of birth, old age and
death and in virtue of the bliss of bathing in the flowing ocean
of *nirvāṇa* without conditions or residue. However, devoidness
498 will, for the reason given, inevitably destroy anyone who conceives of it contrary to the special interpretation given. That is
why devoidness destroys anyone who wrongly grasps it and
why those of feeble insight are incapable of grasping it at all.

> 12 For this reason the mind of the enlightened one was
> averse to teaching the Truth, realizing how difficult it
> would be for those of feeble insight to fathom it.

For this reason the Truth, understood as the absence of being in things, destroys the person of feeble insight and small mind because he grasps it falsely. So it is that, having realized how difficult it would be for those of feeble insight to fathom the Truth, the mind of the enlightened one, of the illustrious Buddha, after awakening to supreme and perfect enlightenment and after beholding the realm of all beings and the surpassing depth of the Truth, was averse to teaching the Truth, though gifted with special knowledge of the great means to do so.

As is said in the *sūtra*, 'It occurred to the illustrious one in
the very moment of his perfect enlightenment: I have attained
the deep, hidden Truth, radiant even in its depth, unreasoned,
beyond the reach of reason, subtle, to be known only by one
wise and learned. If I were to reveal its radiance to others and
they were not to understand it, that would be fruitless and the
end of me; my thought would be still-born. As I achieved the
499 joy of seeing the sweet Truth alone in a remote forest I should
remain to savour it.' And so on.

The interpretation of the four truths

So, in this manner lacking insight into the incontrovertible nature of the two truths,

> 13 You again perpetrate falsities concerning devoidness.
> The dire consequences you allege do not apply to us,
> nor do they make sense of devoidness.

The dire consequence you cast at us was: 'If the entire everyday is devoid of self-existence, nothing can come to be nor cease to be. It follows inexorably that, for you, the four Buddhist truths do not hold.'[1] Such an allegation, hurled because of a lack of due insight into the nature of the two truths, and because of ignorance of the nature of devoidness, and of its meaning and purpose, it does not make sense applied to our understanding of devoidness.

It does not, therefore, make sense at all. In the way you allege this dire consequence of devoidness, you make a charge against and calumniate, you attack and repudiate devoidness, but your accusation is not logically relevant to our position. Your allegation derives from wrongly foisting the meaning of non-existence onto the idea of the absence of being. But we do not declare the meaning of non-existence and of absence of being to be the same; rather absence of being has the same meaning as dependent arising (*pratītyasamutpāda*);[2] so this fault in the idea of devoidness does not make sense.

500 It is not merely that these dire consequences, as stated, are not relevant to our view, but more than that, the entire structure (*vyavasthāna*) of Buddhist doctrines becomes more intelligible. Expounding this Nāgārjuna said,

> 14 All things make sense for him for whom the absence of being makes sense. Nothing makes sense for him for whom the absence of being does not make sense.

For the one for whom the devoidness of self-existence in all things makes sense, for him everything (*sarvam etad*), in the sense in which we have explained it, makes sense. Why? Because we elucidate dependent arising as devoidness of self-existence.

As the *Anavataptahradāpasaṁkramaṇa Sūtra* has it: 'Whatever is born of conditions is not truly born; and it does not arise as self-existent. Whatever depends on conditions is said to be devoid of self-existence. Whoever comprehends the absence of self-existence is free of delusion.' As the *Prajñāpāramitā-sūtra* puts it: 'All putative elements of existence are devoid, because they lack self-existence.'

It follows that our devoidness makes sense, is luminous and relevant for him for whom dependent arising makes sense. And the four Buddhist truths make sense for him for whom

[1] P. 223, 1.

[2] This permits the translation of *pratītyasamutpāda* as 'the truth of things'.

dependent arising makes sense. Why is this? Because it is precisely what arises in dependence that constitutes unregenerate existence (*duḥkha*), not what does not arise in dependence. What arises in dependence, because not self-existent, is devoid of being. Given afflicted or unregenerate existence, it makes sense that it comes to be and ceases to be and that there is a way leading to its cessation. And so the clear grasp of unregenerate existence, the elimination of its arising, the intuitive experience of its cessation and the inner realization of the way, all make sense.

501 If the truths about unregenerate existence and the clear grasp, and so on, of them obtain, then the spiritual attainments (*phala*)[1] make sense. Given spiritual attainments it makes sense that there are those who are on the way. Given those who are on the way abiding in the spiritual attainments, the Buddhist community makes sense. If the Buddhist truths truly obtain then the Buddhist Truth (*dharma*) makes sense. Given the Buddhist Truth and the Buddhist community, the idea of an enlightened one makes sense too. Therefore the three jewels[2] make sense. All things whatsoever (*padārthāḥ sarve*), whether of this world or of the realm beyond which are realized in the Buddhist discipline, will make sense. Moral and immoral conduct and their consequences, spiritual well-being and downfall and all everyday practical transactions will make sense.

So it is that 'Everything makes sense for him for whom the absence of being makes sense.' For him for whom the devoidness of self-existence in all things makes sense, for him everything in the world, as we have explained it, makes sense (*yujyate*), that is, coheres in living sense (*saṁpadyate*). However, for one for whom devoidness, as we expound it, does not make sense, because he does not understand the dependent arising of all things, the entire world makes no sense. In what way it does not make sense Nāgārjuna will demonstrate in detail.

In sum, our case is flawless and is established without contradicting any principles. Your view is very unsubtle and shortsighted, contradicts principles and is full of difficulties. You are too obtuse to discern clear faults and merits.

[1] Cf. p. 225, 3.

[2] i.e. the Buddhist Truth, the community of monks, and the Buddha.

The unintelligibility of the opponent's concept

502 15 You, who bring down your own errors on us, though mounted on a horse, forget that you are.

It is as if someone mounted on a horse, but forgetting that he is, falsely accuses others of the crime of stealing it. Similarly, you, though mounted on the horse of the theory of devoidness – understood as the dependent arising of all things – do not perceive this because of your overhasty repudiation, and revile us.

Nāgārjuna explains what these faults of the opponent are, which he does not recognize in himself but accuses the proponent of devoidness of:

16 If you discern the true being of things[1] as their self-existence, then you must regard things as having no causes or conditions.

If you consider that things are, ontically (*vidyamāna*), self-existent, you ignore their causal conditions. You regard things, however differentiated into inner and outer, as having no causal conditions, as having ontically no causal conditions, as being beyond cause (*nirhetuka*). But if you suppose anything can be beyond causality,

503 17 You must reject the notions of cause and effect, of agent, means and act, of coming to be and ceasing to be and of spiritual attainment.

Why is that? If you suppose a water jug to be self-existent, what would be the function of the clay and the other causal conditions of such an ontic self-existent, as they would not be causal conditions. It is unintelligible for an effect like a water jug to have no cause (*hetu*). If there were no cause, then, as the potter's wheel and the other tools, the making of the water jug, the potter himself and the actual creation of a vessel in the shape of a water jug would be non-existent, coming to be and ceasing to be would be non-existent. But if nothing comes to be nor ceases to be how can there be spiritual attainment? If you suppose that things are self-existent you discard the entire set of notions having to do with cause and effect; thus, supposing things are self-exixtent, this entire set of notions can make no sense for you. For us, however, who hold the view that

[1] *Sadbhāva*. Candrakīrti glosses this as factual or ontic (*vidyamāna*).

things are devoid of self-existence, this entire set of notions is logically intelligible. Why is that? Because

Absence of being as the middle way

> 18 We interpret the dependent arising of all things as the absence of being in them. Absence of being is a guiding, not a cognitive, notion, presupposing the everyday. It is itself the middle way.

This dependent arising, which is the manifestation of seeds, consciousness and all such things in dependence on causal conditions, is the non-arising of things in the self-existent sense. And the non-arising of things in the self-existent sense is the
504 absence of being in things. As the illustrious one said: 'Whatever is born of conditions is not truly born; it does not arise as self-existent. Whatever depends on conditions is said to be devoid of self-existence. Whoever comprehends the absence of self existence is free of delusion.' And in the *Laṅkāvatāra Sūtra*, 'It being accepted, o Mahāmati, that nothing comes to be of itself, it is my teaching that all the putative elements of existence are devoid of self-existence', and so on. In the *Dvyardhaśatikā*, 'All putative elements of existence are devoid because, ontically, they are without self-existence.'

This very absence of self-existence is a guiding, not a cognitive, notion presupposing the everyday (*prajñapti-upādāya*).[1] Absence of self-existence itself, as it presupposes the everyday, is a guiding, not a cognitive notion. It is the components – wheels and so on – which, being presupposed, are, for practical purposes, referred to as 'a chariot' (*rathaḥ prajñapyate*). That to which the guiding expression refers, as it presupposes its own component parts, does not come to be self-existently. It is this not coming to be (*anutpatti*) self-existently (*svabhāvena*) which is absence of being. This absence, characterized as not coming to be self-existently, is known as the middle way. What does not come to be self-existently does not exist. But because what does not come to be self-existently cannot cease to be, it is not non-existent. Therefore, because it avoids the dual dogmas of existence and non-existence, the absence of being in things, understood to mean that all things without exception

[1] 'Everyday' is not in the text, but by analogy with the chariot, it is the everyday (*saṁvṛti*) world which the term *śūnyatā* must presuppose if it is to function effectively, as 'chariot' presupposes wheels, axle, and so on.

do not arise self-existently, is said to be the middle way or the middle path. It follows that the absence of being as a guiding, not a cognitive, notion which presupposes the everyday and which is the middle way, is the preferred interpretation of the dependent arising of all things.[1]

All elements of existence are devoid

505 Considering this in all its aspects:

> 19 There is no element of existence whatsoever which does not arise dependently; and so there is no element of existence whatsoever which is not devoid of self-existence.

There is absolutely no putative element of existence whatsoever which arises free of conditions. As is said in the *Catuḥśataka*: 'There is never non-dependent existence of anything whatsoever under any circumstances; again, there is never eternal existence of anything whatsoever under any circumstances. Infinite space and other non-composite elements are thought to be imperishable by ordinary people. Thoughtful people do not discern objects for such expressions as they are used ordinarily.' And the illustrious one said, 'The wise man comprehends the elements of existence as dependent; he does not take refuge in ultimate dogmas. He knows the elements of existence have causes and conditions; it is not the nature of the elements to be uncaused and without conditions.' That is to say, 'There is no element of existence whatsoever which does not arise dependently.'

As what arises in dependence is devoid of self-existence, there is no element of existence which is not devoid. Therefore our thought, that all elements of existence are devoid, is not open to the fault charged by our opponent. But he is the proponent of the view that things have self-existence.

Devoidness essential to the intelligibility of the four truths

> 20ab If all things are not devoid, nothing can come to be nor cease to be;

And, then, if there is neither coming to be nor ceasing to be, necessarily

[1] That is, of the way things truly are.

506 20cd It follows that, for you, the four Buddhist truths do not obtain.[1]

Why? Because,

21 How will unregenerate existence come to be if it is not dependent on conditions? Unregenerate existence is said to be perishable and what is perishable cannot have its being in itself.

If something is self-existent it cannot arise dependently; what does not arise dependently cannot be perishable. After all, a sky-flower, which does not exist ontically, is not perishable. The illustrious one said that unregenerate existence (*duḥkha*) was perishable. 'Whatever is perishable, is unregenerate existence.' And from the *Catuḥśataka*: 'Suffering, certain suffering is born of the perishable and there is no happiness in it. Therefore the perishable as such is known as unregenerate existence.'

If it is supposed that things are self-existent, there can be nothing perishable. Which is to say, on the supposition that there is self-existence in things, unregenerate existence makes no sense. Nor is it merely unregenerate existence that makes no sense; on the supposition that things are self-existent, its arising (*samudaya*) as well makes no sense. Nāgārjuna expounds this:

22 Why should something which exists in itself already be brought into existence once again? If devoidness of self-existence is repudiated unregenerate existence cannot come to be.

507 The thought is that unregenerate existence does arise, and therefore there is unregenerate existence, and, as is said, there is a cause of its arising. Therefore, if one repudiates the devoidness of unregenerate existence and supposes that it is self-existent, the idea of a cause of unregenerate existence is meaningless because there would be no purpose in its coming to be a second time. And so for one repudiating devoidness, arising does not make sense either.

Further, an end (*nirodha*) to unregenerate existence is not comprehensible either for one who supposes that unregenerate existence is self-existent.

Nāgārjuna expounds:

[1] Cf. p. 223, 1. Nāgārjuna turns the opponent's own objection into an argument against him.

23 There is no end to unregenerate existence which is self-existent. Because of your obsession with self-existence you preclude the possibility of cessation.

If unregenerate existence were self-existent, how could there be an end to it as self-existence does not terminate? Thus, because of your obsession with self-existence, having seized on the idea and persisting in it stubbornly, you preclude the possibility of an end to unregenerate existence.

Now Nāgārjuna expounds how the Buddhist path (*mārga*) as well is unintelligible for the exponent of the self-existence view.

24 The realizing of a path which exists in itself, is not intelligible. Again, a path which is to be realized cannot exist in itself as you think.

508 If all things were self-existent then the path too would be self-existent in the same sense; but a path is by definition unrealized. Why would one realize it a second time? As Nāgārjuna puts it, 'The realizing (*bhāvanā*) of a path which exists in itself is not intelligible.'

If you concede that a path is to be realized then indeed the Buddhist path could not be self-existent. The meaning is, because of the nature of effect and cause. Again the realization of the way is commended for the purpose of ending unregenerate existence and eradicating its origin. According to the argument developed, the proponent of the self-existence view must realize:

25 If there is no unregenerate existence and no origin or nor end to it, what way can there be leading to its cessation?

There can be no cessation of unregenerate existence because of whose cessation the way, as what is attained, is realized. It follows that the Buddhist path is not intelligible. In sum, the four Buddhist truths cease to exist for those who hold that things are self-existent.

Now Nāgārjuna expounds how, for such, there can be no clear knowledge, no overcoming, no inner acceptance, and no final realization of the Buddhist truths.

Devoidness essential to intelligibility of enlightenment

26 If the lack of clear knowledge is self-existent how can

there ever be knowledge? Surely what is self-existent is unchanging.

509 If it is supposed that at one time there is self-existent ignorance of unregenerate existence but that later there is perfect comprehension (*parijñāyate*) of it, that does not make sense. Why not? Because surely the self-existent is unchanging. Surely it is common experience that the self-existent is immutable and is not subject to change, like the heat of fire. As there can be no change in what is self-existent it is not logically possible that there can be knowledge of unregenerate existence of which there was, earlier, self-existent ignorance. Thus, perfect comprehension of unregenerate existence is not possible either.

And as the perfect comprehension of unregenerate existence is not possible, so:

> 27 Overcoming, final realization and inner realization of the path make as little sense for you as did perfect comprehension and the four spiritual attainments.

Overcoming (*prahāṇa*) of the origin of unregenerate existence and final realization (*sākṣātkaraṇa*) of its cessation are meant by the dual expression 'overcoming and realization'. 'Inner realization' (*bhāvanā*) is of the Buddhist path. It makes no sense because perfect comprehension of unregenerate existence is not possible for you. The eradication of an origin, which, because the self-existent is indestructible, is indestructibly self-existent, is not intelligible. Realization and attainment are to be understood in the same way.

It is not only perfect comprehension and so on which is not possible according to the theory of self-existence. For, 'the four spiritual attainments make as little sense as did perfect comprehension'.

As a self-existent perfect comprehension of an uncomprehended unregenerative existence does not make sense, so the attainment of having entered the stream, which earlier did not exist, cannot possibly exist later. As for the attainment of entering the stream, so, it should be recognized, there can be no attainments of once-returning, not-returning and enlightenment.

It is not merely that, like perfect comprehension, these spiritual attainments make no sense, but the realization (*adhigama*) of them makes no sense either.

510

> 28 How could it be possible, for one who holds to the self-existence of things, to realize a certain attainment which exists in itself as unrealized?

Because it is the nature of the self-existent not to be born nor to perish, it is not logically possible, if one assumes self-existence, that there should be subsequent realization of things whose inherent nature it was earlier to be unrealized.

> 29 If the attainments do not exist, those who strive for and exist in them do not exist. If the eight spiritual categories[1] do not exist, the Buddhist community does not exist.
>
> 30 If the four Buddhist truths do not hold there is no Buddhist Truth. If the Buddhist Truth and community do not exist, how can there be an enlightened one?

The meaning of these two verses is as explained previously.

Further, on the assumption of self-existence in things,

> 31 It follows for you that the enlightened person is not dependent on enlightenment. It follows for you that enlightenment is not dependent on an enlightened person.

511 If there were an ontic existent (*bhāva*) called a self-existent enlightened person, a *buddha*, he would not be dependent on enlightenment (*bodhi*), on awareness that is omniscient; he would not even be related to it. As was said, 'The self-existent is not created nor is it dependent on anything other than itself.' That is, there would be enlightenment without anyone being enlightened; enlightenment would have no basis and be unrelated to anyone becoming enlightened.

Further,

> 32 One whose inherent nature is to be unenlightened, can never, according to you, even though he strives to be awakened, achieve enlightenment in the career of the *bodhisattva*.[2]

This means that because being enlightened is self-existent, there could be no enlightenment for one whose nature is to be unenlightened, even though he strives for enlightenment in the true career of the *bodhisattva*, because it is impossible for one whose nature is unenlightened to alter fundamentally.

Devoidness essential to the intelligibility of moral action

Further,

[1] Cf. p. 225, 4. [2] Cf. p. 227, 1.

33 No one will ever achieve good or ill: what can be attained if things are not devoid of self-existence? The self-existent is not produced by action.

On the assumption of the self-existence of things, bringing about good or ill is not intelligible. What can be attained in the non-devoid? It is not logically possible to bring about anything which, by nature, is not devoid of self-existence, because the non-devoid is factually in existence.

Further,

512 34 Though, for you, there are moral consequences apart from a good or ill act; yet for you there are no moral consequences deriving from a good or ill act.

If a moral consequence (*phala*), whether desirable or undesirable, not deriving from a good or ill act, is self-existent, then it would exist regardless of good or ill. In so far as for you there are moral consequences without good or ill, then, for you moral consequences born of good or ill are not possible; the accumulation of good or ill merit would be meaningless. 'For you there are no moral consequences deriving from a good or ill act.'

However, if you imagine that moral consequences exist deriving from good or ill acts, Nāgārjuna explains that these cannot be non-devoid of self-existence (*aśūnya*).[1]

35 If, for you, moral consequences derive from good or ill acts, how can they, being produced from good or ill, be non-devoid?

The meaning is that they will be devoid of self-existence because produced in dependence, 'like a reflection'.

What is more, all personal everyday transactions (*saṁvyavahāra*) without exception, like going, doing, cooking, reading, standing, originate in dependence. If you consider them to exist in themselves then you repudiate the dependent arising of things; if you repudiate that then you preclude the possibility of all personal everyday transactions. Nāgārjuna expounds:

513 36 By precluding all personal everyday transactions, you preclude the absence of being in the dependent arising of things.

The word 'by' is adverbial, related to the verb 'preclude'.

[1] i.e. having their being in themselves, or, existing apart from cause in time.

Further,

> 37 For one repudiating the absence of being in things,
> nothing whatsoever could be achieved through action;
> an act would not need to be actually carried out and an
> agent would exist without effecting anything.

If things were not devoid of an inherent nature they would have to be self-existent. In that case nothing can be achieved by anyone, in any way, on behalf of what is self-existent, because it already exists. No one makes the openness of space. An act would not enact anything. There would be an act, the agent of which did not effect anything. But this is not the way things are; therefore things are not non-devoid of self-existence.

Further,

> 38 On the thesis of self-existence all things will be unborn,
> immutable and imperishable; they will be without
> diversity of states.

If things were self-existent, then, because the self-existent
514 is uncreated and ineluctable, the totality of creation would be unborn and imperishable; being unborn and imperishable all things would be unchanging. For the proponents of non-devoidness all things do not arise in dependence, are without a diversity of states and are unrelated to causal conditions.

It is said in the *Pitāputrasamāgama Sūtra*: 'If anything were non-devoid, Buddha would make no statement about it; for it is certain that whatever exists of and through itself is immutable and unvarying and neither grows nor diminishes.' And the *Hastikakṣya Sūtra* says: 'If there were a self-existent reality at all the Buddha and his followers would dwell there; but an immutable reality is not achieved and a wise man does not exist beyond all phenomena.'

515 For the theory of self-existence it is not only personal everyday transactions which are unintelligible, but also moral and religious striving. Nāgārjuna expounds:

> 39 If things are non-devoid there can be no eradication of
> the afflictions, no action to end unregenerate existence
> and no attainment of the unattained.

That is, if the totality of things is non-devoid – self-existent – then what is unattained is purely and simply unattained and no unattained moral fruition could ever be attained; any action to end unregenerate existence which had not existed previously could not exist now; an eradication of the afflictions which did not exist earlier could not exist later. All this being so it follows that, on the theory that each thing has its being in itself, everything in this world (*sarvam etad*) fails to make sense. So:

> 40 One who sees all things as arising in dependence, sees unregenerate existence and its origin, its cessation and the path to its cessation as they truly are.

That is, one who, with perfect clarity, sees absence of self-existence as the mark of the dependent arising of all the putative elements of existence, he sees the four Buddhist truths as
515.12 they really are in truth (*yathābhūta, tattvataḥ*).

XIX

Nirvāṇa

The problem

519 Some argue:

1 If everything is devoid of self-existence, nothing can come to be or cease to be; from the total extinction or cessation of what, then, is *nirvāṇa* thought to result?

Nirvāṇa has been described by the illustrious one as twofold for those persons who lead a chaste life, who are practising the discipline leading to perfect realization, and who are committed to living according to the Truth: namely, a *nirvāṇa* with a residual base and a *nirvāṇa* without a residual base.

On the one hand, *nirvāṇa* with residual base (*sopadhiśeṣa*) is conceived as resulting from the total extinction (*prahāṇa*) of the basic afflictions – ignorance, desire and the rest. What is called the base is adherence to personal existence, is being based in that. By the term base is meant the five possessive factors of personal existence which give rise to the existential fiction (*ātmaprajñapti*) of the personal self. The base is the residue. Only a base which is residual is a 'residual base'. *Nirvāṇa* with a residual base means continuing to exist conjoined with a residual base. What kind of *nirvāṇa* is this? It consists of nothing more than the bare factors of personal existence freed from the deceptive afflictions such as the belief in a substantial personal self; it is like a town from which all criminal gangs have been purged. That is *nirvāṇa* with a residual base.

520 In the second case, the *nirvāṇa* in which there are not even the bare factors of personal existence is *nirvāṇa* without a residual base (*nirupadhiśeṣa*). Where the residual base has vanished, it is comparable to a town from which all criminal gangs have been purged and which is itself destroyed.

In this connection it is said, 'The body has collapsed, ideas and perceptions gone. All feeling vanished, all dispositions quiescent and consciousness itself non-existent.' And thus, 'Through a body even to which one does not cling, one still has some feelings; *nirvāṇa* is the coming to an end of the discursive mind as of a light.'

So it is that *nirvāṇa* without residual base is attained by the cessation (*nirodha*) of the factors of personal existence.

How can this twofold *nirvāṇa* be made comprehensible? If there is to be *nirvāṇa*, both afflictions and the factors of personal existence must cease to be. However, if everything in the world is devoid of being (*śūnya*), nothing whatever can either come to be or cease to be. How then can afflictions and the factors of personal existence come to be, whose ceasing to be would constitute *nirvāṇa*? Hence things are self-existent (*vidyate svabhāva*).[1]

521 To this we reply: If we assume that things are self-existent, then

> 2 If everything in the world is *not* devoid of being, nothing can come to be or cease to be. From the total extinction or cessation of what, then, is *nirvāṇa* thought to result?

As the self-existent is ineluctable (*anapāyitva*), if the factors of personal existence and the afflictions are self-existent, how could there be cessation of them, a cessation which must precede *nirvāṇa*? For this reason it is the proponents of the reality of things (*svabhāvavādinaḥ*) for whom *nirvāṇa* is not logically possible. The proponents of the absence of being in things, however, do not argue for a *nirvāṇa* characterized as the cessation of the afflictions and the factors of personal existence and so they are not guilty of this error; it does not constitute a reproach for them.

Statement of the Mādhyamika position

But, if the proponents of the absence of being do not accept a *nirvāṇa* understood as the cessation of the afflictions and the factors of personal existence, how do they conceive the nature of *nirvāṇa*?

Nāgārjuna says,

> 3 *Nirvāṇa* is said to be what can neither be made extinct, nor realized, through action, what neither terminates nor is everlasting, what neither ceases to be nor comes to be.

That is, *nirvāṇa* is neither something which can be extirpated,

[1] Thus far the orthodox Buddhist opponent.

like desire, nor something which can be realized through action, like the fruit of moral striving; nor again something which terminates, like such things as the factors of personal existence, nor is it something imperishable like what is not devoid of being. *Nirvāṇa* is said to be what, in its own nature, neither comes to be nor ceases to be; its nature is the coming to repose, the stilling of all named things (*sarvaprapañcopaśama*).

If *nirvāṇa* is not of the nature of a named thing (*niṣprapañca*), what of the concept of the afflictions, whose elimination is
522 supposed to constitute *nirvāṇa*? What again, of the concept of the factors of personal existence, whose cessation is supposed to constitute *nirvāṇa*? So long as these conceptions (*kalpanā*) prevail, there is no attainment of *nirvāṇa*. It is only by the dissipation of all named things that it is attained.

Let it be, one might object, that in *nirvāṇa* there are no afflictions and no factors of personal existence; but then they exist prior to *nirvāṇa*, and from their dissipation there is *nirvāṇa*.

Our rejoinder to that is: This way of taking the problem should be abandoned because things which are real in themselves prior to *nirvāṇa* cannot be, at a later time, non-existent. For this reason this conception must be given up by those seeking *nirvāṇa*. Nāgārjuna will say,[1] 'The ontic range of *nirvāṇa* is the ontic range of the everyday world. There is not even the subtlest difference between the two.' This being so, it should be realized that in *nirvāṇa* there is no extinction of anything whatsoever, nor any cessation of anything whatsoever. *Nirvāṇa* is of the nature of the utter dissipation of reifying thought (*kalpanā*).[2] As it has been said by the revered one, 'There is no annihilation of the elements of existence; elements of existence which do not exist can never exist; if one reifies, thinking "this exists" or "this does not exist", coursing so, afflicted existence will not come to rest.'

The meaning of this verse is this: In the perfected state (*nirvṛti*) of *nirvāṇa* without residual base, there are none of the putative elements of existence, understood as individual life, actions and afflictions, nor any factors of personal existence, because they have totally disappeared. This is agreed to by
523 proponents of all schools. That is to say, the putative elements

[1] *Kārikā* 20, p. 260 and note 1.

[2] This is often taken to mean 'imaginings'. Throughout this passage it means attributing real existence to what words like *kleśa* and *skandha* refer to: it means reification. This is, in the Mādhyamika view, the aboriginal error.

of existence of the everyday world do not exist in the perfected state. They are like such things as the fear of snakes, as which rope is mistakenly perceived in the dark, but which vanish when there is light. Such things are never real. Nor do the putative elements of existence, understood as individual life, act, afflictions and such things, at any time whatsoever truly exist in the everyday world of birth and death (*saṁsārāvasthā*). The rope as it is in the darkness, is not, in reality (*svarūpataḥ*), a snake, because its factual, real (*sadbhūta*) snakeness is not apprehended by sight and touch either in darkness or in the light of day.

If it is asked, 'How, then, can there be an everyday world of birth and death (*saṁsāra*)?' The answer is: Things which do not really exist appear in fact to do so to ordinary, immature people who are in the grip of the illusory notions of 'me' and 'mine', just as non-existing hair, flies and so on do to those with diseased eyes. Buddha said, 'If one reifies, thinking "this exists" or "this does not exist" coursing so, afflicted existence will not come to rest.'

The assertion of being, the ontological thought that true being is found in individual things, is the view of the school of Jaimini, of Kaṇāda, of Kapila and of all the others right down to the Vaibhāṣikas. The assertion of non-being is the view of the cynics who are rooted in a way leading to calamity. There are the others,[1] the proponents of the non-existence of the states of past and future and of innate dispositions which are meaningfully related and intelligible, but who for the rest are proponents of being; and there are proponents of non-being who deny the ultimate reality of the empirical contents of the mind but who assert their contingent reality and who assert also an ultimate reality, and so are proponents both of being and of non-being.[2] For those coursing so, afflicted existence and the cycle of birth and death will not come to rest.[3]

524 There is the verse: 'A man suspecting he has taken poison faints even when there is no poison in his stomach. Swayed by the care of me and mine, eternally he comes and dies without real knowledge of his self.' In this sense it should be understood that in *nirvāṇa* there is no cessation nor extinction of

[1] The Sautrāntika school of Buddhism.

[2] The Yogācāra school of Buddhism: briefly, external objects are unreal, but consciousness is real.

[3] In this paragraph Candrakīrti discounts all the major philosophical views current in the Indian tradition at his time with respect to the problem of being and non-being.

anything whatever. And therefore *nirvāṇa* is nothing but the ending of all reifying thought (*sarvakalpanākṣayarūpam eva*). To quote the Ratnāvalī: '*Nirvāṇa* is not utterly non-existent, for then how could it be the guide and substance of a way (*bhāvanā*)? *Nirvāṇa* is said to be the end of the distinction between existence and non-existence.' To those who, not effectively understanding that *nirvāṇa* is the achievement of ending all reifying thought, falsely imagine *nirvāṇa* to be something which positively exists, or does not, or does both, or neither,[1] the following *kārikās* are addressed.

The first theory: nirvāṇa *is ontic*

> 4 *Nirvāṇa* is not ontic,[2] for then it would follow that it was characterized by decay and dissolution. For there is no ontic existent not subject to decay and dissolution.

525 In this matter there are some who are committed to the idea that *nirvāṇa* exists ontically (*bhāvataḥ*). They argue in this way. There is a real something (*padārtha*), which is of the very nature of cessation. It is the definite termination to a personal flow of consciousness (*saṁtāna*) which arose from actions deriving from the afflictions. It is analogous to a real dam in a stream of water. That is *nirvāṇa*. An element of existence which by nature is non-ontic is never observed to be an effective agent of this kind. But it is merely the end of the thirst to attain the experience of joy, that is called dispassion, cessation, or *nirvāṇa.*[3] A mere termination is not capable of being an ontic existent. As it has been said, '*Nirvāṇa* is release from the everyday mind, like the going out of a light.' But it is logically impossible that the going out of a light could be a real thing.

There is this reply to that:[4] It should not be thought that the termination of thirst is thirst-termination. Rather the end of thirst came about *in* something called *nirvāṇa* which is a real element of existence (*dharma*) and it is this that is properly thirst-termination. The light is merely a simile. This example should be understood to mean that the release from the everyday mind takes place *in* something which exists.

Nāgārjuna now investigates the theory that *nirvāṇa* can be determined as an ontic existent. *Nirvāṇa* is not an ontic existent. Why not? Because it would follow that it would be

[1] These four possibilities are discussed, and rejected one after the other in *Kārikās* 4 to 16, pp. 251 to 258.

[2] *Bhāva.*

[3] An interjection by the Sautrāntika school.

[4] Another Buddhist school, the Vaibhāṣika.

subject to decay and death, decay and death being invariably the character of ontic existence. Therefore, such could not be *nirvāṇa*. He means that that would make *nirvāṇa* like consciousness and the other factors of personal existence which are subject to decay and death. Explaining the impropriety of the attributes, decay and death, he said: 'no ontic existent is not subject to decay and dissolution'. Anything not subject to decay and dissolution is something which cannot possibly exist ontically for example the 'sky-flower', which is not subject to decay and dissolution.

Further:

526 5 If *nirvāṇa* were an ontic existent it would be compound, because no ontic existence whatsoever exists anywhere which is not compound.

If *nirvāṇa* were an ontic existent it would be compound (*saṁskṛta*)[1] like consciousness and the other factors of personal existence because these are ontically existent. Whatever is not compound cannot be an ontic existent as for example the horns of a donkey. Formulating this contrary proposition Nāgārjuna says: 'No ontic existent whatsoever exists anywhere which is not compound.' The expression 'anywhere' refers to place, time, or philosophical argument. The expression 'no ontic existent whatsoever' refers both to the subject realm and the object realm. This is his meaning.

Further:

6 If *nirvāṇa* is an ontic existent how then could it be beyond all dependence? No ontic existent whatsoever exists which is beyond all dependence.[2]

If, as our opponent thinks, *nirvāṇa* is an ontic existent then it would be dependent, that is, it would be based on its own set of causes. But *nirvāṇa* is not considered to be dependent in this way; rather it is considered to be beyond all dependence.

[1] Literally 'co-effected'. All phenomena are co-effected or arise conjointly. It was agreed among all Buddhist schools that *nirvāṇa* was not *saṁskṛta*.

[2] *Anupādāya* – literally 'non-dependent'. Upādāya is a key term in the Mādhyamika vocabulary. It covers all of the forms of relatedness, but emphasizes dependence. Often, as here, it means both causal dependence and logical dependence (a distinction Indian philosophers do not regard as essential); at times it probably means logical dependence only, in contrast to the term *pratyaya* which often means causal, or at least some form of real, temporal, dependence. The use of these two technical terms is not, however, in our sense, precisely consistent.

If *nirvāṇa* is an ontic existent, how could it be beyond all dependence? Beyond all dependence is precisely what it would not be, because of its being an ontic existent as in the case of consciousness and the other factors of personal existence. Nāgārjuna puts this into the form of the contrary proposition, saying: 'No ontic existent whatsoever exists which is beyond all dependence.'

The second theory: nirvāṇa *is ontically non-existent*

527 In this matter one might argue: If indeed *nirvāṇa* cannot be an ontic existent because of the unacceptable consequence which has been urged, then *nirvāṇa* can only be non-existent because it is merely the end of personal existence (*janma*) which arises from the afflictions. We reply that this too is illogical:

> 7 If *nirvāṇa* is not an ontic existent will it be an ontic non-existent? But if there is no ontic existent, there is no ontic non-existent either.

If *nirvāṇa* is not accepted as an ontic existent, that is, if '*Nirvāṇa* is an ontic existent' is repudiated, does *nirvāṇa* then become an ontic non-existent? The meaning is that *nirvāṇa* will not be an ontic non-existent. To say *nirvāṇa* is the non-existence of the afflictions and personal existence would mean however that *nirvāṇa* was merely the perishability of personal existence and the afflictions. Therefore, to say, 'It is merely perishability and nothing else which is the non-existence of personal existence and the afflictions' would entail that *nirvāṇa* would be mere perishability. But this is not commonly accepted. To say, 'Liberation follows naturally without effort' does not make sense.[1]

Further:

> 8 If *nirvāṇa* is an ontic non-existent, how could *nirvāṇa* in that case be beyond all dependence? Because what is ontically non-existent is not beyond all dependence.

Here 'ontic non-existence' or 'perishability' convey meaning (*prajñapyate*) only by their logical dependence (*upādāya*) on the ontically existent; because donkeys' horns and such things are not perceived to be perishable. A subject of predication (*lakṣya*) has meaning only in dependence on its predicates
528 (*lakṣaṇa*), and predicates have meaning only as based in a

[1] *Nirvāṇa* is not merely the natural termination of a natural process.

subject of predication. That is, predicates and the subject of predication are meaningful only in so far as they are reciprocally dependent. How could there be perishability without something ontically existent as the subject of predication? Therefore 'ontically non-existent' too conveys meaning only in logical dependence. And so, if *nirvāṇa* is ontically non-existent, how could it, in that case, be beyond all dependence? Dependent is exactly what *nirvāṇa* would be, if it is ontically non-existent; it is like the argument concerning perishability. Elucidating this very point clearly, Nāgārjuna said, 'Because what is ontically non-existent is not beyond all dependence.'

But if the ontically non-existent is not beyond all dependence, how can such ontically non-existent things as the son of a barren woman be dependent? Who said that such things as the son of a barren woman are ontically non-existent? It was said earlier: 'If something is not established as ontically existing, the ontically non-existent cannot be established. It is being predicatively other than an ontic existent which people call ontic non-existence.'[1] And so there is no ontic non-existence of such things as the son of a barren woman.

There is a verse about this: 'Space, rabbits' horns and the son of a barren woman are spoken of as unreal, as phantasies concerning ontic existents.' Here too, it is to be understood that these are merely imagined contradictions (*kalpanā pratiṣedhamātra*) of ontic existence but are not conceptions of the ontically non-existent because nothing real corresponds to them. 'The son of a barren woman' is literally nothing but mere words (*śabdamātra*). The object of this expression is never perceived as something which could be either ontically existent or non-existent. How could it make sense to think in terms of ontic existence and non-existence for something which by its very nature cannot be experienced (*upalabhyate*)?[2] Therefore the son of a barren woman is not to be thought of as ontically non-existent. And so it has been established that there is no ontic non-existent which exists beyond all dependence.

The Mādhyamika principle re-stated

Here one might interject: If *nirvāṇa* is neither an ontic existent nor an ontic non-existent what then is it? The reply of the revered, perfected ones runs:

[1] P. 158, 5.

[2] A self-evident principle in Mādhyamika; from it the profoundest consequences follow.

529 9 That which, taken as causal or dependent, is the process of being born and passing on, is, taken non-causally and beyond all dependence, declared to be *nirvāṇa.*

The expression 'process of being born and passing on' means either merely arising and passing away, or the succession of birth and death. This process of being born and passing on may be understood as based on a complex of causes and conditions (*hetupratyaya*) as the long and the short; or may be understood as things being dependent on what is outside themselves, like light from a lamp or a sprout from a seed. In any case it is certain that whether understood as dependent on something outside itself (*upādāya*) or as originating from causes (*pratītya*) it is the ceasing to function (*apravṛtti*) of this continuous round of birth and death, due to its being taken as uncaused or as beyond dependence, that is said to be *nirvāṇa*. However, what is nothing more than a ceasing to function cannot be conceived of as either ontically existent or non-existent. Thus *nirvāṇa* is neither ontically existent nor ontically non-existent.[1]

Again there are those for whom character dispositions (*saṁskāras*) continue through successive lives. Their view is that origination and destruction are rigidly dependent on causes and that the absence of cause, that is, of these character dispositions, is said to be *nirvāṇa.*

Or there are those for whom it is the person (*pudgala*) which persists through successive lives. For these the person is indefinable either as perishable or imperishable. Being born and passing on is based on the person as substratum and it
530 functions only as so dependent. This being born and passing or., which functions only in dependence as a substratum, in the moment it no longer so functions, being no longer dependent, is known as *nirvāṇa.*

As the mere ceasing to function of either the person or the character dispositions cannot be conceived as either existent or as non-existent, it follows that it makes sense that *nirvāṇa* is neither existent nor non-existent.

Further:

10 The teacher[2] enjoined the abandonment of both

[1] As this definition fits all fictions – sky-flowers, and so on – equally well, how tell them from *nirvāṇa*? In Mādhyamika thought fictions are 'mere words', inefficacious in striving for enlightnment, whereas *nirvāṇa is* efficacious, being the notion which conduces to enlightenment.

[2] Buddha.

existence and non-existence. Therefore it makes sense that *nirvāṇa* is neither existent nor non-existent.

Concerning this the *sūtra*[1] says: 'All those, o monks, who long for deliverance from what is real by means of something which is itself either real or unreal, they lack perfect insight. Both these are to be renounced: a longing for something real or existent and a longing for mere non-existence.' But it is not *nirvāṇa* that the illustrious one urged should be given up; it is rather not to be given up. 'Therefore, it makes sense that *nirvāṇa* is neither existent nor non-existent.'

The third theory: nirvāṇa *is both an ontic existent and an ontic non-existent*

Then there are those[2] for whom *nirvāṇa* is of the nature of the ontically non-existent because personal existence and the afflictions do not exist in *nirvāṇa*. Yet *nirvāṇa* itself has the formal character of an existent because of the nature of such. Therefore it is both existent and non-existent. For those for whom it is of the nature of both, *nirvāṇa* is not logically possible. Expounding this Nāgārjuna said,

531 11 If *nirvāṇa* were both existent and non-existent then final release would be both existent and non-existent, and that does not make sense.

If *nirvāṇa* were of the nature of both the ontically existent and non-existent then final release (*mokṣa*) would be both ontically existent and non-existent. Hence both the reality of character dispositions in a personal existence and their disappearance would constitute final release. But it is not intelligible that character dispositions as such are the final release; and that is why Nāgārjuna says, 'that does not make sense'.

Further:

12 If *nirvāṇa* were both existent and non-existent then it could not be beyond all dependence because both the existent and the non-existent are dependent.

If *nirvāṇa* were of the nature of both the ontically existent and non-existent then it would presuppose a dependence on a complex of causal conditions, that is, it would not be beyond

[1] Possibly *Udāna*, iii, 10.

[2] The Vaibhāṣika school presumably, which provided the first theory also.

all dependence. Why? Because both the ontically existent and non-existent are dependent. If it is agreed that the ontically non-existent is dependent on the ontically existent for its meaning and the ontically existent is dependent on the non-existent for its meaning, then both of these, the existent and non-existent, are clearly dependent and not beyond all dependence. This is the result if *nirvāṇa* were of the nature both of the existent and non-existent. But neither is this the case nor does it make sense.

Further:

> 13 If *nirvāṇa* were both existent and non-existent how could it be uncompounded, as both the existent and non-existent are compounded?

532 That is, the ontically existent is compounded because it is in conjunction with the complex of its own causal conditions; the ontically non-existent is compound because it has its being in conjunction with dependence on the ontically existent and because of the doctrine that death and old age are dependent on birth. And so, if *nirvāṇa* were to be in its true nature both existent and non-existent then it would not be uncompounded, but would be rather compounded. And because it cannot be thought of as compounded it is not intelligible that *nirvāṇa* is, in its true nature (*svarūpa*), both existent and non-existent.

Well, if *nirvāṇa* itself could not be, in its true nature, both existent and non-existent could the ontically existent and non-existent both be in *nirvāṇa*?

But neither is this intelligible. Why? Because:

> 14 How could *nirvāṇa* be both existent and non-existent? Both cannot exist in the identical place and respect simultaneously, as with vision and darkness.

There is no co-existence in one self-identical *nirvāṇa* of two mutually incompatibles as the existent and the non-existent. Hence the question: 'How could *nirvāṇa* be both existent and non-existent?' The thought is that it could most emphatically not be.

The fourth theory: nirvāṇa *is neither an existent nor a non-existent*

How it could make sense to say that *nirvāṇa* is neither existent nor non-existent, Nāgārjuna now proceeds to expound, saying,

15 There is the dictum, '*Nirvāṇa* is neither existent nor non-existent.' If the existent and the non-existent were established fact, this dictum would be proved.

533 If there were something called 'the existent' then, by distinguishing *nirvāṇa* negatively from it, one could make the claim (*kalpanā*), '*Nirvāṇa* is *not* an existent.' If there were something which was 'the non-existent', then by distinguishing *nirvāṇa* negatively from it, *nirvāṇa* would be definitely not non-existent. Where however, there is neither 'an existent' nor 'a non-existent', there can be no negation of them. Therefore the claim that *nirvāṇa* is neither existent nor non-existent is clearly logically impossible and does not make sense.

Further:

16 If *nirvāṇa* is emphatically neither existent nor non-existent, by whom is it claimed, 'it is neither existent nor non-existent'?

If it is argued that *nirvāṇa* is neither of the nature of the existent nor of the nature of the non-existent, by whom, in such case, is it claimed that *nirvāṇa* is such as to have the nature of neither of these? By whom is it grasped, by whom revealed? Is there someone then in *nirvāṇa* so constituted that he can succeed in this? Or is there not? If there is, then one would hold that there is a personal self (*ātman*) even in *nirvāṇa*. But this one does not accept, because there is no self detached from the factors of personal existence. But if there is not, by whom is it determined that *nirvāṇa* is of such a nature? And if one says that the one who so determines it is still based in the everyday world (*saṁsāra*), such a one must determine this either by conceptual or by intuitive knowledge. If it is supposed that he does it by conceptual knowledge (*vijñāna*), that is illogical. Why? Because conceptual knowledge is the grasping (*ālambana*) of objects as signs (*nimitta*), and in *nirvāṇa* there are no objects as signs whatsoever. So *nirvāṇa* is not grasped through conceptual knowledge as such.

Nor is it known by intuitive knowledge (*jñāna*). Why? Because *nirvāṇa* supervenes in virtue of an intuition which becomes aware of the absence of being in things. And it is precisely the nature of such an intuition that it does not arise ontically (*anutpādarūpa*). How can the statement, '*Nirvāṇa* is neither existent nor non-existent' be comprehended by what does not, in its essential nature, exist? For intuition of the
534 absence of being, by its very nature, is beyond the world of

named things. Therefore that '*Nirvāṇa* is neither existent or non-existent' cannot be claimed by anyone at all. This statement is unintelligible as it cannot be comprehended, nor clarified, nor made.

Rejection of the four theories in principle: the Mādhyamika conclusion

Nāgārjuna, explaining that, as the four theories do not obtain in any way with respect to *nirvāṇa*, so they do not obtain with respect to the perfected one who has attained *nirvāṇa*, said,

> 17 One does not conjecture if the illustrious one still exists subsequent to his decease, or does not exist, or both exists and does not exist.

As was said earlier: 'One who holds the crude notion that the perfectly realized one "exists" must speculate "he does not exist" after his enlightenment.'[1] In this sense one cannot conjecture whether the perfected one exists or does not exist subsequent to his decease; then, because neither of these alternatives obtains one cannot conjecture that both do; and because both do not obtain, one cannot conceive or conjecture that neither obtains.

It is not only concerning the illustrious one after his decease that one does not conjecture in the fourfold way, but as well,

> 18 One does not conjecture if the illustrious one is existent during his lifetime or is non-existent, is both or neither.

535 Why this is neither to be argued for nor conjectured was expounded in 'The Perfectly Realized One'.[2]

Precisely for this reason:

> 19 There is no specifiable difference whatever between *nirvāṇa* and the everyday world; there is no specifiable difference whatever between the everyday world and *nirvāṇa*.

This is why one does not conjecture of the illustrious one that he exists or does not exist, neither while living nor even after achieving ultimate freedom (*parinirvṛta*). And so there is no specifiable difference at all between the everyday world

[1] P. 203, 13 [2] Chapter XVI, pp. 203–4.

(*saṁsāra*) and *nirvāṇa* with respect to one another, because, on being thoroughly investigated, they are basically of the same nature. And the illustrious one has said the same thing. 'The everyday world, o monks, which consists of birth, decay and death, is the highest existence.' That is comprehensible just because there is no specifiable difference between the everyday world and *nirvāṇa*.

Thus,

> 20 The ontic range[1] of *nirvāṇa* is the ontic range of the everyday world. There is not even the subtlest difference between the two.

But it is not only the indistinguishability of the everyday world from *nirvāṇa* that makes it impossible to ontologize the notions of termination and beginning,[2] but also,

536 21 The theories concerning *nirvāṇa* as existence after decease have to do with the termination and beginninglessness of existence, and all presuppose the notions of termination and beginning.

These theories are impossible because the everyday world and *nirvāṇa* are in essence one (*ekarasatva*), namely, to be, by nature (*prakṛti*), at peace (*śāntatva*). These fourfold views proceed on the analogy of the notion 'after his decease' in this way: 'the perfected one exists after his decease', 'the perfected one does not exist after his decease', 'the perfected one both exists and does not exist after his decease', 'the perfected one neither exists nor does not exist after his decease'. These four views presuppose an analogy between decease and *nirvāṇa*.

And then there are these views concerning the end of personal existence (*loka*):[3] 'existence has an end', 'existence is without end', 'existence is both with and without end', 'existence neither has nor has not an end'. These views are based on the supposition that there is such a thing as 'end'. In the first case the theory supports the view that personal existence has an end, supposing existence has an end because of not believing in the future birth of world and of the self. Similarly,

[1] *Koṭi*. Frequently translated 'limit'. The argument concerns the beginning and end of personal existence (*loka*) but this is not merely an argument concerning limits in time; it concerns the nature of *saṁsāra* and *nirvāṇa* which is such that theories using the concepts of beginning and end are simply inapposite.

[2] I.e. termination of *saṁsāra* and beginning of *nirvāṇa*.

[3] Not 'the' world, but 'world' in the sense of personal existence, i.e. existence interiorized by the assumption of a self.

believing in future birth, the argument is that existence is without end. Both believing and not believing the argument proceeds in its both-and mode. By double negation the argument then runs 'existence is not either with or without an end'.

The four arguments which presuppose the notion of a beginning are: 'existence is without a beginning' (*śāśvata*), 'existence has a beginning', 'existence both has and has not a beginning', 'existence neither has nor has not a beginning'. In this case, believing in a previous birth of personal existence or the self, the argument is that existence is without a beginning; but not believing in this, that existence has a beginning; both believing and not believing, the argument is that it both has and has not a beginning; neither believing nor not believing, that it neither has nor has not a beginning. These arguments are based on the notion of 'beginning'.

537 How could these theories be made intelligible? If anything whatsoever were real in itself then, by ontologizing the categories 'existent' and 'not existent', these theories would apply. As, however, it has been made clear that there is no specifiable difference between *nirvāṇa* and the everyday world, so:

> 22 As elements of existence are, as such, devoid of being, what is there which can be without an end, or have an end? What can both have and not have an end, neither have an end nor not have an end?
>
> 23 What is self-identical, what is other? What is without beginning, what has beginning? What both has and has not beginning? What has neither beginning nor no beginning?

These fourteen insoluble problems (*vyākṛtavastūni*) are not intelligible if you suppose that things have self-existent natures. It should not be forgotten that, one who, having foisted (*adhyāropya*) on things this notion that they have self-existent natures, affirms or denies it and, having fabricated these theories, insists upon them stubbornly, will be hindered, by this stubborn insistence, on the narrow path which leads to the city of *nirvāṇa* and will be fettered in the cycle of unregenerate existence.

At this point one might object: If *nirvāṇa* is as you negatively define it, then the Truth propounded by the illustrious one for the purpose of achieving the liberation of all existence will have been created to no purpose. This Truth, which is suited as the answer in any walk of life, was created by the illustrious one who, in virtue of his infinite compassion, attends with love all beings of the three worlds as one attends a beloved only son, who incontrovertibly knows the inner disposition of the entire creation as it really is and who follows the mass of creatures in their wanderings.

We rejoin: If there were anything at all called 'Truth'
538 (*dharma*) which in its own nature was absolute (*svabhāvarūpataḥ*), there would be those who were the bearers of this Truth and there would be some ultimate being called the illustrious Buddha, its teacher. This is the way it would be.

As however,

> 24 Ultimate beatitude is the coming to rest of all ways of taking things,[1] the repose of named things; no Truth has been taught by a Buddha for anyone, anywhere.

How can the above objection affect us? Because here the meaning is that the very coming to rest, the non-functioning, of perceptions as signs of all named things, is itself *nirvāṇa*. And this coming to rest being, by its very nature, in repose, is the ultimate beatitude (*śiva*). When verbal assertions (*vācas*) cease, named things are in repose; and the ceasing to function of discursive thought is ultimate beatitude. Again, the coming to rest of named things by the non-functioning of the basic afflictions, so that personal existence ceases, is ultimate beatitude. The coming to rest of named things as a result of abandoning the basic afflictions and hence of totally extirpating innate modes of thought (*vāsanā*) is ultimate beatitude. Again the coming to rest of named things through not seizing on objects of knowledge or on knowledge itself, is ultimate beatitude.[2]

When the illustrious Buddhas are in *nirvāṇa*, the ultimate beatitude, which is the coming to rest of named things as such,
539 they are like kingly swans in the sky, self-soaring in space or in the nothingness of space on the twin wings of accumulated merit and insight; then, it should be known, that, because they do not perceive objects as signs, no rigid 'Truth' whatsoever either concerning bondage or purification has been taught either among or for any gods or men whatsoever.

As it is said in the *Tathāgataguhya Sūtra*, 'During that night,

[1] *Sarvopalambhopaśama*. It is not merely that ways of *thinking* about things change in *nirvāṇa*, but that the everyday way of *perceiving*, or '*taking*', things ceases to function.

[2] This paragraph, Candrakīrti's pithiest account of *nirvāṇa*, turns on the notion of 'the coming to rest of named things' (*prapañcopaśama*), as though the turmoil of a world in time were a distortion arising from human passions.

o Śāntamati, in which the perfected one became perfectly enlightened with the unsurpassed, perfect enlightenment, during the night in which he passed totally into *nirvāṇa*, not one syllable was uttered nor used by the perfected one, neither did he address anyone, nor will he. Yet all creatures, according to their propensities, perceive the voice of the perfected one as it issues forth in the various dialects of their homelands; for them it takes special forms, "this revered one is teaching this doctrine for our benefit", or, "we are hearing the doctrine of the perfected one". But, in truth, the perfected one indulges neither in ontologizing thought nor in phantasies because, o Śāntamati, a perfected one is freed from all ontologizing thought, all flights of phantasy, all innate thought patterns, and from everything with name.' To quote, 'Inexpressible, beyond language are the elements of existence, tranquil, pure and devoid of being; one who knows them so is called a Bodhisattva, a Buddha.'

But, one might object, if the Buddha has taught no truth at all to anyone whatsoever at any time, how is it that the various scriptural admonitions have been taken as meaningful?

We rejoin: This arises only from the imagination of people who are dreaming and who are deep in the slumber of ignorance. 'This revered one, lord of gods, demons and men in all the three worlds, has taught this doctrine for our sakes', they think. The illustrious one said, 'The perfected one has his
540 being as a reflection of the pure, passionless truth; he is not ultimately real in himself nor is he perfected; he is beheld as a reflection in all worlds.' This is explained in detail in the treatise on *The Secret of the Sayings of the Perfected One.*

And so, as there is no true doctrine concerning *nirvāṇa*, how can the existence of *nirvāṇa* depend on the existence of such a doctrine? Therefore it is established that even *nirvāṇa* does not exist (*nāsti*). It was said by the illustrious one: '*Nirvāṇa* is no-*nirvāṇa* the lord of existence taught; a knot tied by infinitude itself and loosed even by the same.'

And again, 'O illustrious one, an enlightened one cannot arise for those who believe that elements of existence come to be and cease to be. O illustrious one, there is no final triumph over everyday existence for those who search persistently for *nirvāṇa* as something existent. Why? O illustrious one, *nirvāṇa* is the cessation of all perceptions as signs, the coming to rest of all activity overt and covert.

541 'Therefore they are deluded people who, having taken up the spiritual life in some popular religious order, have fallen

into a heretical view and persistently seek for *nirvāṇa* as existent – as oil of sesame is pressed from sesame seeds or butter churned from milk. Those who strain for a *nirvāṇa* as the everlasting extinction of all elements of existence, these I say are self-deluded heretics. The saintly wise man, one truly realized, does not bring about either the coming to be or the ceasing to be of any element of existence whatever; nor does he claim to possess or to indubitably cognize any element of existence whatever – ' and so on.

Glossary

agṛhīta uncomprehended; incomprehensible
atīta what is past; the past
advaya non-duality; absence of pairs of opposites; an indicator of the truth of things
(sam)adhigama attainment, realization
adhipateya decisive factor, one of the four types of causation examined
adhyāropa foisting distorting ideas onto things; especially the transfer or imputation of the idea of entitative existence to everyday 'things'. Cf. *samāropa*
adhvā a sector of a trajectory or traverse
adhvajāta path of movement; trajectory
anantara immediately preceding (factor), one of four types of causal condition
anapāya indefeasible; ineluctable
anapekṣa unrelated; independent
anavasthā groundlessness in an argument, i.e. infinite regress
anavasthāyitva instability; changeableness
anāgata what is not yet realized; the future
anātman lack of an inherent self-nature
anitya non-permanence, a characteristic of everything ontic
a-niścaya a negative assertion making a cognitive claim
anutpatti non-arisal in time, a corollary of dependent origination
anubhava experience; unmediated knowledge, denied, of course, by Mādhyamika
anumāna inference, one of the traditional means of valid knowledge; also an entire argument
anupalabdha not experienced; inexperienciable
anupalambha having no sense of; not perceiving
anupaśyana contemplation; way of regarding
anupādāya beyond dependence; cf. note 2, p. 252
anta end (not in space but) of individual existence in time; an extreme view, dogma
anya (wholly) other; really discrete
anyatva otherness (definitional and entitative)

anyathā otherwise; differently
anyathātva otherwiseness, i.e. becoming other; alteration
anyathābhāva the being or becoming of otherwiseness, i.e. alteration
aparokṣa not mediated
apavāda verbal denial of existence to something which has been asserted to exist
apekṣa any relation; (discursive or real) dependence
apratītya non-dependent, either logically or really or both
a-pravṛtti the ceasing to function as
a-prasaṅga what does not follow logically
abhāva non-existent; not ontic; a non-entity; what can be negatively predicated of *bhāva*
abhijñā supernatural power achieved through the discipline of meditation
abhidhātavya what is to be designated by words
abhiniveśa stubbornness; pertinaceous holding to a view
abhyupagama presupposition; acceptance of something as real
ayoniśa uncaused; groundless (real and logical)
avasthita determinate; constituted; invariable (of time)
avācya indefinable
avācyatā the inexpressible (in a strictly discursive or logical sense)
avidyamāna non-factual; inexistent
avidyā primal ignorance, i.e. unawareness of the truth, either the Buddhist or Mādhyamika truth depending on the context, but most frequently the deeply buried assumption that the world really consists of entities in temporal, spatial and causal relationship
aviparīta inerrant; incontrovertible; veritable (common description of the Buddhist path)
avisaṁvādaka free of contradiction
avyākṛtavastūni the (fourteen) topics on which the Buddha declined to take a stand (cf. pp. 202ff); they are not so much unanswerable questions, as non-questions
avyāvartana ineluctable, incontrovertible
aśubha what is not good, i.e. bad
asat non-existent
asattva non-existence
asaṁbaddha incoherent; not meaningful
astitva ‘it is’-ness; is-ness; being-ness; being
asthita variable (of time)
asvabhāva not self-existent
ahamkāra the pervasive I–me sense which sustains the everyday world and which is delusively made into an object and taken to be the ‘self’. It is inseparable from *mamakāra*, the pervasive sense of mine
āgama (1) approaching, arriving; (2) authoritative (traditional) scripture

ātman inherent self-nature, most often, but not always, with reference to the (putative) self of a person; subject of perceiving, thought to exist independently of the activity of perceiving; Mādhyamika holds that *ātman* is never experienced; it is a false conceptualization of the I-me sense

āpadyate it follows or ensues, as of a consequence in an argument

āyatana basis of cognition, both sense faculties and their corresponding objects

ārya a wise man, i.e. one who has inseen the Buddhist truths, especially in the Mādhyamika sense; often a synonym for *yogī*

āryasatya one of the four 'truths for the wise', i.e. the truths concerning *duḥkha*, the Buddhist truths (the 'holy' truths)

ālambana objective basis ('cause') of perception; the seizing on something in perception

āśraya base, substrate, to which predicates may be assigned, or which is the peculiar ontic *sine qua non* of another thing

itaretara reciprocal; mutual

iṣyamāna being conceived or postulated; one who is conceiving or postulating

ukta asserted as a considered view

(an)utccheda (non)terminating in time

utcchedadarśana nihilism or naturalism; the view that all things perish without re-birth. Mādhyamika is at pains to distinguish itself from this view

(an)utpāda (non)arising in time; the weakest possible sense of 'coming to be'

utpatti (caused) origination; arisal in time

upacāra figure of speech; metaphor

upapatti appropriateness (of an argument); conclusive argument; reasoning; Mādhyamika denies that there can be an *upapatti* of anything in the world; yet the higher truth is said to be distinguishable by *upapatti*

upapattiniyukta not in accord with reason

upapattiviruddha contrary to reason, the basis for condemnation of any view

(na)upapadyate (it does not happen) it happens; it is (not) possible; it is (not) thinkable; it is (not) intelligible. Perhaps the commonest technical term in the *Prasannapadā*; it is the ultimate condemnation of an argument or point of view. Cf. *(a)yuktam*

upalabhyate taken to be real in perception or in pragmatic belief; immediately experienced

upalabdhi, upalambha perception; taking things in a certain way

upalambhopaśama the coming to rest of ways of taking things
upaśama serene coming to, or being at, rest, said of the manifold of named things when it enters into the middle way, i.e. into the world of an enlightened one
upasthāna moving into the presence of; penetration
upādātā appropriator; appropriative perceiver
upādāna seizing on; appropriating; appropriative perceiving; the five *skandhas*
upādāya based upon, presupposing, in both a discursive and a real sense
upāya the practical wisdom to make the truth relevant to any situation
upālambha finding fault with; refutation

ekatva identity ('one-ness')
(an)ekārtha (non)self-identical; (non)invariant; (not) of one meaning; (non)indifferentiable

karaṇa (the act of) effecting; instrumental; a means
karaṇatva cause; efficaciousness
kartā the doer, agent
kartṛka of or by a productive agent
karma act; deed; effect; object
kalpanā elaborative thought-activity; the elaborations themselves, which imply an (usually unrecognized) ontological claim. The dissipation of *kalpanā* is said to be *nirvāṇa.* Conception or thesis
kāraka doer; agent subject; productive agent
kāraṇa material cause; direct cause
kārya what is to be done; effect
kurvāṇa effecting something actually, i.e. carrying out an act
kṛtaka made, artifacted, 'created', said of all things that arise in time from causes
kevala abstract; constructed by thought
kriyā generative force (in causal explanation); the performance of an act; an act; (a specific) activity
kleśa affliction. There are varying lists but Nāgārjuna invariably deals with only three which appear to be structurally self-contained: *rāga* – possessive desire; *dveṣa* – aversion; *moha* – the illusion that everyday things are ontological entities. Bondage takes the form of an individual blend of these three
kṣaya wasting away; coming to an end
khapuṣpa sky-flower; along with 'horns of a rabbit', 'horns of a donkey', 'son of a barren woman', the commonest paradigm of mere verbal sound which refers to nothing real; '*nirvāṇa*' also refers to nothing real (ontic); so the interpretation of Mādhyamika turns on this difference

(a)gata (not) gone; (not) traversed
gati going, walking
gantavya space to be traversed
gantā one moving; mover; what is in motion
gantum to move, i.e. motion
gamana moving; movement
gamikriyā the activity 'motion'; motive activity
gambhīra deep, profound; frequently used of Buddha's words to imply a hidden or secondary level of meaning
gamyate 'it is being moved', i.e. it moves, or, movement
gamyamāna the act of being in motion or of being traversed; being in traverse
gṛhyate perceiving or taking something to be as . . . (often falsely)
graha grasping for, seizing on, an idea; belief; holding to a meaning; comprehension
(sam)grahana the concrete act of believing something
grahītā the one who believes

cakṣu the eye; eyesight
citta mind as enduring entity apart from its 'contents'; consciousness. Cf. *vijñāna*; the faculty and activity of discursive thought
caitasa equivalent of *caitta*
caitta content of the mind (*citta*)

tattva not 'ultimate reality', as Mādhyamika repudiates such notions; rather the truth of things, i.e. the way the world gives itself to one on the middle way; the way things are in truth
tattvacintā understanding or conception of the way things really are
tathatā the so-ness or thus-ness of things, i.e. the way things are in truth
tathāgata a perfectly realized one; defined as the truth of all things, as the one of perfect attainment, a term commonly reserved for the historical Buddha
(a)tathya (not) real in the everyday sense
tarka disputation which assumes there is proof in argument
timira darkness; partial blindness due to a morbid inflammation of the eye; the most frequent analogy for the normal human condition
tulya of the same kind; comparable
tṛṣṇa thirst for existence; in the context of the four *āryan* truths it is given as the origin of all afflicted existence

darśana the act of seeing; vision both as sense perception and as ultra-rational intuition *diśyate* sometimes explicit, discursive teaching, presupposing the possibility of conceptual explanation. Sometimes a pointing to, an indirect teaching

duḥkha the unenlightened state, unregenerate existence coterminous with primal ignorance (*avidyā*) and the everyday (*saṁvṛti*); afflicted existence in contrast to *nirvāṇa*

dūṣaṇa vitiating faultiness; inadequacy

dṛṣṭi a way of looking at things; a thesis in metaphysics; an ideology

deśa space

doṣa a (logical) flaw or difficulty; undesirable, often unacceptable consequences (mostly, but not always, logical) of advancing a thesis

doṣaprasaṅga the entailment of (usually) logical faults; discursive absurdity; dire consequence (of a point of view) maybe because heretical, maybe because an affront to common sense

draṣṭavya object of vision

draṣṭā the one who sees; the subject of the act of seeing

dvaya duality; pairs of opposites, a pervasive mark of the everyday

dveṣa aversion ('hatred') one of the three basic afflictions; correlated to what one holds to be bad

dharma a many-faceted term. Most frequently one of the several score of the (putative) 'elements of existence', the ultimate, simple reals propounded by the Buddhist schools Mādhyamika is attacking. Also attribute; good; good deed; and of course the Buddhist Truth

dharmatā the quintessential nature of the *dharmas*; the truth of things

dhātu primal element; there are six: earth, air, water, fire, space and consciousness

(a)nānārtha (in) variant; (not) of various meanings

nāstika a naturalist or 'nihilist'; one who holds that the perishability of all things is the truth of things

nāstitā, nāstitva is not-ness; non-being; 'it is not'-ness; not-isness

nitya what is not perishable, the enduring

nimitta (perceived) sign; characteristic; cause; a pervasive mark of the everyday: each perceived particular points to and implies a complex of other particulars. *Nirvāṇa* is said to be without *nimitta*

niyama inherent regularity; law

nirapekṣa unrelated; lacking (discursive or real) dependence

nirākaraṇa rejection; repudiation (of an argument)

niruddha come to an end

(a)nirodha (non)perishable

(a)nirgama (not) departing; (not) moving away from

nirmukta separated from

nirvartaka bringing forth; causing

nirvikalpa beyond, or not the result of, thought construction

nirhetuka being without cause; being without effect, i.e. non-causal; lacking a basis in reason
nivṛtti cessation
niṣidha rejection; repudiation
niścaya an assertion with cognitive claim
niścīyate it is clear, it is decided (said at the conclusion of an argument)
niḥsaraṇa exhaustion or extinction (of theories); Candrakīrti glosses it as 'ceasing to function' (*apravṛtti*)
nītārtha (of canonical *sūtras*) intended for those who have been brought to a comprehension of Buddha's truth. Cf. *neyārtha*
neyārtha (of canonical *sūtras*) intended for those who are yet to be guided to a comprehension of Buddha's truth. Cf. *nītārtha*
nairarthya meaningless; pointless
nairātmya lacking a self, or substance; as a doctrine it is virtually synonymous with the sceptical aspect of Mādhyamika
nyāya an argument; a train of thought; a line of reasoning

pakṣa the proposition to be proved in a syllogism; an argument. Cf. *pratijñā*
pakṣadoṣa an invalid argument
padārtha an everyday thing or its name
para other; the other
parataḥ of, or from, another
parabhāva other-existence; existence-as-other; existence-in-dependence-on-other
parapratijñā adversary's or counter argument or thesis
paramārtha the higher, 'surpassing' truth or realm; sometimes close to 'higher reality', but 'reality' is not appropriate to Mādhyamika
paramārthasatya may be synonymous with above or may be the truth or true account of the higher realm. There is no direct verbal access to the higher realm, but ordinary language, used by enlightened ones, can point the way there
paraspara reciprocal (usually logical)
parasparāpekṣā reciprocal dependence of both concepts and things (there is, ultimately, no difference)
parikalpa unfounded supposition; imputation, the spontaneous activity of the mind which generates the seemingly real everyday world
parikṣaya dissolution; dissipation (intransitive)
parijñāna clear, i.e. realized knowledge; perfect comprehension
parimāṇavattva measurability (e.g. of time)
paryāpta adequate; conclusive (in argument)
paryudāsapratiṣedha a negation which accepts implicit affirmation
pudgala 'person', not a 'self', but the pragmatic supposition of a subject

of mental acts and of moral or unmoral deeds. The strict Buddhist must regard this view as a heresy

pṛthaktva difference; separateness as individual

pṛthakbhūta existing independently, i.e. as an ontic self-existent

prakṛti aboriginal nature of a thing

prajñapti in general a term or a way of talking which is pragmatically tenable and useful; a term or a way of talking which guides toward the surpassing comprehension or awareness; an existential hypostatization

prajñaptyupādāya a *prajñapti* making use of the language and ideas of the everyday (all *prajñaptis* do)

prajñaptisatā mode of existence as a *prajñapti*

prajñapyate in this and other causative forms the verb *prajñā* means to convey ideas successfully; to speak and think sensibly about, or to make sense out of something

prajñā the realized awareness which follows liberation from the afflictions

pratijñā the assertion or thesis to be established in a syllogism

prajñāpāramitā the consummate awareness of the way things are, which *is* the way they are; awareness which surpasses or transcends the everyday mode of awareness; it is not any kind of 'wisdom', it describes the way of an enlightened being

pratipakṣa an adversary thesis; an antithetical concept or statement

pratipadyamāna proceding on the way

pratibandha logical opposition

pratipādana the propounding or establishing of a view

pratibādh to reject totally

pratibimba a reflection (in a mirror), a recurring analogy to emphasize the radical dependence of the higher truth on ontic factors

pratītya dependent, relative, usually in a temporal series

pratītyasamutpāda 'dependent origination'; in Nāgārjuna's thought 'non-dependent non-origination', i.e. the absence of being in things, the way things are in truth

pratyakṣa direct, unmediated perception; includes intuition and introspective observation; the model is perception through the external sense organs; the first of the traditional 'valid' means of knowing

pratyaya condition, the most general term for 'cause'; conditionedness is defined as the reciprocal dependence of cause and effect. Chapter III, 'Enquiry into Conditions', examines four types of cause and attempts to show that they are unintelligible. 'Condition' is an anti-causal notion

pratyayatva being a condition; causal efficacy

pratyukta an answer which negates

pratyutpanna what is arising here and now; the present

pratiṣedha repudiation; the commonest term for negating or rejecting an opponent's thesis

prapañca the world of named things; the visible manifold

prapañcopaśama the coming to rest, or repose, of the manifold of named things. The preferred formulation of the 'middle way'; usually interchangeable with 'dependent origination', 'absence of being in things' and *nirvāṇa*

prapañcopaśamaśiva the serenity, or beatitude of the coming to rest, or repose, of the manifold of named things

pramāna a means of knowledge. Most Buddhist schools accept only two: perception and inference; Nāgārjuna accepts two more: authority and analogy, for everyday purposes because they help to describe every man's world, but, of course, he repudiates all means of cognition as, in truth, unintelligible

prameya object known, or content or knowledge. Such Mādhyamika holds to be inseparable from a conventional language; in truth, there are no predicable contents of cognition

prayogavākya connected statement; syllogistic argument

pravṛtti actual functioning; factual emergence (arising)

prasaṅga connection, (logical) consequence; the exposure of the unacceptable consequences (often, not always, the absurdity) of a point of view

prasaṅgaviparīta logically corrupt; internally contradictory

prasajyapratiṣedha in Candrakīrti's usage a negation for *prasaṅga* purposes, i.e. for the purpose of confuting an opponent, but which does not commit the speaker to any affirmation implied in the negation

prasanna clear, serene

prasannapada lucid (clear-worded)

prasiddhi a conventionally accepted view; a presupposition in argument

prahāṇa orthodox term for the elimination or destruction or overcoming of ignorance and the other afflictions

prāpti an essential relationship, an effective interaction, between two discrete existents. Mādhyamika rules this, of course, unintelligible

phala fruit (of a deed); result; consequence; effect. An attainment on the way of the Buddhist monk

bodhi the state of enlightenment; the illumined mind

bhād total, not merely discursive rejection

bhāva anything which has existed or can exist; entity, 'thing' in the everyday world; an ontic existent whether particular or universal; substance or predicate; the nature of something, a *dharma*

bhāvajāta the world of 'created', i.e. everyday, things

bhāvanā inner realization of a way

bhāvarūpa of the nature of an ontic existent

bhinna (logically) disjoined; incompatible (of predicates)

madhyama literally 'middlemost'; commonly meaning 'middle' but not in the sense of 'in between' but rather 'of a different order'
madhyamā pratipad middle way. This is not a way or a mean mid-way between two extremes; it is a way which repudiates both being and non-being in allowing the true nature of things to prescence
mamakāra the pervasive sense, not necessarily conscious, of 'mine'; inseparable from the sense of I-me, *ahamkāra*
māyā magic trick; common analogy for the world, understood as the seeming interplay of seeming entities which are, however, devoid of an entitative nature and thus incapable of real interaction
mārga path; a prescribed discipline; not to be mistaken for the middle way (*madhyamā pratipad*) which is realized enlightenment, not a specific discipline
mithyā delusive; false
mṛṣā false; unreal; illusory
mokṣa liberation; final release; emphasizes the happening within personal experience
moṣa stolen; 'not what it pretends to be'; every attribute which gives the appearance of being *owned* by its subject is stolen, is a *moṣa-dharma*. Of course all attribution in the everyday way is *moṣa*
moha illusion, both specific content and pervasive structure of the everyday as which it is one of the three basic afflictions

yathābhūta as (things) are really; the true as-ness of things; often synonymous with *tattva*
yathāsthita as something, by its nature, is
(a)yukta (in)coherent; (un)tenable; (not) making sense; (not) logically defensible (i.e. absurd; the ultimate condemnation of an argument). Cf. *upapadyate*; sometimes synonymous with *upapatti*
yukti reason; appropriate argument
yuktividhura destitute of reason and intelligibility
(na)yujyate it (an idea or an argument) is (in)coherent, does (not) make sense; logically (in)defensible
yogī one who is enlightened, who is free of the afflictions of everyday existence, who sees the truth of things, who is on the middle way. The term *yogī* takes the place, in the *Prasannapadā*, of the more religious term *bodhisattva*

rakta the one who desires; the one who is inflamed
rahita separated from; devoid of
rāga desire, one of the three basic afflictions; thought of an an inflammation of the mind

rūpa concrete form (external body or mind content); object of perception
rūpakāraṇa the material basis of the objects of perception

lakṣaṇa distinguishing mark or characteristic attribute; definition
lakṣya what is to be characterized or defined; the 'subject' of attributes
labhyate perceived; seized upon inwardly or externally
loka world; often world as it is for personal existence; hence, sometimes, an individual destiny
lokavyavahāra transactions (frequently verbal) of unenlightened people which make up the everyday world
lokasaṁvṛti the everyday world as sustained by belief in the reality of the person
lokasaṁvṛtisatya usually a pleonasm for the above
lokottara what is beyond *loka*; the unworldly
laukika worldly, adjective of *loka*; the socially conventional in idea and speech; the secular (mundane) as opposed to the monk's life; the phenomenal (samvṛtic) as opposed to the trans-phenomenal (paramarthic)

vaktavya how something should be spoken about; a definition
vartamāna existing so as to function fully or naturally
vastu real object in the external world
vastumātra real
vastusvarūpa the true nature of real things
vāc assertive, predicative, allegedly cognitive use of words
vikalpa conceptual mind activity; hypostatization
vikalpanā a (usually untenable) presupposition
vicāryamāṇa critical investigation; the Mādhyamika dialectical analysis of a thesis
vijñāna consciousness, perception, cognition; sometimes opposed as perceptual consciousness, a 'pure' act of consciousness, to *jñāna* a normal act of cognition; sometimes conceptual knowledge as opposed to intuitive knowledge (*jñāna*)
vitarkaṇa discursive thinking
(na)vidyate there is (not); there exists (does not exist); something can(not) be encountered within the common sense world; something is (not) real
vidyamāna existing (in fact)
viparīta perverted, false (as a belief); one who is perverted, i.e. in error
viparyāsa faulty concept; false belief, i.e. misbelief
vipratiṣiddha contrary
vibhāga distinction based on a (putatively) real difference, most commonly between a pair of reciprocally dependent concepts

viruddha incompatible, contradictory; *parasparaviruddha* reciprocally contradictory
virudhyate it is incompatible with; it is opposed to
virodha incompatibility; contrariety
viṣaya object, either in the mind or in the public world
viṣayasvabhāva things as they are in themselves
viśeṣa reifying distinction; distinguishing attribute (wrongly) predicated of things; a mere verbal qualification
viśeṣaṇa act of predicating a *viśeṣa*; the distinguishing predicate
viśeṣyabhāva the subject of which the distinctions hold
(a)vyabhicāritva (in)variableness
vyatirikta apart or separate from (really and logically)
vyatireka separateness (real and logical)
vyavadāna purging of, purification from, the basic afflictions (*kleśa*)
vyavasthā principle or rule
vyavasthāna constitution, nature
vyavasthita constituted; established (by argument); existing
vyavahāra the everyday in its interpersonal, transactional aspect, usually emphasizing the importance of speech
vyākhyāta fully explained; accounted for

śakti energy specific to an activity
śānta at peace; as, in truth, things are not produced by causes and are neither in being nor not in being, they are said to be at peace
(a)śāśvata (non)eternal
śāśvatadarśana eternalism; the view that the elements of existence are imperishable
śiva final beatitude; a non-technical reference to *nirvāṇa*
śubha what is good
śūnya before Nāgārjuna Buddhist orthodoxy held all putative entities of the everyday (including contents of the mind) to be *śūnya*, i.e. to be devoid of being; only the constituents of things – *dharmas* – were truly existent. The Mādhyamika school holds that the constituents of things are no less devoid of being or self-existence, i.e. are *śūnya*. But this is not to say they are non-existent or unreal. In its full use *śūnya* means 'lacking both being and non-being'
śūnyatā the truth of things, i.e. the absence of both being and non-being in any putative ontic existent; the distinctively Mādhyamika understanding of 'dependent origination' and enlightenment; it is the preferred discursive term for *dharmatā* and *tathatā*
sākṣād unmediated
sākṣādkaraṇa unmediated realization or experience
(a)sat (non)being; (not) in existence; (not) true, i.e. false
satattva co-existence

satkāyadṛṣṭi the view (or dogma) that the person has the reality of a substance
sattva existence-ness; factualness
satya truth or reality: indefinably ambivalent or above the distinction. Cf. *āryasatya*
satyadvaya the duality of 'truth'; the two 'truths' (or realities): the everyday world (*saṁvṛti*) and the realm of the surpassing truth (*paramārtha*). The two terms are not precisely isomorphic, *saṁvṛti* implies the everyday *world, paramārtha* is often the surpassing truth *about* the world; but sometimes it is synonymous with the 'realm of *nirvāṇa*'
sādhana the process of (putatively) establishing a thesis
saddharma the Buddhist Truth
sadbhāva indisputable existence; 'fact'
(a)sadbhūta (not) factually real
sādhya what is to be established in an argument
sādhyasamatva identity of premise and conclusion; a circular argument
samāropa the use of ordinary language in a special sense; an overlay of meaning; the only way of talking about the truth of things
saṁkalpa spontaneous mental activity seen as essentially volitive
saṁkleśa individual, i.e. concrete *kleśa*; state of being afflicted
saṁjñā the process of perception and idea-formation (as a *skandha*). A notion or appellation
saṁtāna a karmic series which is the basis of the belief in person
sampadyate coheres in lived sense
(a)sambhava (im)possible either logically or really or both; potential
sammoha befuddlement; being in the grip of *moha*
saṁvidyate an intensification of *vidyate*
saṁvṛti the wholly obscured; the false, delusive everyday world of personal existence, of politics, of history. The rule of predicative assertion though this is ultimately without sense
saṁvṛtya in the everyday sense; in the everyday world (adjective to *saṁvṛti*)
saṁsāra birth–death cycle; afflicted existence; everyday life seen as the antipode of *nirvāṇa*
saṁskāra in a general sense, any complex of forces operative in the everyday world; in a special sense, such a complex as a character disposition of a person; one of the *skandhas* and second of the twelve causal factors of afflicted existence
saṁskṛta compounded, i.e. not pure, not self-existent. All ontic entities *and* qualities are *saṁskṛta*. In a special sense co-extensive with *saṁvṛti*, the everyday
sahabhava simultaneity or conjunction ('co-existence')
(a)siddha (not) being actual; something (not) functioning as what it is supposed to be

siddhānta tenet, dogma
siddharūpa concrete, realized
siddhi establishment of an existential or a cognitive claim; (established) existence
sukha happiness, usually in the everyday, illusory sense
sopapattika in accord with reason
skandha a constitutive factor of personal existence, cf. footnote, p. 98. *Skandhas* exhaust the psycho-physical individual but are the basic categories of the everyday world as well
sthāna rest
sthiti state of rest
svataḥ of itself or himself or themselves
svatantra self-contained; self-sufficient; independent; conclusive
svatantrānumāna self-contained argument; an inference grounding in premises considered tenable
svabhāva self-existent (entity or nature); against the view that the everyday world is constituted of self-existent entities and natures the entire Mādhyamika attack is directed; only *tattvam* – the truth of things – is self-existent, but, of course, in a quite different sense
svarūpa own most, or true, or intrinsic, nature of anything
svalakṣaṇa a simple, ultimate element of reality, given, unmediated, in sensuous or mental intuition; it is neither a subject nor a predicate but is self-characterizing (a notion repudiated, naturally, by Mādhyamika)
svasaṁvitti unmediated self-awareness

hetu the ground or reason, the 'because' in the Indian syllogism. But also the 'material' or 'efficient' cause, one of several kinds differentiated
(a)hetutaḥ (not) of or from a cause
hetupratyaya causal condition; a condition of the nature of *hetu*; causes and conditions
hetudoṣa invalid reason

Bibliography

Some suggestions for those interested in the thought of Buddhism, but who depend on readily accessible books and journals in English, French and German. For more exhaustive information two bibliographies are recommended:

1 Karl Potter, *The Encyclopedia of Indian Philosophies*, vol. 1, Bibliography, Motilal Banarsidass, Bombay, 1970.
2 A. K. Warder, *Indian Buddhism*, pp. 519-66, Motilal Banarsidass, Bombay, 1970.

Mādhyamika texts

Prasannapadā (various chapters in French, German or English)

	Chapters
1 J. W. de Jong, *Cinq Chapitres de la Prasannapadā*, Paul Geuthner, Paris, 1949.	XVIII to XXII
2 E. Lamotte, 'Le Traité de l'acte de Vasubandhu', *Mélanges chinois et bouddhiques*, vol. 4 (1936), pp. 265-88.	XVII
3 Jacques May, *Candrakīrti Prasannapadā Madhyamakavṛtti*, Adrien Maisoneuve, Paris, 1959.	II, III, IV, VI, VIII, IX, XI, XXIII, XXIV, XXVII
4 S. Schayer, *Ausgewählte Kapitel aus der Prasannapadā*, Polish Academy of Sciences, Krakow, 1931.	V, XII, XIII, XIV, XV, XVI
5 S. Schayer, 'Feuer und Brennstoff', *Rocznik Orientalistyczny*, vol. 7 (1931), pp. 26-51.	X
6 T. Stcherbatsky, *The Concept of Buddhist Nirvāṇa*, Leningrad, 1927. Reprint. Mouton, The Hague, 1965.	I, XXV

Madhyamakakārikās (Nāgārjuna) (English)

1 Fred J. Streng, *Emptiness* (Appendix), Abington, Nashville, 1967.
2 Kenneth K. Inada, *Nāgārjuna*, Hokuseido, Tokyo, 1970.

Vigrahavyāvartanī (Nāgārjuna) (English)
Freely Translated and also expounded by S. Mookerjee in *The Nava Nalanda Mahavira Research Publication*, vol. 1, pp. 7–41.
Translated by K. Bhattacharya, 'The Dialectical Method of Nāgārjuna', *Journal of Indian Philosophy*, vol. 1, no. 3, Nov. 71, pp. 217-61.

Ratnāvalī (or *Ratnamālā*) (Nāgārjuna)
The portions recovered in Sanskrit translated by G. Tucci in the *Journal of the Royal Asiatic Society of Great Britain and Ireland*, 1934 and 1936.
Translated from the Tibetan in *The Precious Garland and the Song of the Four Mindfulnesses* by Jeffrey Hopkins, Harper & Row, New York, 1975.

Suhṛllekha (Nāgārjuna) (English)
Translated by L. Kawamura from the Tibetan in *Golden Zephyr*, Dharma Publishing, Berkeley, 1975.

Die Mittlere Lehre des Nāgārjuna, Max Walleser, Heidelberg, 1911. Contains a translation from Tibetan of Nāgārjuna's *Kārikās* and a putative auto-commentary, the *Akutobhayā*.
Nāgārjuna's Philosophy as Presented in the Mahāprajñāpāramitā Sūtra by K. Venkata Ramanan, Charles E. Tuttle, Tokyo, and Rutland, Vermont, 1966. Translated from Chinese, this Sastra is attributed doubtfully, and on internal evidence improbably, to Nāgārjuna.
Entering the Path of Enlightenment (Śāntideva's *Bodhicaryāvatāra*), trans. Marion L. Matrics, Macmillan, London, 1970.

Śikṣā Samuccaya (Śāntideva) (English)
Translated by Bendall and Rouse, Motilal Banarsidass, Bombay, 1971 (reprint).

Śataśāstra (Āryadeva)
Translated from the Chinese by G. Tucci in *Pre-Dignāga Buddhist Texts On Logic from Chinese Sources*, University of Baroda, Gaekwad, 1929.

Prajñāpradīpaḥ (Ch. I) (Bhāvaviveka) (German)
Translated by Y. Kajiyama in *Wiener Zeitschrift fur die Kunde Sud und Ostasiens*, vols VII (1963) and VIII (1964).

Some Mahāyāna sūtras

The Perfection of Wisdom in Eight Thousand Lines and Its Verse Summary, translated from Sanskrit by E. Conze, Four Seasons Foundation, Berkeley, 1973.

The Laṅkāvatāra Sūtra, translated from Sanskrit by D. T. Suzuki, Routledge & Kegan Paul, London, 1959 (reprint).
The Holy Teaching of Vimalakīrti, translated from Tibetan by Robert A. F. Thurman, Pennsylvania State University Press, 1976.
The Śūraṅgama Sūtra, translated from the Chinese by Charles Luk, Rider, London, 1966.

The corpus of the early Buddhist texts is available in English in
1 *The Sacred Books of the Buddhists*, Luzac, London.
2 The Pali Text Society, Translation Series, Luzac, London.

Anthologies

E. Conze (ed.), *Buddhist Texts Through the Ages*, Bruno Cassirer, Oxford, 1954.
H. C. Warren (trans.), *Buddhism in Translation*, Atheneum, New York, 1963.

Books about Mādhyamika

K. Inada, *Nāgārjuna*, Hokuseido, Tokyo, 1970.
T. R. V. Murti, *The Central Philosophy of Buddhism*, Allen & Unwin, London, 1955.
R. H. Robinson, *Early Mādhyamika in India and China*, University of Wisconsin, Madison, 1967.
T. Stcherbatsky, *The Conception of Buddhist Nirvāṇa*, Mouton, The Hague, 1965 (reprint). Includes a translation of Chapters I and XXV of the *Prasannapadā*.
F. Streng, *Emptiness*, Abingdon Press, Nashville, 1967.

Buddhism in general

E. Conze, *Buddhism – Its Essence and Development*, Bruno Cassirer, Oxford, 1951.
E. Conze, *Buddhist Thought in India*, Allen & Unwin, London, 1962.
E. Conze, *Thirty Years of Buddhist Studies*, University of South Carolina Press, Columbia, S.C., 1968.
N. Dutt, *Mahāyāna Buddhism*, Mukhopadhyay, Calcutta, 1973.
Erich Frauwallner, *Die Philosophie des Buddhismus*, Akademie Verlag, Berlin, 1969.
Erich Frauwallner, *History of Indian Philosophy*, Motilal Banarsidass, Bombay, 1973.
K. N. Jayatilleke, *Early Buddhist Theory of Knowledge*, Allen & Unwin, London, 1963.

David J. Kalupahana, *Buddhist Philosophy – A Historical Analysis*, University of Hawaii, 1976.

E. Lamotte, *Histoire du Boudhisme Indien*, Publications Universitaires, Louvain, 1958.

Satkari Mookerjee (ed.), *The Nava-Nalanda-Mahavira Research Publication*, Nalanda, vol. 1, 1957.

R. H. Robinson, *The Buddhist Religion*, Dickenson Publishing, Encino, Ca., 1970.

T. Stcherbatsky, *The Central Conception of Buddhism*, Susil Gupta, Calcutta, 1923.

T. Stcherbatsky, *Buddhist Logic* (2 vols), Dover, New York, 1962 (reprint).

D. T. Suzuki, *On Indian Mahāyāna Buddhism*, Harper & Row, New York, 1968.

A. K. Warder, *Indian Buddhism*, Motilal Banarsidass, Bombay, 1970.

M. Winternitz, *Geschichte der Indischen Literatur*, 2 vols, Koehler Verlag, Stuttgart, 1968 (reprint).

Papers of special relevance

E. Conze, 'The Ontology of the Prajñāpāramitā', *Philosophy East and West*, vol. 3, no. 2, July 1933, pp. 117-29.

Douglas D. Daye, 'Mādhyamika' in C. S. Prebish (ed.), *Buddhism a Modern Perspective*, State University of Pennsylvania Press, 1975, pp. 39-93.

J. W. de Jong, 'The Problem of the Absolute in the Madhyamaka School' and 'Emptiness', both in *Journal of Indian Philosophy*, vol. 2, no. 1, Dec. 1972, pp. 1-17.

Nathan Katz, 'An Appraisal of the Svātantrika-Prāsaṅgika Debates', *Philosophy East and West*, vol. 26, no. 3, 1976, pp. 253-66.

B. K. Matilal, 'Negation and the Mādhyamika Dialectic', in *Epistemology, Logic and Grammar in Indian Philosophical Analysis*, Mouton, The Hague, 1971, pp. 146-67.

Jacques May, 'La Philosophie bouddhique de la vacuité', *Studia Philosophia*, vol. 18, 1959, pp. 123-37.

Shasan Miyamoto, 'Voidness and the Middle Way', *Studies on Buddhism in Japan*, Tokyo, vol. 1, 1939, pp. 73-92.

T. R. V. Murti, 'Nāgārjuna's Refutation of Motion and Rest', *Philosophical Quarterly*, vol. 9, no. 3, October 1933, pp. 191-200.

Harsh Narain, 'Śūnyavāda: A Reinterpretation', *Philosophy East and West*, vol. 13, no. 4, 1964, pp. 311-38.

Louis de la Vallée Poussin, 'Madhyamaka', *Mélanges Chinois et Bouddhiques*, vol. 2, 1933, pp. 1-59.

R. H. Robinson, 'Some Logical Aspects of Nāgārjuna's System', *Philosophy East and West*, vol. 6, no. 4, Jan. 1957, pp. 291-308.

R. H. Robinson, 'Did Nāgārjuna really refute all philosophical views?', *Philosophy East and West*, vol. 22, no. 3, July 1972, pp. 325-31.

S. Schayer, 'Das mahāyānistische Absolutum nach der Lehre der Mādhyamikas', *Orientatische Literatur Zeitung*, vol. 38, 1935, pp. 401-15.

S. Schayer, *Ausgewählte Kapitel aus der Prasannapadā*, Einleitung, pp. vi-xxxiii, Polish Academy of Sciences, Krakow, 1931.

Mark Siderits and J. Derwin O'Brien, 'Zeno and Nāgārjuna on Motion', *Philosophy East and West*, vol. 26, no. 3, 1976, pp. 281-99.

Mervyn Sprung, 'The Mādhyamika Doctrine of Two Realities as a Metaphysic' in M. Sprung (ed.), *The Problem of Two Truths in Buddhism and Vedanta*, Reidel, Dordrecht, 1973.

Mervyn Sprung, 'Non-Cognitive Language in Mādhyamika Buddhism', in L. Kamamura and K. Scott (eds), *Buddhist Thought and Asian Civilization*, (Herbert Guenther Festschrift) Dharma Publishing, Berkeley, 1977.

Mervyn Sprung, 'Being and the Middle Way', in M. Sprung (ed.), *The Question of Being*, Pennsylvania State University Press, 1978.

Mervyn Sprung, 'The Problem of Being in Mādhyamika Buddhism' in *Developments in Buddhist Thought*, Canadian Council for the Study of Religion, Waterloo, 1979.

Frederick J. Streng, 'The Buddhist Doctrine of Two Truths as Religious Philosophy', *Journal of Indian Philosophy*, vol. 1, no. 3, 1971, pp. 262-71.

Journals

Academic journals with the highest concentration of papers on Buddhist thought.

1 *Philosophy East and West*, University of Hawaii.
2 *Journal of Indian Philosophy*, Reidel, Dordrecht.
3 *Journal of Buddhist Philosophy*, State University of New York at Buffalo.
4 *Wiener Zeitschrift fur die Kunde Sud- und Ostasiens*, Brill, Leiden.
5 *Mélanges Chinois et Bouddhiques*, Institut Belge des Hautes Etudes Chinoises, Louvain.

[redacted]

[redacted]